ABORIGINAL
SELF-DETERMINATION

ABORIGINAL SELF‑ DETERMINATION

Proceedings of a conference held
September 30 – October 3, 1990

Edited by Frank Cassidy

 co-published by
Oolichan Books
and

The Institute for Research on Public Policy
L'Institut de recherches politiques

1991

Copyright © 1991 by The Institute for Research on Public Policy

ISBN 0-88982-111-9 Oolichan Books
ISBN 0-88645-138-8 (IRPP)

Canadian Cataloguing in Publication Data
Main entry under title:
Aboriginal self-determination

Co-published by the Institute for Research on Public Policy.
Proceedings of a conference held at the
University of Toronto, Sept. 30 – Oct. 1-3, 1990.
Includes bibliographical references.
ISBN 0-88982-111-9 (Oolichan). — ISBN
0-88645-138-8 (IRPP)

   1. Native peoples—Canada—Politics and
government—Congresses.* 2. Native peoples—
Canada—Government relations—Congresses.*
3. Native peoples—Canada—Legal status,
laws, etc.—Congresses* I. Cassidy, Frank.
II. Institute for Research on Public Policy.
E92.A26 1991   323.1'197071   C91-091826-0

Cover art: Tom Maracle   73630

Publication of this book has been financially assisted by The Canada Council

Published by
Oolichan Books
P.O. Box 10
Lantzville, BC V0R 2H0

and

The Institute for Research on Public Policy
L'Institut de recherches politiques
P.O. Box 3670 South
Halifax, Nova Scotia B3J 3K6

Typeset by Vancouver Desktop Publishing

Printed in Canada by
Hignell Printing Limited
Winnipeg, Manitoba

Contents

Foreword

In one way, the problems facing First Nations as they work towards greater self-determination are those that confront all self-conscious communities as they attempt to integrate their activities into an increasingly competitive global economy while maintaining the unique activities that define their societies and inform their values. In another more important sense, the First Nations of Canada must overcome the specific burden of historical repression of their inherent rights before they can chart a course towards greater political autonomy and economic self-sufficiency with dignity. This historical burden must also be recognized and understood by other Canadians, as both groups seek to shape the outlines of a new relationship based on mutual respect.

Both the international and the Canadian contexts for aboriginal self-determination were explored in depth at the October 1990 symposium on this subject jointly sponsored by the Assembly of First Nations and the University of Toronto, and are captured in this proceedings volume prepared by Professor Frank Cassidy for publication by The Institute for Research on Public Policy. In addition to an outstanding roster of aboriginal and non-aboriginal speakers, this meeting benefitted from the presence of political leaders such as Ontario Premier Bob Rae. The inclusion of a clear political dimension to the conference reflected the realization that for significant change to occur, a broad base of support must be generated by committed and concerted political action.

The willingness and ability of the Assembly, the University, and the Institute to work together on this project is in itself a demonstration of the cross-cultural collaboration that increasingly is seen as the prerequisite for meaningful reworking of the relationship between aboriginal and non-aboriginal peoples. The Institute looks forward to working with the Assembly of First Nations on future meetings of this sort, and, as a basis for continuing informed and constructive dialogue, will continue its research program on aboriginal issues in such key areas as native entrepreneurship, constitutional/legal change, and self-government.

Likewise, the University of Toronto is committed to an active program of scholarship and research on issues affecting aboriginal peoples. In addition, the University, through initiatives such as the Aboriginal Health Professions Program and the Special Committee of the Academic Board examining the question of access to

ix

professional programs for students of aboriginal heritage, is determined to take practical steps to hasten effective self-determination
among First Nations. The University is grateful in particular to the
Assembly of First Nations for the opportunity to be associated with
this symposium.

For its part, the Assembly of First Nations recognizes that public
education and broader understanding are critical in its own struggle
for constitutional entrenchment of the inherent aboriginal right to
self-government and views this symposium as an important part of
that education process. The opportunity to exchange ideas is useful
and appreciated. By itself, however, it is not enough: the time has
come when actions must replace words. Justice for aboriginal peoples
must come, and the rightful place of First Nations must not only be
recognized but given practical effect. First Nations have explained
and discussed long enough. Now, the other Canadian governments
must acknowledge their obligations and act accordingly.

The symposium steering committee is pleased that The Institute
for Research on Public Policy is publishing the proceedings of this
important meeting and regards the document as a useful contribution
to the ongoing dialogue which alone can show aboriginal and non-
aboriginal Canadians together the way ahead to a society of mutual
recognition and mutual respect.

Monique Jérôme-Forget, President, The Institute for Research on
  Public Policy

Ovide Mercredi, Grand Chief of the Assembly of First Nations

Robert Prichard, President, University of Toronto

Abrégé

D'un certain côté, les problèmes auxquels se trouvent confrontées les Premières Nations, alors qu'elles se dirigent vers l'autodétermination, sont identiques à ceux auxquels doivent faire face toutes les communautés qui prennent conscience d'elles-mêmes et qui essaient de s'intégrer à une économie globale de plus en plus concurrentielle, tout en maintenant le caractère unique qui les définit et façonne leurs valeurs. Par ailleurs, et ceci est peut-être plus important, les Premières Nations du Canada doivent se débarrasser du fardeau que représente la répression historique de leurs droits ancestraux, avant de pouvoir tracer la voie qui les mènera avec dignité vers une plus grande autonomie politique et économique. Ce fardeau historique doit également être reconnu et compris par les autres Canadiens, alors que les deux groupes tentent de préciser les grandes lignes de leurs nouveaux rapports, basés sur le respect mutuel.

Lors du symposium sur l'autodétermination des peuples autochtones, co-parrainé par l'Assemblée des Premières Nations et l'Université de Toronto, qui s'est tenu en octobre 1990, le contexte international et le contexte canadien ont été tous deux explorés en profondeur. Les résultats de cette réflexion sont rassemblés dans le présent volume, préparé par le professeur Frank Cassidy pour être publié par l'Institut de recherches politiques. Cette rencontre a permis non seulement de réunir des conférenciers exceptionnels, autochtones et non autochtones, mais elle a également été honorée par la présence de leaders politiques tels que le premier ministre de l'Ontario, Bob Rae. Le fait d'avoir inclus une dimension politique incontestable à ce colloque est l'indice que l'on a compris que, pour aboutir à des changements importants, il était indispensable de préparer une base solide au moyen d'actions politiques engagées et concertées.

Que l'Assemblée, l'Université et l'Institut soient prêts à collaborer pour mener à bien ce projet est en soi l'exemple même de la collaboration multiculturelle qui est de plus en plus perçue comme étant la condition nécessaire à tout remaniement significatif des relations entre les autochtones et les non autochtones. C'est avec plaisir que l'Institut collaborera de nouveau avec l'Assemblée des Premières Nations lors de rencontres futures de cette sorte et, afin d'assurer la base pour un dialogue continu informé et constructif, il poursuivra ses recherches sur les questions touchant aux autochtones, dans des domaines-clés tels que l'entrepreneurship autochtone, les changements constitutionnels et/ou légaux et l'autonomie de gouvernement.

De son côté, l'Université de Toronto a montré son engagement en créant un programme actif de bourses et de recherches sur des questions relatives aux peuples autochtones. De plus, grâce à des initiatives telles que le Programme sur les professions dans le domaine de la santé pour les autochtones et le Comité spécial du Conseil académique chargé d'étudier la facilité d'accès des programmes professionnels pour les étudiants d'origine autochtone, l'université est déterminée à prendre des mesures concrètes pour accélérer la réalisation de l'autodétermination pour les Premières Nations. L'université est particulièrement reconnaissante à l'Assemblée des Premières Nations de lui avoir fourni l'occasion de jouer un rôle actif lors de ce colloque.

L'Assemblée des Premières Nations, quant à elle, reconnaît que la sensibilisation du public et une meilleure compréhension de la question sont essentiels dans la lutte qu'elle mène pour faire intégrer dans la constitution le droit des autochtones à l'autonomie de gouvernement. Selon elle, ce symposium a joué un rôle important dans ce processus d'éducation, et elle reconnaît et apprécie le fait qu'il a été possible de procéder à cet échange d'idées. Toutefois, ceci n'est pas suffisant : l'heure est arrivée où les paroles doivent céder la place aux actes. Justice doit être faite pour les peuples autochtones : la place qui revient de droit aux Premières Nations doit non seulement être reconnue, mais cette reconnaissance doit être suivie d'effet. Les Premières Nations se sont suffisamment expliquées et ont assez discuté. Maintenant, les autres gouvernements canadiens doivent accepter leurs obligations et agir en conséquence.

Le comité directeur du symposium est heureux que l'Institut de recherches politiques ait accepté de publier les actes de cet important colloque; ce document lui paraît être une contribution extrêmement utile au dialogue en cours qui, par lui-même, peut montrer aussi bien aux Canadiens autochtones qu'aux non autochtones la voie à suivre pour parvenir à une société où règnent la reconnaissance et le respect mutuels.

Monique Jérôme Forget, président, Institut de recherches politiques

Ovide Mercredi, Grand Chef de l'Assemblée des Premières nations

Robert Prichard, président, Université de Toronto

novembre 1991

Introduction

Self-determination, Sovereignty, and Self-government

by Frank Cassidy

Self-determination is the right and the ability of a people or a group of peoples to choose their own destiny without external compulsion. It is the right to be sovereign, to be a supreme authority within a particular geographical territory. Self-government is a term which is often associated and sometimes used interchangeably with the terms self-determination and sovereignty. Such a practice can be misleading, for a group of people can exercise self-government— that is, they can make quite significant choices concerning their own political, cultural, economic, and social affairs—without actually having sovereignty or experiencing self-determination. This might be the case because the form of self-government that is practised in such circumstances is one that is ultimately defined and limited by external forces.

Self-determination, sovereignty, and self-government are for some people dry and ultimately meaningless terms. For others, they are misleadingly loud bullets in the arsenal of rhetoric. Upon occasion, they can be terms which represent great emotion and deep aspiration. This is particularly so when a people are struggling, as the First Nations in Canada are, to assert their independence and identity, to become more self-sufficient and to gain freedom.

As eloquently described by Georges Erasmus, then National Chief of the Assembly of First Nations (AFN), at the beginning of this volume, the idea of First Nations' self-determination is a simple, if powerful, one. Before the Europeans came to this shore, "we had been here for tens of thousands of years," Erasmus explains. The indigenous peoples of this continent were sovereign. We governed ourselves, Erasmus asserts, and, suddenly, people from other lands arrived, claiming it was their land, that they had "discovered" it.

The sovereignty of First Nations was never fully extinguished. It lives today, and it can be the basis for the development of more acceptable and appropriate arrangements between Canadians and First Nations. In fact, if these arrangements stem from a recognition of the inherent right and powers of self-government, we can begin

1

to have the kind of Canada of which all Canadians can be proud and in which all Canadians can prosper.

It is all so simple, Georges Erasmus and other First Nations leaders maintain. It is only a matter of Canada accepting its own Constitution, of accepting Section 35 which recognizes and affirms existing aboriginal and treaty rights. It is only a matter of political will on the part of the provincial and, most importantly, the federal governments. It is all so simple, and yet progress is so slow, it often seems as if it will never come at all.

As Professor Ted Chamberlin of the University of Toronto so eloquently asserts: "While a certain practicality must bear on these issues, there is no mistaking the fact that the peoples of First Nations everywhere are refusing to be practical, if being practical means becoming enslaved to a diminished reality." And, as Maurice Laforme, the Chief of the Mississaugas of the New Credit says: "In striving to achieve our goal of Indian government, we must think of the generations unborn, to ensure that their lives are better than those that exist today." It was with these ideas and feelings as a backdrop, that the Assembly of First Nations decided to join with the University of Toronto to organize the Symposium on First Nations' Self-Determination on October 1, 2, and 3, 1990.

The primary goal for the Symposium was to advance the level of debate with respect to aboriginal self-government issues in Canada. More specifically, the objectives of the symposium were to:
1. establish a common understanding of related issues;
2. promote a constructive and meaningful dialogue among First Nations, the general public, and governments about what is involved in aboriginal self-government;
3. demonstrate that First Nations government is achievable for and beneficial to both First Nations and Canada; and
4. facilitate the implementation of First Nations government in Canada through the identification of concrete solutions and models.

The symposium brought together a diverse range of First Nations leaders, federal and provincial government representatives, scholars, journalists, and individuals from various interest groups. With the help and insights of these participants, the organizers hoped that those Canadians who do not comprehend the aspirations of First Nations would develop a greater understanding and that those who will not accept the implications of these aspirations will realize they may no longer have that luxury. They hoped to foster the movement for First Nations' self-determination, sovereignty, and self-government.

The Sources of Power: What is First Nations Self-Government?

Aboriginal self-government is a contested concept that is expressed in contrasting ways. If First Nations' self-government is viewed from the perspective of a Canadian nation state that asserts undivided paramountcy, then the matter is simply one of defining quite limited, if significant, decision-making powers that reflect this supremacy. From a different viewpoint, if self-government is an act of self-determination, self-government must reflect the sovereign powers of First Nations and, if their relationship with Canada is to continue, these sovereign powers must be recognized as equal to those of Canada. These contending notions are the source of the first set of exchanges in this book.

Gordon Peters, the AFN's Ontario Regional Chief; John Amagolik of the Inuit Tapirisat of Canada; Doris Ronnenberg of the Native Council of Canada (NCC), and Ben Michel of the Sheshatshit First Nation each explain their view of the origins of the powers of First Nations governments. Peters observes that he cannot point to a constitution, legislation, or a source document such as the Magna Carta. "There is only one source of authority," he maintains, "and that is the Creator." There is a natural law and a sacredness to the earth, he says, and that natural law, which is the source of all power, must be respected by everyone. This, then, is the origin of First Nation's self-determination.

John Amagolik's presentation is one that shows the similarity in the views of Inuit and Indian leaders on the matter, a similarity that is often overlooked by observers who stress diversity within the aboriginal peoples' movement. "Our sovereignty," Amagolik asserts, does not come from the Crown or the Constitution. It comes from the people, their history, traditions, and cultures. "Simple as that. It comes from the Creator." Aboriginal people, he suggests, were put in this part of the world "to protect it for future generations."

Again taking a similar stance, the NCC's Doris Ronnenberg notes that the inherent powers of indigenous peoples are recognized in the International Covenant on Human Rights. The Canadian government has signed this Covenant, she reminds us. Ronnenberg also cites Section 35 of the Constitution as a source of power for First Nations governments, and, importantly, she cites the need for an Aboriginal Bill of Rights, "conceived and designed by aboriginal people." All governments, including those of First Nations, must be held accountable, Ronnenberg asserts. The idea of an Aboriginal Bill of Rights is one that will merit more discussion in coming years.

3

Ben Michel is an Innu and a member of the Sheshatshit First Nation. His people have carried on a valiant fight against the NATO low-flying flights which have threatened the wildlife and the environment of their traditional lands in Labrador. Michel struck one of the more militant notes in the symposium when he reminded the participants and audience that there is yet another source of governing powers: an economic one. "If you want Canada to understand you and your right to self-determination," Michel argues, "then it is Canada's economic power that you must destroy."

John Tait, the federal Deputy Minister of Justice, offers in his remarks a different emphasis than Gordon Peters, John Amagolik, Doris Ronnenberg, and Ben Michel. Canadian governments, he suggests, are not as concerned with the sources of power as much as they are with defining precisely what First Nations' self-government is. Tait points to the federal government's "two-track strategy." With this strategy, the federal government remains committed to constitutional entrenchment of the aboriginal right to self-government, while providing a way, through the delegation of federal powers, to create "practical self-governing arrangements." Experimentation with such arrangements will, he hopes, provide an answer to the question: "What is self-government?"

Mark Krasnick, the Government of Ontario's top public servant on First Nations matters, departs from Tait's perspective in an interesting way. Picking up an idea also put forward by Erasmus and others, Krasnick suggests that the Constitution does not necessarily have to be amended to guarantee the right to self-government. Arguing that the source of aboriginal self-government predates Confederation, Krasnick contends that Indian people are essentially federal citizens and that the *Indian Act* could be revised to spell out very limited federal powers in relation to them. In effect, he asserts, aboriginal governments would be what the tribes are in the United States, "domestic dependent nations." As such, they would be entitled to financial and other benefits from the federal government. The First Nations would have the best of both worlds. They would have a large degree of independence and they still would be an important part of Canada.

Krasnick's provocative suggestions provide a basis for the kind of renewed dialogue the Symposium was organized to encourage. In his paper, Richard Price of Alberta is equally thought-provoking as he brings to the discussion the concept of "empowerment" and a comparatively new way of thinking about self-government—"a well-being" approach. In addition, Price picks up on Mark Krasnick's and

Georges Erasmus's theme about the relevance to First Nations in Canada of native Indian experiences in the United States. Price concludes with a recommendation for community-based research, to be done in collaboration with First Nations and in a way that is directly relevant to their needs. This, he suggests, might be a way to help self-government emerge from sovereign, self-determining communities.

Sharing Power: How Can First Nations Government Work?

Greater self-government on the part of First Nations in Canada can emerge in a variety of ways. What are known as land claims agreements might be one route. The courts are another, as is legislation under existing federal and provincial powers. For those First Nations that have already signed treaties, more self-government may be possible through a stronger fulfilment of the terms of such agreements.

Whichever of these routes proves to be a successful and appropriate one, real self-government can only, in the final analysis, arise from within First Nations communities and be accommodated by a renewed and restructured federalism. As events unfold, land claims agreements, judicial decisions, legislation, treaties, federalism, and community-based initiatives will all come into play. Certainly experiences in the United States show this to be the case. First Nations government can work, but, indeed, it is a complex process.

Yukon First Nations leader David Joe opens the dialogue on "Sharing Power." Following the failure of the First Ministers' Conferences, there remain at least two possible avenues for achieving the constitutional entrenchment of self-government, Joe points out. A First Nation or a group of First Nations might pursue a favourable judicial interpretation of Section 35 of the Constitution, or self-government arrangements for specific First Nations could be entrenched in the Constitution as part of land claims agreements. Such agreements are, in effect, modern treaties and, therefore, can be entrenched under Section 35(3) of the *Constitution Act, 1982*.

In contrast to its general statements of support for the concept of entrenchment, the Government of Canada has adopted a position that entrenchment will not take place in the context of a land claims agreement. As a result, Joe argues, the Agreement-in-Principle that has been concluded in Yukon provides only for a constitutional guarantee committing Canada and the Yukon territorial government to enter into negotiations on self-government with any Yukon First Nation which so requests. The agreements that result will not be entrenched, but, Joe maintains, they may be one of the more pragmatic means of making self-government work at this time.

Ian Johnson and Allan Paul bring attention to another way of introducing greater self-government, an option that is receiving close, if hesitant, scrutiny from many First Nations. This is the legislative route, a route that relies on the sharing of federal and provincial powers instead of the recognition of First Nations' inherent powers. Rather than a "debilitating debate over jurisdiction," Johnson, the Chief Self-Government Negotiator for the United Indian Council of Chippewas and Mississaugas, suggests that First Nations should use existing federal and provincial authorities and regimes to support the expansion of self-government. Co-management and co-existence, he argues, will be the keys to achieving many of the goals of First Nations in the near future.

The federal government's community-based self-government policy lends itself to the approach Johnson describes. It provides for federal legislation as a vehicle for making self-government happen. The Alexander First Nation signed an agreement based upon this policy a few years ago. Alexander has used the resulting funds to research various models of self-government. Reflecting the hesitancy that many First Nations feel about this route to self-government, Paul, the former Alexander Chief, urges people to have an open mind. He describes First Nations government as "a sleeping bear." When this bear wakes up, he suggests, it must start rebuilding its energy and thinking about how it is going to survive. If federal funding will allow it to do so, fine; but the Alexander First Nation, he maintains, will use federal policy to seek not delegated authority but a recognition of sovereignty. "We are not looking at it as Indian Affairs does," Paul says. "We're looking at it as tribal members."

Many First Nations have already made treaties with Canada, Daniel Bellegarde of the Federation of Saskatchewan Indians points out, and these treaties are a manifestation of sovereignty as well as a guarantee of self-government powers. No country is entirely sovereign, Bellegarde argues. To varying degrees, compromises are made, and through such compromises "a nation can act in a sovereign way to give up part of its sovereignty, and enjoy the protection of another power." This is what many First Nations did when they signed treaties, but Canada, he contends, has not lived up to many of the promises it made in return. Canada, Bellegarde asserts "is campaigning to 'municipalize' our lands and communities under provincial

6

control and to call this 'self-government,' when it is really delegated local administration." As an alternative, he calls for a Treaty Commissioner to monitor and assure the just implementation of the treaties.

Self-government may be seen as a reflection of sovereignty and self-determination, but it is important to understand that many First Nations also believe, as Bellegarde and the Federation of Saskatchewan Indians do, that some forms of self-government can be a denial of sovereignty. Some leaders, such as Sharon McIvor of the Native Women's Association of Canada, go even further and question the legitimacy that concepts such as self-government have for First Nations.

"I have . . . come to the conclusion that the terms we're speaking of are non-aboriginal terms," McIvor argues. This is particularly true about the concept of power, she contends. "Power" is not a concept that reflects the culture or traditions of aboriginal people. The idea of responsibility for "the way we live" is a much more appropriate one, McIvor maintains, and it points to the only real way that aboriginal peoples can obtain greater control over their lives—by taking responsibility for their own communities and the pressing issues in their everyday lives.

If First Nations self-government is going to work, then there must be strong support from various parts of the Canadian public as well as appropriate and pragmatic routes to its further development. Dick Martin of the Canadian Labour Congress and Doreen Quirk of the Federation of Canadian Municipalities express such support. "We recognize that the concept of power-sharing must be firmly routed in the principle of self-determination," Martin notes, but he cautions that it is important for non-aboriginal people to learn to distinguish between providing support for, as opposed to direction to, indigenous peoples. Quirk expresses similar sentiments and offers the expertise and advice of her Federation, while noting that a local government or municipal model of self-government may well be a much more limited one than most First Nations are seeking.

Ironically, the process that the federal government offers as part of its community self-government process may well lead to a model for self-government that can be most closely compared to a municipal one. As explained by George Da Pont of the Department of Indian Affairs and Northern Development, this process, which enables specific First Nations to move beyond the *Indian Act*, is but one of several ways that First Nations can attain more self-government. Other federal initiatives involve a review of the *Indian Act*, which

7

might result in major changes to it. It is also important to recognize, Da Pont points out, that current *Indian Act* powers can be exercised more creatively by First Nations. "The Government of Canada," he declares, "is committed to moving on all fronts to achieve greater autonomy and self-sufficiency for First Nations."

It is interesting to note that Da Pont and other federal spokespersons carefully avoid using the words "self-determination" and "sovereignty." Instead, they talk about "greater autonomy" and "decision-making" power. Given this reluctance to address key issues in a way that many First Nations find satisfying, it is not surprising that there is increasing attention to the experiences of tribes in the United States. As Charles Wilkinson notes, these experiences are worthy of scrutiny, but he also points out that First Nations in Canada may have a real advantage because of the "knowledge and sophistication" of their leadership.

Despite rather unsuccessful efforts of First Nations to achieve a recognition of their self-governing powers through the processes of Canadian executive federalism, Richard Simeon of the University of Toronto argues that it is the Canadian tradition of federalism which may well provide some solutions. The "essential message of federalism," he notes, "is that it is a regime of multiple loyalties, each of which is legitimate." In a federal system, the central political task is to achieve balance, accommodation, and compromise between contending powers.

Aboriginal self-government based upon the inherent powers of First Nations is "fundamentally consistent" with the constitutional structure of Canada, Simeon asserts. The drive of First Nations for recognition and self-determination is not a threat, he concludes. Rather it is an opportunity for all Canadians to build a better and more just political order.

Implementation: How Will First Nations Government Happen?

If self-government is going to reflect sovereignty and lead to greater self-determination, the sources of First Nations' powers and the sharing of powers between First Nations and Canadian governments must be expressed in practical arrangements that grow out of nation-to-nation relationships. Dan Christmas of the Union of Nova Scotia Indians outlines one set of arrangements. These arrangements would be rooted in the Mi'kmaq tradition of a three-tiered level of government. The Grand Council, called the "Sante Mawi'omi," is envisaged as "the Crown in right of the Mi'kmaq" in whom is vested Mi'kmaq sovereignty and statehood. Political associations or tribal councils, termed as Mi'kmaq regional authorities (MRAs), would perform advisory and technical functions for the bands, autonomous self-governing institutions. The heads of the MRAs would become automatic members of the House of Commons. Christmas terms these "practical, workable options that are worthy of serious debate and consideration."

The Mi'kmaq perspective raises several direct challenges for the federal and provincial governments or, as the Mi'kmaq call them, "settler governments." So, too, do the negotiation and implementation of land claims agreements in Yukon and the Northwest Territories. The implementation of real aboriginal self-government, of forms of self-government that personify self-determination, is no easy matter in a Canadian political and social order that systematically ✳ denies the right of self-determination and treats it as a threat rather than an inextinguishable entitlement.

As Matthew Coon-Come maintains: "Something is rotten in the state of Canada." Coon-Come describes how his people, the Cree of northern Quebec, signed their land claims settlement "under the duress of losing our lands, our way of life." Now, several years later, there are serious questions about Canada's good faith in implementing the agreement and about the erosion of many of the gains stemming from it, particularly because of the giant Hydro Quebec James Bay II project. Canada, Coon-Come notes, is a signatory of the international covenant on civil and political rights, and it should live up to that commitment within its own boundaries.

As Victor Mitander of the Council for Yukon Indians notes, the First Nations in the Yukon are intending, as the Mi'kmaq and James Bay Cree are, to base self-government on their traditions and culture. Mitander also points to some very clear implementation needs: comprehensive and sustained training programs, appropriate mechanisms and levels of funding, and the establishment of independent monitoring agencies. "There is a long history in which the federal government Department of Indian Affairs bureaucrats have never produced any good for our people, nothing but suffering," Mitander notes. "The time has come to stop talking and studying Indian problems and issues. The time has come for concrete action, positive action."

Bill Erasmus of the Denendeh National Office expresses similar, if somewhat more pessimistic, sentiments. Noting that the Dene have been trying to spell out the practical dynamics of a working relationship with Canada since 1973, Erasmus admits that, "to date, we have very little to report of any good standing." Land claims negotiations are based on policies that call for the extinguishment rather than the recognition of aboriginal rights. In actuality, Erasmus observes, these policies are a form of coercion, as First Nations are placed in a situation where they are forced to trade away their inherent rights for explicit benefits from the Government of Canada. "There is no degree of meaningful dialogue on sovereignty," Erasmus notes, "because in their view it does not exist."

Michael Whittington, the Chief Negotiator for the federal government in Yukon, makes an effort in his presentation to address many of the issues that are raised by Mitander and Erasmus. The federal government, he suggests, is moving ever more rapidly to recognize the relationship between self-government and land claims matters. In addition, he notes that financial self-sufficiency has to be the ultimate goal for Canada and the First Nations.

Adam Zimmerman, Chairman and CEO of Noranda Forest Products, also points to the importance of money, specifically capital, if self-government is to be implemented successfully. He indicates several concerns as well as a caution regarding First Nations self-government. Self-government needs to be more precisely defined, Zimmerman asserts, so other Canadians know what to expect when they are dealing with First Nations. And, he adds, First Nations must be realistic: "However much any of us might yearn for the old days, they are not going to come back, they cannot be repeated and the best any of us can hope for is a gradual change."

My own paper in this section outlines a nine point program for improving the relationship between Canada and First Nations and bringing about a much fuller degree of self-government. The paper calls for wholesale changes to the federal government's land claims policy, a much firmer and more aggressive recognition of aboriginal and treaty rights on the part of Canada, a repeal of the *Indian Act*, the abolition of the Department of Indian Affairs, and several other measures. It expresses my hope that soon the Ministers of the Crown will realize they can no longer talk of *giving* aboriginal peoples the right or powers to govern themselves. No one, not Canada nor any provincial government, needs to or can give them what they already have—the right to self-determination, in the fullest sense of the phrase.

The Road to Self-Determination

The leaders of First Nations governments talk about self-government in the light of sovereignty and self-determination. They are eager to negotiate and reach accommodations based upon mutual recognition. Canadian officials are also ready to negotiate and reach agreements, but theirs is the language of extinguishment rather than recognition, and for them, self-government is the exercise of clearly circumscribed powers, circumscribed by *their* governments and in terms of *their* sovereignty. A dialogue between these two perspectives is not always present or possible, but, somehow or another, the debate goes on, and the road to self-determination remains as a promise, if not a well-marked thoroughfare.

There are signs of hope, nevertheless. Premiers such as Tony Penikett of Yukon and Bob Rae of Ontario provide some of that hope. Tony Penikett comes right to the point. "I represent a government that is committed to aboriginal rights, aboriginal title, and aboriginal self-government, in principle and in practice, because they are right and because they work." The federal government, he asserts, has it in its power to explicitly entrench the aboriginal right to self-government in the Constitution and it should simply do so.

"The hangup about sovereignty," Premier Rae contends, "is something we have to deal with." He notes that no sovereignty in the world is absolute today. In Canada, Ontario is recognized as being sovereign in some areas of jurisdiction; the federal government is recognized in others. There is no legitimate reason why First Nations governments cannot have their inherent powers demarcated and recognized in those jurisdictional fields in which they need to operate to meet the needs of their people. The federal and provincial governments have created too many "road blocks," Rae claims. They have to stop playing "constitutional ping pong." It is not "beyond our creativity, or our power, if we have the political will to do it," he concludes.

There is no question that Tom Siddon, the federal Minister of Indian Affairs and Northern Development, strikes a different note in his speech. The contrast to Penikett and Rae is apparent in the Minister's definition of self-determination. It means, he suggests, "*giving* native people the capacity to develop and implement their own solutions to their special political, social, and economic problems." (Emphasis added.) The Government of Canada, he asserts, wants "a new relationship" with First Nations. In the short term, the best hope for this relationship lies in legislative change that takes place with a recognition on the part of First Nations that they "must respect the laws of this country and the rights of its non-native citizens."

George Watts and Elijah Harper take strong issue with Siddon's perspective. "How could Mr. Siddon's statement represent what Canadian people are thinking?" Watts asks. "It is outright colonialism. It can't be seen in any other vein." Watts warns that violence may well be the unwelcome wave of the future, unless there is a meaningful consideration of self-government by the Canadian people and, most importantly, by the Government of Canada. Harper questions the idea that the federal government has been listening to First Nations, and he calls for First Nations to be united in relation to the common issues that mark the road to self-determination.

Towards A National Agenda

How will First Nations make progress on their journey to greater self-government and the realization of self-determination in the near future? How will they make sure that their sovereignty, their inherent rights, will be recognized and honoured? As Georges Erasmus notes, the papers in this collection provide a basis for providing fuller answers to these questions. These papers are supplemented by several background readings.

Donald Smith recalls another conference on aboriginal issues at the University of Toronto over fifty years ago. Joe Sanders and Brian Slattery focus on the further definition of the concept of sovereignty and on the clarification of how this concept is related to self-determination and the historical evolution of relations between First Nations and other Canadians. Charles Wilkinson provides an outline of the development of native sovereignty as a legal concept in the United States. The AFN provides a detailed critique of federal government land claims policies. Lawrence Courtoreille describes the relationship between the treaty-making process and self-determination. Frank Cassidy provides a synthesis of the growing literature on aboriginal governments and indicates some of the directions for future research.

In his final remarks, Georges Erasmus outlines the organizing strategy that will help the Assembly of First Nations and other aboriginal organizations with a national mandate to move towards a recognition and fulfilment of self-determination, sovereignty, and self-government. The first item he addresses is the need to foster and support much more involvement of women.

12

It is necessary, Erasmus suggests, to develop a commonly shared national agenda, "a program on sovereignty and land rights." Erasmus concedes that it is not realistic at this point to think there can be one national organization for women, Metis, Indians, Inuit, and other groupings who each currently have their own associations, but, he notes: "We are strongest when we are united. We are strongest when we have a single agenda."

First Nations self-determination, sovereignty, and self-government must come from within. They also need to be understood, recognized, and valued by other Canadians. To accomplish this goal, Erasmus urges a strengthening of First Nations alliances with women's organizations, the churches, labour, environmentalists, and others. Such alliances are part of the national agenda that will guarantee "the kind of recognition and the kind of Canada we all should have."

Georges Erasmus' words need to be taken seriously by all Canadians, aboriginal and non-aboriginal. We need a new national agenda to take us to the year 2000. We need to ensure First Nations justice and recognition. There will never be real self-determination, sovereignty, and self-government in Canada until we all enjoy these rights. Non-aboriginal Canadians must come to grips with our history of colonialism. Once we do so, we can join in a true partnership with First Nations to finally create one Canada based upon respect for the self-determination of all peoples. This is the national agenda that emerged from the First Nations Self-Determination Symposium.

As the editor of this volume, I would like to thank several people for their help and confidence. Heather Neufeld has been a joy to work with, as she efficiently and competently assisted me on just about every part of the book. I also want to thank Sena Paradis, Darcy Dobell, Barrie Keefe, and Rebecca Printup for their help and, especially, my editor Rhonda Bailey at Oolichan for her excellent work.

I deeply appreciate the confidence of the Assembly of First Nations and the University of Toronto. At the AFN, Georges Erasmus, Neil Sterritt, and Rose-Ann Morris each did a great deal to bring this project to fruition. Professor Ted Chamberlin of the University of Toronto was especially encouraging. As the key organizer of the symposium, Rose-Ann Morris should get special recognition for her extraordinary effort to bring together such an interesting and informative group of people.

I would like also to thank the authors of the contributions to this collection, who spent a considerable amount of time on their papers.

At the School of Public Administration of the University of Victoria, John Langford and Doreen Mullins were consistent and generous in their efforts to help me get time to do this work. Special thanks are in order for Rod Dobell, past President of the Institute for Research on Public Policy, for his support from the beginnings of my work on this project.

Finally, I would like to thank my wife, Maureen, whose confidence, advice, support, and strength are always present.

The Self-Determination Symposium was an exciting event, and the following members of the Symposium's Steering Committee deserve recognition:

Celia Asselin, Department of Indian Affairs and Northern Development

Ted Chamberlin, University of Toronto

Judy Gingell, Council for Yukon Indians

Dave Keenan, Council for Yukon Indians

Luc Laine, Reserve Indienne des Huron-Wendat

Simon McInnes, Department of Indian Affairs and Northern Development

Chief Allen Paul, Alexander First Nation

Rene Paul, Alexander First Nation

Stuart Paul, Tobique Indian Band

Gordon Peters, Chiefs of Ontario

President R. Prichard, University of Toronto

Mark Stevenson, Ontario Native Affairs Directorate

Sylvia Thompson, Chiefs of Ontario

Chief Leonard Tomah, Woodstock Indian Band

Al Torbitt, Winnipeg, Manitoba

George Watts, Nuu-chah-nulth Tribal Council

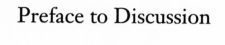

Preface to Discussion

Maurice Laforme

Chief
Mississaugas of the New Credit

My name is Maurice Laforme, Chief of the Mississaugas of New Credit. I am sixty-eight years old. I should have been seventy-two, but I've been sick. I welcome you to the Mississauga Nation territory.

It's a pleasure to see the Assembly of First Nations symposium being held in our traditional territory. I would like at this time to give you a brief background on the Mississauga Nation history. We are five bands located primarily in south-central Ontario. The Mississaugas of New Credit are located in southwestern Ontario. Our neighbours, the Six Nations of the Grand River share our lands with us.

The people of the Mississauga Nation cared enough for the white settlers who came to this area to share some of our land with them. We agreed to co-exist with them peacefully, and help them survive and feed themselves in this new land. As all the native people in the world, and more particularly Canada, have experienced, our white friends helped themselves to all our land. Because of this, the Mississauga Nation was forced to split up and seek lands in different locales of the province of Ontario. We are now separated geographically. In some situations, by great distances. The geographic separation is the only separation we allow today.

Our spirit of unity and tradition, culture and spirituality has at times in the past been set aside, but it has never been forgotten. Throughout history, we have rekindled our unity to confront very common issues as the need arose. Today, yet again, we stand united within a historical alliance with our friends and neighbours to the north, the Chippewa Nation. Our unity at this point in history is as strong, if not stronger, than it has ever been. We will never again permit ourselves to become separated. Our spirit lives forever, and we will endure any attempt to break it.

This unity represents itself in our alliance known as United Indian Councils of Mississauga and Chippewa Nations. We rekindled this alliance in 1986 to support one another in both our common and individual treaty and land claims. We have a number of treaties particular to this area and many land claims, which are presently "in the system," as Tom Siddon would say.

One of the things we have been working on together is our claim to the City of Toronto. We have undertaken considerable research into the treaties that deal with the area surrounding this city dating

17

back to 1787. Our research shows clearly that our ancestors were hoodwinked out of this land, and the government itself recognized that the treaties were invalid and fraudulent. Through the hoodwinking process, the white settlers introduced alcohol to the Indians, and this alcohol has a very devastating, and sometimes fatal, effect upon our First Nations. But the Indians are still one jump ahead of them. We introduced them to tobacco. It might take a little longer, but it is just as lethal.

Within the context of our larger claim, we have a special claim to the Toronto islands, which were never surrendered and have been expressly set aside from each treaty we signed with the Crown. The Toronto islands and much of the Toronto lakeshore is Mississauga land. One specific land claim is that of the Mississaugas' New Credit just down the road here. We have a validated claim to two hundred acres of land along the Credit River in Mississauga, Ontario. Once they had our land, they even wanted our name. Well, at least they asked us for that.

One result of our rekindled alliance is the United Indian Council of Mississauga and Chippewa Nations proposal to form our own government. While we know we have the inherent right to govern ourselves, and we wish to seek constitutional protection of this right, we feel it necessary to proceed without that constitutional protection. We are very much in support of the efforts of native leadership across the nation to secure this right. We will work together with any and all First Nations to achieve such an end.

We very much want to share with everyone our knowledge and experience if it is so desired. We are now into the negotiations phase of our Indian government proposal, and it is safe to say we have already learned many things about the government of Canada on a few occasions we have sat across the table from them.

In my personal experience, I always felt that the white man felt he knew more than the Indians. That he was smarter. One day in Toronto last week a young Indian lad was leaning up against the lamppost down on Yonge Street and this well-dressed executive came along with his briefcase and he saw the young Indian lad and he said: "Hey Indian, what time is it?" And the young guy looked at him and he says: "How did you know I was Indian?" He says: "I just guessed." "Well," he says, "guess the goddamned time too then."

In striving to achieve our goal of Indian government, we must think of those generations yet unborn, to ensure that their lives are better than those that exist today. Our Indian governments must begin to prepare for the continued existence of natives as a people, to protect our heritage, culture, and traditions while making better the lives of our people today.

With that, on behalf of the Mississauga Nation, the Mississaugas of New Credit, and the United Indian Council of Mississauga and Chippewa Nations, I welcome you to our territory and more particularly to the Assembly of First Nations symposium.

Ted Chamberlin

Professor of English and Comparative Literature
University of Toronto

I would like to welcome you on behalf of the University of Toronto. I bring greetings and good wishes from the President of the University, Robert Prichard.

Just over fifty years ago, in 1939, the University of Toronto sponsored with Yale University a Conference called "The North American Indian Today." In the half century since that conference, the University of Toronto as an institution has not exactly been at the forefront in this field . . . though individuals within the University have played important roles in developing greater understanding about issues affecting aboriginal people.

In the past few years, there have been several collective initiatives at the University of Toronto that deserve mention, each of them in different ways involving First Nations: a conference on Indian history organized by the Department of History two years ago; a native women's symposium organized by the Women's Studies Program at New College last spring; a Special Committee of the Academic Board established on direction from the Governing Council to look into the question of access to professional degree programs for students of aboriginal heritage; and the Aboriginal Health Professions Program, which has been in place for nearly five years under the direction of Dianne Longboat.

There is much more to do, and we all hope that this Symposium will be a beginning . . . not only of new initiatives at the University of Toronto, but also, and most importantly, of genuine self-determination among First Nations.

The symposium had its beginnings in a conversation I had with the National Chief of the Assembly of First Nations, Georges Erasmus, on the morning after the failure of the last of the mandated First Minister's meetings on constitutional entrenchment of aboriginal rights in March, 1987. It seemed to us then, and it became even more

19

apparent a few months later with the signing of the Meech Lake Accord by the Prime Minister and the Premiers, that ignorance and stupidity were winning out; and that the University of Toronto, being (at least theoretically) in the business of encouraging knowledge and wisdom, might have a role to play . . . but *not* on its own, since the knowledge and wisdom that the University tends to favour often has a decidedly European character about it, which, for this subject at least (and in my opinion for many other things as well) needs to be put in perspective by the wisdom and knowledge of the first peoples of this country. The idea of a jointly sponsored conference was reinforced by a resolution of the Assembly of First Nations in June of 1988 to participate in a series of events leading up to 1992. And so this began.

"Columbus did not discover a New World," wrote the West Indian historian Philip Sherlock. "He established contact between two worlds, both already old." There is a reminder in those wise and knowledgeable words. The sovereignties of the peoples of the First Nations of this country are simple, durable, ancient, and permanent facts of life in this land. Or more precisely, they're not simple at all, any more than the political, cultural, and spiritual heritages of European and other settlers are simple. But they are permanent realities, for all of us; and we ignore them at our peril.

They didn't used to be ignored. In the early days of settlement, when the beginnings of what became British (and later Canadian) Indian policy were being established, the realities of all this were much clearer. William Johnson, the architect of that policy, wrote in the mid 1700s about how "many mistakes arise from erroneous accounts made of Indians. They have been represented as calling themselves subjects, although the very word would have startled them, had it ever been pronounced by any interpreter. They desire to be considered as allies and friends."

And so they were . . . but erroneous accounts have a habit of coming back into currency, and so do habits of ignorance. We are here to ensure that we do not slip further into antagonism and enmity, and that we get the interpretations right this time round.

It's time to get down to business. It is *outstanding business*, as Harry Laforme, Indian Commissioner of Ontario, reminded us all recently, picking up on the by now ironic title of a publication of the Department of Indian Affairs from the early 1980s. It's *unfinished business*, as Lloyd Barber, until recently the President of the University of Regina, called it in a speech delivered in Yellowknife in the early 1970s, when some of the students I teach in first year university were

20

not even born. We cannot leave to yet another generation this embittering, debilitating legacy of disinterest and distrust. Here's a passage from Lloyd Barber's speech.

> Native people are seriously talking about a distinctly different place within Canadian society, an opportunity for greater self-determination and a fair share of resources, based on their original rights. No doubt this will require new and special forms of institutions which will need to be recognized as part of our political framework . . .
>
> The old approaches are out. We've been allowed to delude ourselves about the situation for a long time because of a basic lack of political power in native communities. This is no longer the case, and it is out of the question that the newly emerging political and legal power of native people is likely to diminish. We must face the situation squarely as a political fact of life, but more importantly, as a fundamental point of honour and fairness. We do, indeed, have a significant piece of unfinished business that lies at the foundations of this country.

This is why this symposium is beginning with the foundations of First Nations self-government. It is also why this symposium *must*, if we are to get out from the shadows of ignorance and stupidity, be *just* the beginning.

I want to make a couple of final points. The first is that it is foolish, and insulting, and ultimately very dangerous, to assume that people do not mean what they say. When the people of the First Nations speak of their sovereignty, they *mean* something; and what they mean, whether we understand it or not, has always been a central, albeit sometimes not a particularly convenient, part of the history of this land.

Furthermore, the ultimate sanction for First Nations self-government goes much deeper than our European-based historical and constitutional arrangements, important though these may be. The ideals of sovereignty which will ultimately inform the realities of First Nations self-government flow from the individual and collective integrity of the people of the First Nations themselves; and this integrity is dependent upon deeply held spiritual values and beliefs. It would be a very serious mistake to ignore this, even though it may not fit into our categories of social, economic, and political progress.

Finally, it is worth keeping in mind that the ideals and the realities of self-determination, troublesome though they may be to those who wish for tidier resolutions, provide the *only* way of transcending the debilitating logic of mutually exclusive alternatives, such as separation or assimilation, that have plagued aboriginal affairs in so many countries for so many years. For the people of the First Nations, it must not be a matter of choosing between drowning or being marooned on an island, but a matter of choosing which of several ways to take advantage of living by the shore, with access both to the land and to the sea.

While a certain practicality must bear on these issues, there is no mistaking the fact that the peoples of First Nations everywhere are refusing to be practical, if being practical means becoming enslaved to a diminished reality. The ideals of self-determination, which we are here to discuss, represent the perennial determination of the people of the First Nations to shape realities according to images of their own material and spiritual aspirations. And these new realities will be *possible* for aboriginal people *everywhere*, once enough people are convinced that they are *inevitable somewhere*. The somewhere can be, and should be, right here in this country.

Georges Erasmus

National Chief
Assembly of First Nations

This symposium has been a long time in coming. It is really interesting how it is happening at this particular junction in our history. For some people, it seems that our issues are complicated, because everywhere I go, I hear from people: "What is it you mean?" It does not seem to make a difference who or how important, or what kind of positions these people have, they all ask the same questions. It might be a minister in a very important government. It might be a head of a very large corporation. Or it might be people on the street who are very supportive. They want to know where we are going.

For the indigenous people of the Americas and in particular of North America, our answers lay in the relationships that we created with the European peoples that came here. We rely on our version of what happened, which is still kept alive today in every indigenous community across Canada and North America.

Our version of what happened is that we had an agreement that we would allow the Europeans to come to this part of the World. They would set up their own institutions. They would live amongst us. And they would not have to live under the institutions of the indigenous nations.

We had been here for tens of thousands of years. It is important for people to realize that. The exercise of sitting down on a nation-to-nation basis was not a new phenomenon to indigenous people.

For thousands of years before any contact with the European people, we had been doing this amongst ourselves, and anytime that we would make agreements amongst ourselves, they were always extremely sacred. Our spiritual leaders would be in the forefront of the agreements that were being made. Sometimes these agreements were about territorial boundaries that had been created between people who had fought amongst themselves. Sometimes they were about the burying of the hatchet amongst ourselves.

I am a Dene. In our history, we have a very important time, internally amongst the Dene. One day we came to an important point in our history and we made peace internally and there were many days of celebration. We knew what we were doing. Likewise with our surrounding neighbours, the Inuit to the north and to the east. We had a pretty good idea where our boundaries were.

Near Coppermine, right now, there is a historical site, called Bloody Falls. It plays an important role in the history of the Dene and the Inuit. It is a very important boundary. We both respect it.

South of us there was a very powerful Cree Nation, and, because of pestilence and plague from White settlers, they started moving west and north and at one point started to take over the territory of the Dene. Way into the territory of the Dene they advanced. We fought. We started regaining our territory. We brought them back down south. We reached a treaty between the Cree and the Dene. We named the great river the Peace River, to show the boundary between the Dene and the Cree. Even to this day, you go to that particular river and you will find there is a very important line there. A very few Cree live north of that boundary, and very few Dene live south of that particular boundary. That is the history of all First Nations all throughout America. We knew what we were doing, when we sat down with other nations.

It absolutely befuddles me, after the Dene defended their territory for tens of thousands of years, why, when a few missionaries, whether they were bishops or not; a few bureaucrats, with a document that had already been drafted up somewhere else; and a few policemen came to the territory of the Dene, that we would all of a sudden consciously decide that from then on we would give up the sovereignty of our people. We would extinguish the title of our people, and so from then on either a man or woman being in the right family from Great Britain would have all this authority over us.

That did not happen; it was not how it happened. In fact, when the Treaty party came to our area, they did not even mention land. Over and over, they explained to the Dene everything would be the same as it always had been. It would continue on the way it always was. People asked: "You mean we will be able to live on the land like we always did?" "Absolutely," was the answer. "We will make the decisions like we always did on our land, we will be able to hunt when we wish, we will be able to roam around?" "Absolutely guaranteed," was the answer. "Well, what is this all about?" we said.

You said you wanted permission for White people to pass through here, and White people to come live amongst us. This is the version of the treaty that the Dene have. You don't need any radical to come along and tell you this. You can get the oldest. You can get the most peace-loving of the Dene. You can get the youngest of the Dene. They will tell you this same version.

I have had the privilege of travelling amongst the First Nations, here in the United States, Australia, Europe, Siberia, throughout the Soviet Union, and all the northern countries, and I realized that the same thing that had been done to the aboriginal people here had been done to people elsewhere. When it was expedient to recognize the aboriginal people—that they were powerful, meaningful, and with military strength—these people were treated more as equals. Indeed, we were allies in the European Wars that happened here on the soil of aboriginal people. By and large the record shows that we were on the victorious side, although it would be hard to prove that nowadays, by the way that the Canadian government recognizes our rights.

The record all across Canada is that indigenous people, whether they signed treaties or not, obviously had sovereignty. To even question whether or not indigenous people were sovereign is beyond me.

So we lived life differently. We were not that interested in materialistic things. We were far more preoccupied with being good human beings, more sensitive to the environment and all elements of our populations. Our elders played a role. Young people were important. Women had a large share of power. Yes, we hunted. We fished. And we made all our own tools. We didn't need a factory somewhere that made us depend on it. We were self-sufficient.

So, because we lived this way for tens of thousands of years, is that to mean we lost our sovereignty because we had a different vision of why human beings are alive? Because we believed that not only is there only one Creator, but that he is present in all things alive and all things in the universe, we lost our sovereignty? So someone can stick a flag on a small portion of our land, and that's it? Sovereignty has been transformed, by some fool who didn't even know where he was? Throughout all of his life, he never realized where he had actually gone.

Even today, we are called Indians, as if we live in India, as if we had citizenship rights in the state of India. All nonsense. When does it end? Yes, it was stupid for Columbus to believe he was in India. Yes, it was stupid for the European people to come here and stick a flag in this part of the country or world. Europeans have not been here for five hundred years, but there are descendants living here calling themselves Canadian. So Quebecers would be most indignant if anybody stuck a flag on their territory and said—forget it, that's it, you are nonexistent. We don't like the way you live, we don't think it means that you have sovereignty.

This particular view of history, it is not only of the Dene. Talk to the Innu. Talk to the Haida. Talk to the Nisga'a. The process that was set down in the *Royal Proclamation* seems a lot fairer in retrospect than what we have today. At least then, the territory that was being exploited was where treaties for land had been signed with First Nations.

It seems the longer the descendants of the European people lived amongst us, the more power hungry they became, and the more they left their morals behind them. So at one point, in 1867, they actually developed an *Indian Act* that started to restrict the First Nations people to plots of land, all across Canada. Canadians should not feel in any way that they have any ability to look to South Africa and be critical.

The extraordinary thing about Canadians is that maybe one in a thousand realizes what you have done to the indigenous people. You wonder why we have poverty. When you look at the land base, the indigenous people have provided 6,350,000 square miles of land. Excluding the possible land settlements in the Northwest Territories and Yukon, and excluding the James Bay agreements, the reserve base is 10,000 square miles of land. That is what is left.

There is no justice. There is no equality. It's not fair. It does not make any difference how you look at it, it's not fair. You can look at it on a per capita basis. You can look at it on the basis of the original agreements. There is virtually not a single reserve, outside of what has been established in the last few years, that is fully still intact, because the Canadian government was not satisfied with taking 99.9 percent of the land. Anytime it needed land—for bridges, highways, railway passages, hydro line right-of-ways—it took it from reserve land. During that period of time when we could not even get off our reserves without a pass. Thank god, I lived in the part of the world where our people were not accepting reserves.

The Department of Indian Affairs was virtually handing out the little remaining land as fast as it could, hardly ever with any compensation. That is why there is something like one thousand specific little claims in this country that have to be dealt with.

So our vision of the world is this, and we do not think it is strange. We certainly don't think it's bizarre. Our territory all across this country was settled peacefully, because we thought we were dealing with honourable people. Remember, you always paraded your religious leaders in front of us, always did that, always knowing it meant something on our side of the table. We certainly didn't know what it meant on your side of the table.

So we say very simply the sovereignty of the indigenous people was never fully extinguished. That is the case for the Micmacs, on first contact. It is the case of the Dene and Inuit on last contact, and it is the case where we have treaties, and it definitely is the case where there are no treaties. We say the treaties themselves are acts of sovereignty when First Nations were at the table. It was government activity that was going on and as I said earlier, that was certainly not new to us.

We would like an end to the repugnant proposals forever coming from Canada, that we must accept some kind of delegated authority that started from some Sovereign in Europe. That the indigenous people have absolutely no sovereignty left; nothing, it's a blank sheet. The eraser was so complete, there is not even a faint remnant of the sheet. We don't intend on accepting that. We don't even intend to contemplate that. That is not acceptable.

Canadians would not accept that from any other situations in the world. Are we in Kuwait? Why did we bother with what was going on with Saddam Hussein? Why were we concerned with the institutions of a people that are being obliterated completely and taken away, when we can't even see right in front of us? Nowhere can you go, where you don't have indigenous soil. You are doing this to people here.

What kind of recognition do we have for aboriginal languages in this country? Nothing! In fact, you force us, we are expected to operate in French and English. Even in places in this country where we are majorities, where we have lived tens of thousands of years, we are forced into a situation where we have no land rights. And somebody comes there, from Southern Canada, or anywhere. They squat there, and in two or three years, they have some kind of land rights. Immediately right beside them, you might have the Inuit that have used the territory for over ten thousand years. That doesn't mean anything, doesn't mean anything at all.

26

Canada's policies for recognition of the rights of aboriginal peoples, whether they are land rights or rights to govern ourselves, are based on nineteenth century outdated modes of thinking. They are narrow, legalistic arguments, not based on any kind of common sense. They are not even based, at all, on any kind of policy that says we the Indian and Inuit have our land rights and sovereignty recognized, that we should have enough territory, enough control over our resources, both subsurface and surface, that we would pay our own way, that our land would provide for us, and once again we would have dignity. The same thing should be there for all First Nations.

We, the aboriginal people, think there are exciting solutions, but it seems we are talking to ourselves. South of us in the United States, the government has reviewed the treaties that were signed with First Nations there. It has come away from the treaties, accepting, to a certain extent, the First Nations view of the world and what happened.

The concept of government-to-government and nation-to-nation relations in the United States has become reasonably well accepted. So, too, has the concept that the First Nations there did not extinguish all of their original sovereignty.

It is also fairly well established that the United States has not crumbled because it has recognized that the indigenous people there continued to enjoy some of their original sovereignty. We don't think that this notion is a problem for Canada either. We don't see a problem for Canadians and the Canadian government, if they would recognize that the source of sovereignty for Canada is two-fold. Something that was brought over, but also something that was from the indigenous people who were here for tens of thousands of years. Something that is still alive.

So we don't ever put ourselves in the same situation as people who are separatists in this country. In fact, we have done everything we could to deter these people and slow these people down and to suggest that we can work together for a single state with proper power-sharing that would be acceptable to Quebec, the rest of the non-native people that have come here, and to First Nations.

We believe we can work out an acceptable arrangement. How would we implement it? Amongst the First Nations we have a lot of work to do. Thanks to the divide and conquer tactic, thanks to the policy of Canada never recognizing that we are collectives and that we are not simply little communities scattered throughout this part of the world, we must once again reorganize our peoples. We must again act as nations.

27

Our political organizations don't reflect ourselves as the indigenous nations that we are. We don't seek sovereignty for every little community. We seek sovereignty of a people in the collective. It's not every Dene community that is sovereign. It's the Dene as a collective that retains the right to be self-determining. It is the same with the Haida, the Mohawks and the rest of us.

Our preference for a solution is to sit across the table and to arrive at agreements that are acceptable to both Canada and to First Nations. Short of that, we will continue to research our rights, be they an aboriginal right, treaty right, or our right to govern ourselves. We expect that will lead to legal confrontation and that we will end up in courts.

The ironic thing is that one of the most progressive institutions in Canada now happens to be the Supreme Court of Canada. I don't really believe that they are out there on dangerous ground. I believe like most people in the legal profession, particularly those who are involved in such important decisions, as judges of appeal, that they are basically being conservative and staying on very safe ground. When they make decisions like the *Sparrow* decision—saying we have an aboriginal right to fish, first access to fish, and that all of Canada's policy should be based on recognition and the affirmation of the right, that they can't even define the right—they are on very safe ground.

The only reason why the judges look as if they are out there dragging along the rest of the non-native population, particularly politicians, is because the Canadian population is represented by people with completely out-of-date, uneducated views, totally uninformed and certainly not progressive.

The kind of powers that would probably be acceptable to us are those that provinces already have in their areas of sovereignty. Canada lends itself very easily to what indigenous people want. We already have a division of sovereignty. We already have a situation where the federal government has clear powers, S. 91 powers, and provinces have clear powers, S. 92 powers, many in which they are absolutely paramount and sovereign. Not another government anywhere in the world can interfere with their legislation. That model lends itself very nicely to what First Nations always told the people in this country. You already have federal powers, and provincial powers. Let's look at First Nations powers. And we will have three major forms of government. Three different types of sovereignty. Two coming from the Crown, one coming from the indigenous people, all together creating one state.

Canada can look to the world and say: "Look what we have done.

We have combined the sources of sovereignty with a people that have been here for tens of thousands of years. We now have recognition that says aboriginal title can live. We don't have to extinguish it and we have shared power and shared land, so that indigenous people can govern themselves." It all makes sense. So that's the challenge before indigenous people. That's the challenge before the people living here.

We have not been well served by Canadian governments. Some amongst us argue that until we do away with the Department of Indian Affairs, we will never have progress. Maybe they are right to suggest getting rid of Indian Affairs. I don't know what happens to people working there. Maybe they get tired. You can start with somebody that doesn't have one racial view in their head, put them in that department for a period of time—where they are controlling a whole group of people, where they are in a kind of dictatorship relationship, where most of them are non-native people working over native people and they have vast control over our lives—and I guess something happens.

Being rational human beings, I suppose we must come up with a rationale. Every time you get a pay cheque and every time you come home at night you must be able to have some rationale as to why you have done what you have done. Why you took this band council resolution and why you thought you had the authority to either let it go through, or to disallow it. Why you thought for that distant community over there. Why you had the right to play God in their lives.

That department must go. The *Indian Act* must be greatly changed, and most of it must go. But it must be done in a way in which indigenous people are in charge of what is going on.

There is a debate in this country on how, legally, if we had the political will, we could move ahead. Do we need to change the Canadian Constitution? No, it is not necessary. Section 35 of the Canadian Constitution already has a section that deals with modern treaties, and it has already recognized and affirmed treaties all across the country. The United States provides us with models. If you interpret the treaties as being nation-to-nation, with First Nations having a large degree of their internal sovereignty still remaining, move ahead and implement that. If the political will is there, it would not necessarily be a disadvantage to have a First Ministers meeting that would lay out clearly areas of jurisdiction that are inherently with First Nations.

I personally don't see the need for that, and I also have a lot of mixed feelings about what it would take to convince Canadian Governments to push through an amendment that would in their eyes be recognizing sovereign powers to indigenous people and not be undermining their governments.

So I believe there is a tremendous onus on the Federal Government. Constitutionally they have the ability to move. They have the ability to recognize that indigenous peoples still retain a large degree of their sovereignty. Whether or not we have every province in the country on board, we should begin to move.

We should begin to move very quickly. Certainly the Federal Government has no excuse in the northern parts of this country where we don't have provincial governments slowing us down.

The Canadian Government cannot sit on its hands and wait for constitutional conferences to return. I argue that there is absolutely no need to do so at all. All that is needed is the political will to use the vehicles that are there now, and we can very quickly implement the kind of recognition that the indigenous people in this country want and fully deserve.

Sources of Power:
What is First Nations Self-Government?

Gordon Peters

Ontario Region Chief
Chiefs of Ontario

I would like to speak of some of the things that we know to be, where our authority and our jurisdiction and our power comes from as a people. I don't think that I can speak of that in terms of a constitution. I can't speak of that in terms of legislation, and I can't direct you to any source document such as the Magna Carta or the Bible or any other document that you could read that would tell you truly where our power comes from.

There is only one source of authority that we have, and that is the Creator, who put us here with a very distinct purpose in mind.

I think you need to understand us as we understand ourselves. The original instructions that we were given as a people and the role we play was to take care of the earth. And there were three other people that were given instructions to take care of certain other things that we needed to survive—the water, the atmosphere (which we call the environment), and light. Those basic elements are the source of power that the Creator has given us, because without those things we cannot exist. The constitution would be meaningless if we couldn't breathe. Legislation would mean nothing if there was no land. In order for us to exist, to survive, we need all of those elements.

For us to understand the original instructions that we were given, it must be part and parcel of our understanding that we are not the Creator as man, but we are simply part of creation. We must live in harmony and share the power with all other beings—the animals, the birds—to keep in tune.

We must understand the legends and stories that we have about the creation of this land and why we call this land Turtle Island—our songs, our dances, our ceremonies—all of those oral things that tell us how we were put here and why we were put here and what we must continue to do in order to remain here. Those songs and those oral ways and those traditions are so strong and so powerful in being able to relate to us our existence that they were some of the first things that the European people tried to diminish, and then to eliminate, so that we would no longer have the connection with the original instruction, so that our authority would then come from the same kind of documents that were being provided for their people.

As we begin to start understanding ourselves again as a people, as we start to deal with our own ceremonies, our own traditions, our

33

own songs, I believe we will again identify for ourselves what is the true source of authority for all peoples, not only the First Nations. I think all people will have to come and recognize that they cannot and will not regulate nature. There is a natural law that we must observe. There is a natural power that is greater than ours as man. Until we recognize that, legislation, constitutions, and all other forms of supposed authority and jurisdiction will be meaningless.

John Amagolik

Former President
Inuit Tapirisat of Canada

I'm supposed to comment on the source of sovereignty, the source of power, where our right to self-determination comes from. My thoughts on that are not complicated and I will deal with them, but first of all I would just like to comment on what went on in the summer of 1990 in Canada. Just like all of you, I suppose, I saw the images when the Oka seige ended and the people walked out of that centre, and I cannot understand why the media and the governments continue to describe the end of the seige as a surrender. I saw no hint of surrender. I saw people walking out of the centre. I heard them say I am going home. I saw some of them start running. I saw them being tackled and captured, but I saw no surrender. I saw no surrender in their faces. I heard no surrender in their voices. And I guarantee you there was no surrender in their hearts. So let's stop calling it surrender.

The Conservative government introduced a motion in the House of Commons to praise the soldiers and call them heroes. I couldn't understand that either. The real heroes were Mohawk people like One Acorn Miller. Those are the real heroes. When aboriginal people protest and challenge Canada, they are taken to court, charged, and put in jail. When we resist, the army and the police are called and we are thrown into jail and we are called criminals. But if we start winning, the governments will go to any lengths to beat us. They will break their own laws, they will break their own policies, they will break their own Constitution — anything. And that's what they have done this past summer. They have put themselves above the law.

A small island in the mouth of the St. Lawrence River with a population of 120,000 people has sovereign power in Canada. Very clear sovereign powers. This is totally acceptable. But when the aboriginal peoples of Canada talk about sovereignty, it's called bizarre. And I'm getting tired of the *Globe and Mail* editorials which keep referring to the Meech Lake Accord. They try to keep telling the Canadian people that the aboriginal peoples lost their best opportunities to do something when the Meech Lake Accord died. This is a lie.

The Prime Minister must now live up to his words. Georges Erasmus and I have been waiting for a phone call from the Prime Minister's office ever since the guns were laid down. We have had no such call. We hope that when he gets back from New York he will pick up his phone and call us, because we are waiting for it.

And people talk about acceleration of the claims process. Acceleration means throwing more money at it. It's not going to work if you are just going to accelerate the extinguishment of our rights. If you don't change the policy, if you just accelerate the existing policy, it's not going to work, because that existing policy is still based on denial and extinguishment. The denial started back five hundred years ago, and the denial continues today. And that denial was clear in the Meech Lake Accord. The Meech Lake Accord attempted to prolong the myth that there are two founding nations in Canada—the English and French. That myth must now die. I hope it died with the Meech Lake Accord.

So the policy must change. The policy of denial and extinguishment must change. I've been talking to a lot of young people this summer. They phone me up, they ask me: "What do you think of what's going on in Quebec?" These are twenty and twenty-five year old young people, and they are all saying the three same words. Three same words keep coming out: "No more surrender."

Now, where does the source of our sovereignty, our power and our right to self-determination come from? It doesn't come from the Crown. It was recognized by the Crown, but it didn't come from the Crown. It doesn't come from the Canadian Constitution. It's recognized by the Constitution, but it doesn't come from there. It doesn't come from Bourassa or Mulroney. It comes from the people, from our history, our traditions and cultures. Simple as that. It comes from the Creator. Because aboriginal people of Canada are convinced that they were put in this part of the world to protect it for future generations. That's our source of power. Very simple.

Doris Ronnenberg

President
Native Council of Canada

As an aboriginal person and elected officer of aboriginal representative organizations, I have been involved in expressing the aboriginal perspective in hundreds, maybe even thousands of meetings with native leaders and federal and provincial officials and First Ministers over the last decade. I think that gives me the necessary background to share with you my thinking on the theme for this panel.

I have been asked to talk about what First Nations government is, and I intend to do that. Simply put, there are at least three major sources from which aboriginal self-government and self-determination spring. The first is from the Creator, who placed us on this continent. The second is the International Convention on Human Rights, which guarantees all people the right to self-determination. And the third is Section 35 of the Canadian Constitution itself. But I want to preface my discussion of those three elements by addressing some of the factors that make it difficult for many non-aboriginal Canadians to understand what we, as aboriginal people, are talking about when we talk about self-determination and self-government. The debate about aboriginal self-determination and self-government is relatively new to most non-aboriginal Canadians, so it is important that it be put on an accurate footing.

To start with, these issues are *not* new to aboriginal Canadians. Self-government and self-determination was the natural state of affairs for the aboriginal people of Canada for at least 39,800 of the last 40,000 years at even the most conservative archaeological estimates. The only new issue is the lack of recognition of those governments in the Canadian political structure since 1867.

Colonial governments chose to ignore existing political systems and imposed their own sense of order on what they called the "New World." So, before we can usefully detail what the sources of power for aboriginal self-government are, we must take a hard look at what is really happening when aboriginal Canadians talk about self-government to non-aboriginal Canadians.

In my experience, the most significant factors in the current situation are the differences in how aboriginal and non-aboriginal people see each other. These differing perceptions often go unspoken and can easily become a kind of unintentional breeding ground for misunderstanding. The first of these perceptions has been the basis of government policy toward aboriginal peoples since long before

Confederation. It is the simple, but incredibly destructive, assumption that aboriginal people are, or will eventually become, extinct. Government policy has always been designed to eliminate—by assimilation—the aboriginal peoples of Canada. Just think of how many times you have read in school text books or heard in documentary films, the phrase "vanishing race" or "disappearing redman" applied to aboriginal North Americans.

To put it another way, how is it that we don't hear the phrase "vanishing Englishman" or "disappearing Frenchman?" Certainly the lifestyle of aboriginal peoples has changed since the days of Pontiac or Tecumseh. By the same token, Brock or Wolfe would be equally uncomfortable with modern Canadian life. In modern Canada, the fact is, the aboriginal population is growing at four times the rate of the general population, while English and French populations are becoming increasingly outnumbered by other ethnic populations.

Yet somehow the notion persists that aboriginal people in Canada are a temporary anomaly in the Canadian mosaic, while French and English are recognized as founding peoples. It is very difficult to convince people who have this "vanishing race" perception locked into their minds that aboriginal people in Canada have the right to ongoing and permanent forms of self-government. On the other hand, aboriginal people are convinced they have an obvious right to self-government because they—unlike the English and French immigrants—belong on this continent, because the Creator placed them here. From an aboriginal perspective, that is a primary "source of power" for aboriginal self-government. Every other race in the world has some specific geographic locale in which they are self-determining and self-governing. For the red race, that locale is, and should be, North America.

The Creator gave us the mandate and the responsibility to live on this continent. To do that successfully, we must obviously have the capacity to make the decisions necessary to exercise that mandate and carry out that responsibility.

The second perception which influences understanding of aboriginal self-government and self-determination is related to a political numbers game. Most of you in this room think of aboriginal people in Canada as a demographically insignificant minority, and you may have seen statistics that aboriginal peoples are only 2 percent of the Canadian population. That particular number is a reflection of the number of aboriginal people in Canada who are registered under the *Indian Act*—somewhere between five and six hundred thousand. A small number indeed next to twenty-five or twenty-six million other Canadians!

By the same token, if we were to count the English and French populations in Canada only on the basis of those whose predecessors are registered as being born in France or England, how many "status" French and English Canadians would we have? Even if we passed a European Bill C-31 and included those descended from French and English passenger lists to the "New World," my guess is that the number would be surprisingly small.

How many people who call themselves French or English in Canada can actually name an ancestor who lived in England or France? Yet the right of those people to govern themselves in the context of an English or French culture is never questioned. In fact, it is constitutionalized! When aboriginal people and their descendants propose they receive the same treatment for their cultural communities, they are asked to "prove" that they are Indian, Inuit, or Métis. The fact is, most aboriginal people in Canada are not now and never will be registered under the *Indian Act*.

Some years ago, the federal Secretary of State commissioned a study on the demographic characteristics of Métis and Non-Status Indian peoples. In the context of his report in 1978, Christopher Taylor estimated that as many as 15 percent of the Canadian population has some aboriginal ancestry.

The point is that if the same criteria that is now applied consistently to English and French people were similarly and equitably applied to aboriginal people, we would comprise at least 15 percent of the population. But if sheer numbers are to determine who can and cannot govern themselves in the future, then we all better start learning Chinese.

The real issue here is not so much a question of numbers as it is a question of the basic human right to self-determination, and that is the second source of power for First Nations governments. Aboriginal people in Canada are unique peoples, distinct on the North American continent. By that fact alone, we have the right to self-determination and to self-government.

Only the most die-hard neo-colonialist would deny that the indigenous people of a country today have the international human right to self-determination. The Canadian government has signed the International Covenant that guarantees those rights. Polls tell us that most Canadians support the principle that aboriginal people in Canada should be self-governing, at least on their own territories. It seems aboriginal people are being asked to wait for Canadian politicians to catch up to public opinion.

And that brings us to a third source of power for aboriginal self-government and self-determination—the Canadian Constitution itself. Aboriginal leaders supported the patriation of the Constitution—which was a long-overdue act of self-determination on the part of the Canadian State—on the constitutionally entrenched condition and promise that Aboriginal and Treaty Rights would be identified, defined, and included in that Constitution. This was the minimum degree of assurance that we required to remove our opposition to patriation and risk the loss of our original nation-to-nation relationshp with the British Crown. This minimum was made necessary precisely because both federal and provincial laws have been, and are being, used to oppress the political aspirations of aboriginal people. Federal and provincial legislation is now suspect as a basis for establishing our self-government.

It is precisely because aboriginal people are perceived by the current political system as being insignificant that the full weight of constitutional law is necessary to counter that perception. To put it simply, if the patriated Canadian Constitution is to be the highest law of the land, then it becomes critically necessary to provide full recognition and to accommodate the political reality of the First Peoples of Canada in that law. Since the Canadian Constitution prefaces its very existence on the supremacy of God, the least it could do is recognize the act of God that placed aboriginal people on this continent.

When the Fathers of Confederation drafted the *British North America Act* of 1867, it never occurred to them to include aboriginal people in the process. Indians were considered to be a vanishing issue at the time. In fact there are only seven words in the original Constitution which even refer to aboriginal people. That wording is in paragraph 24 of section 91, which gives the federal government exclusive jurisdiction to legislate for "Indians and Lands reserved for Indians."

The intent of the original Constitution was to take all legislative and governing powers (except for amending the Constitution) and divide them between the federal government and provincial governments. That is what section 91 and section 92 of the *BNA Act* does. There appears to be no room in the current Canadian Constitution for a third order of government. It appears that every governing power in Canada must derive either from the federal or the provincial governments. For some governments, a third order of aboriginal government would mean destroying the fabric of Canadian constitutional law.

Aboriginal people, of course, do not agree with that assessment. They assert that Section 35 is a full box of existing rights, which provides the constitutional mechanism needed to validate or empower aboriginal self-government. The question remains, however, whether the political will exists in Canada to adopt that position.

In the short time available here, it has not been possible for me to present much detail on the sources of power I have outlined, but I hope it will be enough to generate useful discussion.

Having made these remarks, and keeping in mind Gordon Peters' remarks about openness and frankness, I would like to address an aspect of aboriginal self-government that has not received enough attention.

That is, the need for an Aboriginal Bill of Rights, conceived and designed by aboriginal people.

All governments must be accountable. It is certainly the tradition of our people to hold our leaders accountable.

Ben Michel

Band Council Member
Sheshatshit First Nation

It is important when one is talking about the right of self-determination for peoples that there is a clear understanding. When you are dealing with a sovereign nation and you're trying to get it into a form of de-colonization, or what you perceive to be the de-colonization route, it is very important that we do not fool with ourselves about this very, very important right that all peoples throughout the world, minorities or otherwise, have.

The very source of power in all government institutions or institutions of European norm is the economic source. If you want Canada to understand you and your right to self-determination, then that is what you must destroy in Canada. The economic stability that is within Canada. Don't fool yourselves with ignorance and arrogance about having these rights or pretending to have these rights, or that you are going to be better than the European. That's a lot of nonsense.

We know ourselves. We have worked as a unified community and we're trying very, very desperately to work as a unified people. We number as much as ten thousand. We consider ourselves as an Innu nation. It is important for Canada to realize that, if we are going to actually talk about the right of self-determination. If not, then the Innu people must not adhere to, must destroy, the economic basis of Canada—if Canada is not prepared to listen—we must do that as Innu people.

We have the Hydro lines in our part of the world. Take those out. Take whatever crisis anywhere in the world and use that against Canada. Because what the people of Canada will fear is the price of

40

something going up. Let's not kid ourselves. If Canada is not going to listen, non-violence, civil disobedience actions are only courses by which we can get Canada to address these very important issues.

If we are to consider ourselves as sovereign people, let's not demean the word. Let's use the full privilege and right that sovereignty entails. Don't let Canada destroy this philosophy of people and nation-building. I am not asking for the people or the indigenous peoples throughout this great land to insurrect. What I am asking and telling the people is not to fool themselves. Canada will only listen if you destroy their very power, and that is their economic base. Don't fool yourselves, don't kid yourselves.

If you want to have the right of practising your right to self-determination, act as a responsible people, and, in whatever way or shape or form, destroy the economy of Canada. Do it with dignity and responsibility and put yourself on the line and say I did it and I did it for this reason. Say it to the world in that way. Do not be afraid to be criminalized or to be called a terrorist because you have acted as the very word describes. It is your freedom to choose politically, socially, and cuturally. It is your right to be a self-determining people.

John C. Tait

Deputy Minister of Justice and
Deputy Attorney General of Canada

Background

Over the past decade, one of the primary issues in aboriginal affairs has been self-government—that is, the rights of aboriginal people to exercise control over matters which affect their lives. While self-government issues certainly did not originate in the 1980s, the debate was focused by the process of aboriginal constitutional discussions which took place between 1983-1987 pursuant to the requirements of Part II of the *Constitution Act, 1982* between the federal government, provincial governments, and representatives of aboriginal people. As this process unfolded, it became quickly apparent that its major concentration would be finding a way to entrench self-government rights of aboriginal people in the Constitution.

While many different ideas were advanced and considered by all parties to the discussion, there was, unfortunately, not sufficient consensus to produce a constitutional amendment. The inability to

41

achieve constitutional amendment has invariably been termed as the "failure" of these discussions. It is, however, somewhat unfair to characterize the considerable exchange of views which took place over these years in question as a failure. First, there is no doubt that the process resulted in a better understanding by governments of aboriginal self-government aspirations. Second, the process forced governments as well as aboriginal leaders to think through the logical consequences of their respective positions on self-government. While this may not constitute the degree of progress which everyone envisaged, it is nonetheless a significant step forward.

The comments below are brief observations on how the federal position has developed in response to the dialogue of the 1980s.

The Constitutional Dilemma and the Two-Track Strategy

The demands of aboriginal people for recognition of the right to self-government in the Constitution of Canada raised a series of threshold questions. What was the basis of aboriginal claims to the right of self-government?—aboriginal rights?—treaty rights?—international rights of sovereignty and self-determination? What would be the result of constitutional entrenchment?—sovereign nations?—a third order of government?—provincial or municipal-like institutions or some hybrid? Early in the debate it became apparent that there were many different answers to these questions from the various parties around the table. It also became evident that there was likely no one form of self-government constitutional arrangement that would be applicable to all situations, given the diverse circumstances of the aboriginal people in Canada.

The federal position that emerged on aboriginal self-government was based first and foremost on an understanding of the desire of the aboriginal people to have their rights entrenched in the supreme law of the country. At the 1985 First Ministers' Conference (FMC) on Aboriginal Constitutional Matters Prime Minister Mulroney stated:

> As a Canadian and as Prime Minister, I fully recognize and agree with the emphasis that the aboriginal people place on having their special rights inserted into the highest law of the land, protected—as we all want ours—from arbitrary legislative action. Constitutional protection for the principle of self-government is an overriding objective because it is the constitutional manifestation of a relationship, an unbreakable social contract between aboriginal peoples and their governments.

In order to attempt to reconcile the wishes of the aboriginal people for constitutional recognition of self-government rights with the concerns of governments over the possible consequences of such entrenchment, the federal approach since 1985 has been based on four core elements.

1. Recognition of the right of self-government for aboriginal people within the Canadian federation.
2. The requirement for negotiated agreements between federal and provincial governments and aboriginal communities to elaborate these rights.
3. Constitutional protection of rights of aboriginal people set out in negotiated agreements.
4. No derogation from existing aboriginal and treaty rights.

It was thought that, through entrenchment of a process of negotiations flowing from the recognition of a right, the gap would be bridged between the position of aboriginal groups demanding recognition of an inherent right of self-government, and the position of governments that sought greater definition of that right. At the 1987 FMC the Prime Minister set out the federal position as follows:

> The Government of Canada takes the position that the explicit recognition of the right to aboriginal self-government is an essential prerequisite. Anything less, in our judgment, would be unacceptable to aboriginal organizations and the people they represent.
>
> Furthermore, we favour a strong commitment to negotiate within the Constitution. Only through discussion and accommodation can self-government rights be appropriately defined in order that they receive, in our view, full constitutional protection. Only through negotiations, people talking to people, will we reach greater understanding of one another on this very vital challenge.

In the end result, the various attempts of the federal government, provincial governments, and aboriginal organizations to craft an amendment which would accommodate the various concerns expressed were unable to garner sufficient support to proceed with a constitutional amendment under the general amending procedure. The commitment of the federal government to a constitutional solution, however, remained intact. In the months following the final FMC in 1987, the Prime Minister stated the federal commitment to reconvene an FMC on aboriginal self-government when there were reasonable prospects for success. To this end, Ministers met with both aboriginal leaders and provinces in an attempt to determine if the basis for consensus existed. In 1989 aboriginal issues were

43

identified in the Speech from the Throne as a federal priority for second round constitutional discussions following ratification of the Meech Lake Accord.

As the debate over the ratification of the Meech Lake Accord progressed, it became clear that aboriginal concerns would figure prominently in a solution which might permit all provinces to ratify the Accord. At their meeting on June 9, 1990, First Ministers agreed on a package of amendments which would have, among other things, required an aboriginal constitutional conference to be held within one year after ratification and every three years thereafter, thus providing an opportunity to address aboriginal constitutional concerns. Unfortunately, the Meech Lake Accord and its companion amendments were not ratified by the required number of provincial legislatures in the required time period.

We are now in a situation where the constitutional agenda of the country is stalled for the foreseeable future. The concerns of aboriginal people, along with others, cannot be addressed until a means is found to re-establish the dialogue. In the interim, however, there is much work which can and should be done within the existing constitutional framework.

Early in the aboriginal constitutional process the federal government recognized the need for a two-track strategy—on the one hand pursuing constitutional change while on the other pursuing practical aboriginal self-government arrangements using mechanisms available within existing constitutional structures. A formal process of community self-government negotiations for Indian reserve communities was instituted under the leadership of the Minister of Indian Affairs and Northern Development to enable Indian communities to negotiate new self-government arrangements on a wide range of issues. At the same time, the federal government vigorously pursued the settlement of land claims in the North, which contain many elements of self-government as well as, in certain cases, commitments to negotiate comprehensive self-government agreements.

Additionally, the Prime Minister, in 1985, appointed the Minister of Justice as federal interlocutor for Métis and non-status Indians, and announced a federal commitment to participate in self-government discussions with off-reserve aboriginal people where those discussions have been initiated by the concerned province.

Given the present hiatus in the constitutional discussions, it is fundamentally important that these efforts at non-constitutional self-government arrangements be maintained, both in order to allow aboriginal governments to assume greater levels of responsibility, as well as to gain valuable experience which will assist the constitutional discussions when they begin anew. While non-constitutional solutions may not meet the total aspirations of aboriginal people, their importance should not be downplayed.

Under the *Cree-Naskapi (of Québec) Act* and the *Sechelt Indian Band Self-Government Act*, for example, the bands concerned have been given a wide range of law-making powers, which permit them to exercise authority over numerous matters that directly affect them. The governing *Acts* take precedence over other federal laws in the case of conflict, and band laws similarly prevail over provincial laws that are inconsistent with them. These are extremely significant powers that extend beyond the range of most local governments in Canada. They present an important opportunity for aboriginal communities to assume control now rather than waiting for a constitutional solution.

By working out and experimenting with some of these practical self-government arrangements, all parties will be better placed to answer the question "What is self-government?" when they next assemble at the constitutional table.

Mark Krasnick

Secretary
Ontario Native Affairs Secretariat

The question we are discussing is as follows: "What is the foundation or the basis for aboriginal peoples' right to self-government?" I'll begin with an overview of my argument—which is that the source of aboriginal self-government predates Confederation, and was provided for in 1867 by Canada's founding fathers in the *British North America Act*, now referred to as the *Constitution Act, 1867*. I will contend that the exercise of self-government was, in fact, prevented by federal legislation and the courts.

One of the implications of my argument is that our constitution does not necessarily have to be amended to guarantee the right to aboriginal self-government. The federal government could easily establish a path to self-government, remove the barriers that have been created over the years, and develop a new order in the relationship between the government and aboriginal peoples.

In any discussion of aboriginal sovereignty in Canada, there are three important dates we should keep in mind: 1763, 1867, and 1982. In 1763, of course, we had the *Royal Proclamation*. In 1867, we had

Confederation and the *Constitution Act, 1867*. And in 1982, we had the signing of the new *Constitution Act*. Each of these documents contains important statements about the relationship between aboriginal peoples and the Crown.

The treaties signed prior to 1763 were also important documents in this relationship, but I want to begin with the *Royal Proclamation of 1763*, because it spelled out a special relationship between the Crown and native peoples, and formalized the treaty process.

The *Royal Proclamation* was issued with respect to lands outside the British colonies in North America—lands that are now part of the United States and Canada. And I want to point out how, starting from the same document, interpretations of aboriginal rights evolved very differently in the U.S. and Canada.

In the United States, the inherent right to self-government, or the Doctrine of Tribal Sovereignty, as it is called, has been recognized since the early days of the Republic. It is one of the cornerstones of American Indian law and policy.

The doctrine dates from the early 1800s, and was set forth in a series of landmark decisions by U.S. Supreme Court Justice Marshall. He determined that state governments have no authority over Indian territories, and that the exercise of tribal authority cannot be limited by state law.

In effect, he said, Indian First Nations in the U.S. are "domestic dependent nations." In this context, First Nations have placed themselves under the protection of a more powerful state. But they have not given up their right to self-government or local autonomy.

Just a few years later, the authors of the *Constitution Act, 1867* were facing some of the same issues. Did they want to achieve the same result as in the United States—to make aboriginal peoples domestic dependent nations? Or did they want to achieve something else?

I would argue that they wanted Indian people to be considered domestic dependent nations—on the basis of Section 91 (24). This section, as you know, makes Indian people and the lands reserved for them a federal government responsibility.

I believe this section implies that the Fathers of Confederation did not want Indian people to be considered as ordinary citizens of the provinces—but rather, as "federal" citizens. As I read it, Section 91 (24) does not mean that the Fathers of Confederation believed Indian people could not govern themselves.

There is simply no evidence in the *Constitution Act, 1867* to indicate that its authors did not support aboriginal self-government.

Section 91 (24) gives the federal government the power to regulate

46

aboriginal government. But this means that, outside the *Indian Act* or other federal laws that apply on reserves, such as the Criminal Code, Indian people should be able to make a full range of laws to govern their own communities. Two things happened to frustrate this over the years.

First, the *Indian Act* became highly comprehensive, regulating almost all aspects of Indian life. Secondly, perhaps in line with the assimilationist thinking that prevailed at the time, the courts reinforced the notion that provincial laws generally apply to Indian people and their lands. Section 88 of the *Indian Act* specifically states that provincial laws of general application apply to Indians, except where they are inconsistent with the provisions of the *Indian Act* or treaty rights.

The *Indian Act* covers almost everything related to native affairs. But just in case anything was left out, they added a clause that says, in effect, "Anything not covered by this law is covered by provincial law."

In my opinion, there is a clear and relatively easy way to establish aboriginal self-government in Canada—and one that does not require a constitutional amendment. We must begin with the premise that Indian peoples are federal citizens, and not citizens of individual provinces. We must also embrace the notion that Indian peoples have an inherent right to self-government.

It follows, then, that what would be needed to establish these principles in law is an amended *Indian Act*—revised legislation that does not totally control the affairs of Indian people. The revised Act would simply spell out the federal government's specific areas of authority, such as serious crime and gaming. In particular, changes would be needed to Section 88 of the Act. And there are a couple of options available for changes here.

One option might be to delete Section 88 altogether. This would remove the notion that provincial laws generally apply to Indian peoples and their lands. In effect, it would create a jurisdictional vacuum—which could then be filled by self-government arrangements determined by the Indian people themselves.

Another option would be to rewrite Section 88 to include specific provisions for aboriginal self-government to displace provincial laws. This would maintain the status quo—but only until such time as native peoples displaced the provincial laws by establishing self-government arrangements of their own design.

And, in case anyone is concerned that changing Section 88 would remove protection of treaty rights, let me remind you that treaty rights are now protected in Section 35 (1) of the *Constitution Act, 1982*.

Amending the *Indian Act* could therefore result in the development of aboriginal governments exercising inherent powers—what United States Supreme Court Justice Marshall called "domestic dependent nations." Bringing this concept back to life has tremendous implications, and raises many issues. One implication is that the reserve lands would become enclaves, lands outside provincial jurisdiction. In turn, however, this implies that the provincial governments would have no financial responsibility on reserve lands.

Deciding how to fund services in these federal enclaves would obviously become a major issue. Perhaps changes would be required in the equalization payment system. Money that now goes to the provinces for services on the reserves might have to be redirected straight to the reserves. Border agreements might have to be developed between the First Nation enclaves and the provinces. There would have to be agreements on the purchase of services, where either jurisdiction could benefit from the services offered by the other.

Remember, at Confederation, the federal government and the provinces divided up revenues to ensure that each level of government had a sound fiscal base. The federal government got the indirect taxes. The provinces got revenues from resources.

What would have happened if native peoples had been allowed to develop self-government, as domestic dependent nations? At the time, most Indian peoples had land bases—reserve lands, which could theoretically have provided a permanent means of livelihood and perhaps an income from resources. Over the years, however, Canada's aboriginal people surrendered much of their land base. Perhaps this has altered the balance in resource-sharing envisaged by the Fathers of Confederation.

While the Supreme Court of Canada has already stated that Indian reserves are not exclusive federal enclaves, it is clear that, with proper drafting, enclaves can be created. Another major issue, of course, would be the status of native peoples who live off the reserves, and in particular, who has financial responsibility for them.

What does the concept of domestic dependent nations mean for Canadians, and for the country as a whole? It means that the federal government would have obligations to First Nations that parallel its obligations to the provinces, and obligations similar to those that the provinces have to individual aboriginal people.

In effect, I believe that a new sense of community could well develop in Canada out of all this—that it could change our sense of nationhood to one that involves the First Nations as an integral part of the cultural and legal make-up of our country.

There are, of course, other options to the theory of domestic dependent nations. One is full sovereignty or nation status. But sovereign nations deal with each other much differently than federal governments deal with provinces. And federal obligations to another government are not based on a sense of national community. First Nations that obtained full sovereignty might then have to sue Canada to gain any benefits at all. By contrast, the federal government would have obligations to domestic dependent nations within Canada—obligations that flow from the Canadian concept of equalization and the benefits of a sharing society.

A second option is for aboriginal self-government in Canada to evolve into a form of government that lies somewhere between federal enclaves exercising inherent sovereignty, and the status quo. If this happens, the role of provincial governments in native affairs will increase significantly.

For example, the provinces may have to bear some of the financial burden of providing services to Indian people on reserves. That could mean that, in an era of self-government, there would be equalization payments within provinces as well as national equalization payments.

Prior to the passing of the *Indian Act*, we must remember that native peoples ran their own affairs, and were, in fact, self-governing. The *Indian Act* frustrated their right to make their own laws, by regulating their entire existence.

However, my reading of Section 35 (1) of the *Constitution Act, 1982* is that the *Indian Act* can regulate some aspects of Indian life, but cannot displace those aspects of Indian life that are essential to continuing Indian culture. The *Indian Act* cannot interfere with the culture of aboriginal peoples—such as forcing them to go to Protestant schools or to give up their languages. In fact, that kind of legislation would be unconstitutional.

Clearly, the form of government used by aboriginal people and their traditional ways of organizing their societies and regulating their own affairs go to the very heart of the definition of aboriginal culture. In my opinion, it is unconstitutional for any federal law to interfere with this fundamental right.

Let me conclude with a three-point recipe for the federal government to create an environment where aboriginal self-government can become a reality.
1. Revise the *Indian Act*, to make it much less comprehensive and repressive.
2. Delete or rewrite Section 88 of the *Indian Act*, either to remove

49

or provide for the displacement of provincial laws of general application to Indian lands and peoples.

3. Develop new relationships with native peoples, using the theory that First Nations are domestic dependent nations within Canada, exercising inherent sovereignty.

The federal government has the power to do these three things, and, in so doing, to remedy more than a century of federal and judicial misinterpretation of the *Constitution Act, 1867*. And restoring the option of self-governance to Canada's aboriginal peoples would be restoring a fundamental right that, in my view, Canada's founding fathers intended all along.

A Community-based Approach to Indian Self-government

Richard T. Price
Associate Professor
School of Native Studies
University of Alberta

Introduction

Indian self-government is a hotly debated issue in Canada. In this short paper, I deal with the processes of empowerment for self-government from within Indian First Nations. The examples will be drawn from Alberta Indian communities as they have participated in recent land claims negotiations and in the process of establishing a new school. Secondly, I will deal with a comparatively new way of thinking about self-government, namely a well-being approach. This well-being approach is supplemented by experiences south of the border dealing with the vital connection between institutional forms of self-government and economic self-sufficiency.

My goal in presenting these ideas regarding empowerment and new approaches is to find more concrete ways of expressing with precision the nature and structure of First Nations government. Also, I hope to contribute to the search for a broader basis of foundations for self-governance and to articulate ideas about how aboriginal communities might determine their own destiny within the framework of our democratic society in Canada. My overall focus is on a community-based approach to Indian self-government, and I would like to participate in the collaborative efforts to positively address the diverse self-government research agendas.

1. Empowering Processes Within First Nations Self-Government—Selected Alberta Experiences

Two themes of First Nations self-government—government-to-government relationships and the empowering of individuals, families, and communities—have found recent expression in Alberta Indian experiences.

In other words, several Alberta First Nations communities have been putting into practice their aspirations for self-government and self-determination. As these experiences have evolved, individuals and communities have, in effect, gathered sources of power from within themselves and their communities; they have become empowered as they struggled to overcome the adversities of their situations.

To begin, let me briefly review some background. For most Alberta Indian communities, the legacy of the relationships bound up or encompassed in Indian treaties 6, 7, and 8, continue to be formative for patterns of thought, expression, and action. Ideally, from an Indian perspective, these treaty relationships were to be relationships of mutual respect and partnership, as land was shared and accommodations made to welcome the newcomers to the west. As the Chiefs of Alberta expressed in their Citizens Plus "Red Paper" of 1970, "To us who are Treaty Indians there is nothing more important than our Treaties, our lands and the well-being of future generations" (Indian Chiefs of Alberta, 1970:1).

Many efforts have been expended by the current generation of Indian leaders and communities in Alberta to rebuild a relationship with their treaty partners—the Queen's representatives, the Government of Canada. In the 1980s, Indian peoples in Alberta have often asserted the linkage of the treaty relationship to the right of Indian self-government. More recently, this has been articulated as a government-to-government relationship, or in other words, Alberta Indian peoples wish to be recognized as full treaty partners with the government of Canada. This modern treaty interpretation still requires more research in terms of both oral history, especially with Indian elders and with more conventional sources.

Some of the most striking examples of this quest for a renewed relationship with the Queen's representatives are found in the negotiations to settle specific treaty land entitlement claims. Three Indian First Nations in northern Alberta, the Fort Chipewyan Crees, the Whitefish Lake, and Sturgeon Lake Bands, have successfully negotiated final settlements to outstanding treaty land entitlements with the governments of Canada and Alberta. My research results indicate that an absolutely vital component to the successful conclusion of negotiations was the gradual evolution to *relationships of mutual respect*:

> These negotiating relationships implied attributes of mutual respect and even trust. For example, one person stated 'the Bands insisted on a relationship first before any deals were made'. Another Indian participant put it this way, 'one of the keys is trust so that a relationship can develop' (Price, 1990:14)

52

The land claims settlements had a number of positive benefits for the communities in terms of a mix of land and support for economic and human resource development. These settlement agreements not only lay a firm economic foundation for further advances towards self-determination, but the experience of negotiating them, in and of itself, is a credible statement of putting self-government into practice—of the power of Indian self-government. Moreover, these three bands, as I have argued elsewhere, had a direct impact on the Alberta government's policy on treaty land claims (Price, 1990:14). Also, the negotiating experiences of the Cree Band at Fort Chipewyan in terms of leadership styles, community support, and maintaining flexibility can be viewed as providing important lessons for elsewhere (McCormack 1990:149).

Another different example of an attempt to rebuild the treaty relationship, and an illustration of community renewal from within, comes from the Alexander First Nation, northwest Edmonton. While the Alexander takeover of schooling from the federal government is similar to experiences elsewhere in Canada, there are a few salient features of their experience which make the now Indian-controlled Kipohtakaw School unique. To list a few unique aspects, Alexander's Kipohtakaw School received international recognition for its creativity and programming within several years of its inception, and then went on to host the "National Indian Education Symposium" in 1988. This led to the formation of the "National Indian Education Forum," which represented a grassroots community-based group of educators from across the country, co-chaired by Adele Arcand, the administrator for the Alexander School. This National Indian Education Forum took a leadership role in researching and providing not only an effective critique, but valuable alternatives to the federal government's proposed policy on post-secondary education.

Equally important, however, has been the empowerment and healing of individuals and families within the community itself. Community leadership came often from within the school, stressing such issues as community participation in decision making, quality education, the necessity of individual/family healing, the importance of reconciliation among family clans in the community, and assertion of the need to research traditional forms of self-government. Members of the school staff sought to lead by their example, first by participating in individual and group healing processes themselves. Thus, in many ways, the Kipohtakaw School leadership was a catalyst for change and growth within this First Nation.

One of the key themes emerging from these Alberta experiences was the importance of leadership—a tough-minded leadership struggling to find a balance and harmony with individual members and families from the communities. Most of these leaders had a solid track record of experience outside their own communities. Perhaps more importantly, though, they seemed to be able to maintain a bicultural balance within themselves as self-confident Indians yet having an empathy and understanding for the other persons (and perspectives) from the dominant society. For example, an Indian educator has shared with me and others her insight that "self-government begins within me—in my heart". But her leadership example is not unique, and I continue to be impressed with the Chiefs who lead the Cree Bands at Alexander, Fort Chipweyan, Whitefish Lake, and Sturgeon Lake. I am grateful to them for their sharing of the success stories in the negotiations with governments and within their communities.

2. Philosophical and Institutional Considerations

There is now a growing literature in the field of aboriginal self-government and this is a welcome development. For example, one recent publication, *Indian Government: Its Meaning in Practice* (Cassidy, F. and R. Bish 1989), provides a very helpful analysis of concrete practices of Indian governments in Canada and provides useful suggestions for the future—for example, Canadian federalism and it's potential to incorporate various systems of self-governance. (Cassidy and Bish, 1989:160-162). In preparing for this self-determination symposium, I have come upon two new sources which I believe hold the potential to move our understanding a few steps forward. More specifically, I wish to put forward the well-being principle of self-government, developed by my colleague, Professor Tom Pocklington, at the University of Alberta. Second, I would like to take note of recent research done in the United States regarding the intimate linkage between economic development and Indian political institutions, developed in a recent paper by Professors Cornell and Kalt of the Harvard Project on American Indian Economic Development.

The research of Cornell and Kalt has focused on the economic development success stories and the failures among American Indian tribes and then linked these stories to both political institutions and sociocultural aspects of tribal life and organization. They concluded that effective institutions of self-governance are a precondition to successful economic development. However, the lessons of successful tribes point in certain clear directions for sustainable economic development, namely that Indian structures of self-governance must provide a "hospitable environment for human and financial investment" (Cornell, Kalt, 1990:119). Cornell and Kalt's research indicates that a separation of powers (through legal, cultural, or other means) is necessary to limit political interference with economic development as well as the various forms of political patronage. They point out that all societies, including Indian communities, are faced with "the problem of preventing those who exercise the legitimate powers of government from utilizing such power to transfer social wealth, or additional power, to themselves" (Cornell, Kalt, 1990:110). Specifically, "the task is to limit the role of those in power to that of a 'third party enforcer' rather than a self-interested primary party, in disputes and social decisions over the use of the society's resources" (Cornell, Kalt, 1990:110). In effect, a system of checks and balances is required, if the vital economic self-sufficiency component of self-determination is to be effectively developed.

Pocklington's research finds its roots in the quest of Métis settlements in Alberta for self-determination and his own background in political philosophy. These Métis settlements, although far less populated than Indian reserves in Alberta, have a land base approximately equal to Alberta Indian reserves and are now embarking on the implementation of recent self-government legislation (Bills 33-36, Legislative Assembly of Alberta, 1990). Pocklington defines well-being broadly as encompassing "all the qualities of life that make it better rather than worse" (Pocklington, 1991:127).

Pocklington develops a comprehensive well-being principle of native political self-determination which he states as follows: "Native collectivities should have a legal right of political self-determination to the extent that the recognition of that right promises to enhance the well-being of such collectivities without seriously reducing the well-being either of Natives who are not members of such collectivities or of non-Natives" (Pocklington, 1991:127).

This principle hinges on matters of jurisdiction tailored to the diversity of needs and aspirations of individual aboriginal communities. It also provides a direct connection between those who wish to govern and those who will feel the impact of this new form of aboriginal self-governance. Pocklington then elaborates considerations, which are not meant to be an exhaustive checklist, but rather, examples to illustrate the type of reasoning that is involved in making the case for a well-being approach to aboriginal self-government.

Accordingly, Pocklington asserts that the political arguments for Native self-determination in contemporary Canadian society are strongest (or stronger) where the case can be made along the lines of the following considerations:

- The greater the support for Native self-government by members of the community for which it is contemplated, the stronger the case for it becomes.
- The case for Native self-government is strongest where Native collectivities have a territory within which to exercise their jurisdictions.
- The case for Native self-government is strengthened if the community for which it is proposed is politically healthy.
- Well developed political and administrative skills among a community's members also enhance the case for self-government.
- The argument for greater Native political self-determination becomes more convincing if it is shown that the self-esteem of members of the community in which it is implemented will thereby be enhanced.
- The members of a Native collectivity are better equipped than outsiders to identify the nature and causes of many of their problems, and it is in this respect that the case for Native self-government is strongest.
- Just as there are many cases in which Native collectivities are more adept than outsiders at identifying problems, so too they are often better equipped than outsiders to deal effectively with the problems that confront them.

Pocklington also stresses the importance of representative leadership and the long term goal of economic independence. (Pocklington, 1991:127-132)

Whether one supports the well-being or the political- institutional or treaty and aboriginal rights based approaches to Native self-determination, the essential point is that Indian communities must determine and negotiate their own destinies by acquiring support, first from within their own community, and then from the broader society to make the fundamental decisions that affect their lives. This is what self-governance is about. More conscious efforts can also be made to define Indian self-government in concrete terms.

3. Community-Based Self-Government Research Approaches

In his recent article on Aboriginal Governments in Canada, Frank Cassidy concludes with the comment that in order to make progress on emerging research agendas "Researchers—academic and non-academic, government and independent, aboriginal and non-aboriginal—should communicate more actively. Developing ideas must be shared." (Cassidy, 1990:98). He goes on to outline a number of concrete suggestions for implementation, including electronic networks, conferences, research inventories and publications, and increased financial support.

I would agree with Cassidy's suggestions, and would comment further that the principles for Native Community-Based Research, which were jointly between aboriginal and university researchers, hold some important criteria for collaborative research efforts. Those principles include for example:

- Community-based research must be of perceived benefit to the Native community. The critical requirement is that Native groups decide whether or not the proposed research meets their criteria of benefit, relevance, and utility.
- Community-based research is socially relevant research linking collective analysis with collective action. It has a fundamental goal of building a community's capacity for generating knowledge to solve problems. (Social Sciences & Humanities Research Council of Canada: 1983:2).

The new "Aboriginal Affairs" research funding, which will be made available in 1991/92, through the Social Sciences and Humanities Research Council should open new possibilities for aboriginal economic and self-government research in Canada.

The issue of funding is raised because it has been the source of some problems in the recent past. For example, the Alexander Tribal government and the Native Studies program at my university did develop a proposal in 1989 for a joint research project aimed at determining the long-term human resources requirement for Alexander's self-government process. This project was in the end not funded by the Indian Affairs self-government unit because the federal government's "fast track" timetable did not coincide with the Alexander Tribal government's need for more extensive community discussion and thinking-through processes (e.g. some band members raised legitimate questions about the linkage between Treaty 6 and the current self-government aspirations). Indeed, education and training for Indian band members is clearly a crucial component in the self-determination quest of the Alexander Band and many other Indian bands in Canada (Price, 1991).

All these approaches (whether based in local empowerment processes or university research) have several common and positive themes. First, all recognize there is a tremendous historical, geographic, demographic, and cultural *diversity among aboriginal communities* in North America. Therefore, each aboriginal community must consciously choose its own appropriate institutions of self-governance and then attempt to negotiate specific institutional forms of authority by gaining community and governmental acceptance and recognition. Secondly, while all assert the importance and positive benefits of new forms of Indian self-governance, there is an evolving recognition that a greater degree of precision and definition is required for a proper consideration of Indian self-governance both inside and outside of Indian communities. Community members are now asking tougher questions of their leadership, "Well, what do you mean by self-government? How can we get involved?"

The future for Indian self-government in Canada looks positive when the Indian community leadership is able to respond to this type of questioning of band members, and find processes to build power from within the community and within themselves. In her recent book, Anastasia Skilnyk puts the challenge to individual leaders and community members in the following way:

> . . . if the external, enabling conditions constitute the firewood for the renewal of a people, then the spark to light the fire has to come from within. This spark is the process by which a human being becomes conscious of the responsibility he bears for his own destiny. (Skilnyk, 1985, p. 241).

One of the most encouraging signs of leadership, of both Indian women and men at the 1990 Self-Determination Symposium, were the statements made on the importance of taking the necessary initiatives and responsibilities for their communities and the children yet unborn.

REFERENCES

Alexander (Kipohtakaw) Education Centre, n.d., "Determining Our Own Destiny," Morinville, Alberta, unpublished paper.

Asch, Michael, (1984), *Home and Native Land, Aboriginal Rights and the Canadian Constitution*, (Toronto, Methuen).

Boldt, Menno and J. Anthony Long, (1984), "Tribal Traditions and European Western-Political Ideologies: The Dilemma of Canada's Native Indians," (*Canadian Journal of Political Science*, XVII:3).

Berger, Thomas, (1985), Village Journey (New York, Hill and Wang).

Cardinal, Harold, (1977), *Rebirth of Canada's Indians* (Edmonton, Hurtig).

Cassidy, Frank, (1990), "Aboriginal Governments in Canada: An Emerging Field of Study," (*Canadian Journal of Political Science*, XXIII:1).

Cassidy, Frank and Robert L. Bish, (1989), *Indian Government: Its Meaning in Practice*, (Victoria, Oolichan Books and the Institute for Research on Public Policy).

Cornell, Stephen and Joseph P. Kalt, (1990), "Pathways from Poverty: Economic Development and Institution Building on American Indian Reservations," (*American Indian Culture and Research Journal*, 14:2).

Government of Canada, (1983), *Indian Self-Government in Canada*, Report of the Special Committee, (Ottawa, Queen's Printer).

Indian Chiefs of Alberta, (1970), *Citizens Plus*, (Edmonton, Indian Association of Alberta).

Littlebear, Leroy and Menno Boldt, J. Anthony Long, editors, (1984), *Pathways to Self-Determination: Canadian Indians and the Canadian State*, (Toronto, University of Toronto).

McCormack, Patricia A. and R. Geoffrey Ironside, editors, (1990), *Proceedings of the Fort Chipewyan and Fort Vermilion Bicentennial Conference*, (Edmonton, Boreal Institute for Northern Studies).

Miller, J.R., *Skyscrapers Hide the Heavens*, University of Toronto Press, 1989.

National Indian Education Forum and Alexander School Board, (1990), *Expanding for Educational Horizons, The Final Report of the Post-Secondary Research Co-ordination Project*, (Morinville, Alexander School Board).

Pocklington, Tom and Don Carmichael, Greg Pyrcz, (forthcoming), *Democracy and Rights in Alberta*, (Toronto, Harcourt and Brace).

59

Pocklington, Tom, (1991), *Government and Politics of Alberta Métis Settlements*, (Regina, Canadian Plains Research Centre).

Price, Richard T., editor (1987), *The Spirit of the Alberta Indian Treaties* (Edmonton, University of Alberta).

Price, Richard T., (1990), "Recent Negotiations and Changes to the Alberta Government's Treaty Land Entitlement Policy," (unpublished research paper, University of Alberta).

Price, Richard T., (1991), "Land Claims Negotiation and Settlement: The Political Leadership Challenge of Alberta's Fort Chipewyan Crees," (unpublished research paper, University of Alberta).

Skilnyk, Anastasia M., (1985), *A Poison Stronger Than Love*, Yale University Press.

Slattery, Brian, (1987), "Understanding Aboriginal Rights," (*Canadian Bar Review*, Vol. LXVI)

Social Sciences and Humanities Research Council of Canada, (1983), "Community-Based Research: Report of the SSHRC Task Force on Native Issues," (Ottawa, Social Sciences and Humanities Research Council of Canada).

Sharing Power: How Can First Nations Government Work?

David Joe

Land Claims Negotiator
Council for Yukon Indians

My purpose is to outline various options for power-sharing by First Nation governments and other Canadian governmental structures. Historically, aboriginal peoples and their forms of government were blatantly ignored by European immigrants to North America.

I don't know how I can explain how that has happened. Maybe I can do so by using the analogy of a "stew pot." Imagine, if you would, that you were a guest in someone's country, in someone's tent, and that person invited you in. There was a big stew pot sitting on the table, and the person offered some to the guest. Afterward, much to the surprise of the host, the stew pot was empty.

This analogy is basically about constitutional powers in Canada. All those powers have been divided up between the provinces and the Government of Canada. As we come forward as First Nations to try and understand what has happened, we look into the stew pot—the residual constitutional powers of Canada—and we are advised that, indeed, this pot is empty. Not only that, we are no longer masters in our own house, or certainly not masters within our own tent. Initially we were the host, and now we are not even the guest. We are basically poverty-struck, sitting in a corner somewhere, hoping that the good-will of the sovereign, so-called, might help to invite us to this particular feast.

This process of denial of rights has often led to attempts by contemporary Canadian governments, both federal and provincial/territorial, to enact laws, bylaws, and regulations without the involvement, much less the consent, of aboriginal people. The resurgence of aboriginal activism combined with recent favourable court cases have forced the governments of Canada and the provinces to deal with these century-old issues. This paper will examine aboriginal self-government and the various methods of determining power-sharing in regard to aboriginal self-government.

Entrenchment of Self-Government

Following the failure of the March 1987 First Ministers' Conference to entrench the "right to self-government," there remained at least two possible avenues to achieve the entrenchment of self-government within the context of the Canadian federation. For those aboriginal groups currently negotiating a land claim settlement, there is the possibility of entrenching self-government as part of a land claim agreement within the meaning of Section 35(3) of the *Constitution Act, 1982*. For whatever reason, the Government of Canada is presently maintaining that there will be no constitutional entrenchment of self-government in the context of a land claim agreement. This position is maintained despite assurances by the Prime Minister, Brian Mulroney, following the failure of the First Ministers' Conference, that his government would seek the entrenchment of self-government by whatever means possible.

The second avenue would be to pursue a favourable judicial interpretation of Section 35(1) of the *Constitution Act, 1982*, which would include the right to self-government. Section 35(1) states:

> The existing aboriginal and treaty rights of the aboriginal peoples of Canada are hereby recognized and affirmed.

To my knowledge no aboriginal group in Canada has sought such a declaration despite an apparent willingness by the Courts, particularly in *R. v. Sparrow* [1990] 3 C.N.L.R., and *R. v. Sioui* [1990] 3 C.N.L.R. to broaden the definition of aboriginal rights.

Constitutionally there is no apparent impediment to entrenching self-government in the Yukon and the Northwest Territories. These areas of Canada fall exclusively within federal jurisdiction and obviously meet all the fundamental requirements of the federal proposals respecting "Amendments to the Constitution Relating to Aboriginal Self-Government Proposed by the Federal Government at the 1987 First Ministers' Conference on Aboriginal Constitutional Matters, 26-27 March 1987."

Recognizing that a First Ministers' Conference process is not about to be announced, and the remote possibility of pursuing any of the foregoing options, the aboriginal people are forced to define the eternal questions of: "What do aboriginal people mean by self-government? And how would these governments function?"

In the approximately five hundred years since European contact, there has been little recognition of aboriginal government. Instead, our history in Canada has been one of imposing statutory forms of Band government through various *Indian Acts*. All of these structures and accompanying powers for Band governments have emanated from Section 91(24) of the *Constitution Act, 1867*. A review of these various statutes would clearly demonstrate Canada's reluctance to address progressive forms of constitutional development regarding Canada's aboriginal people. Perhaps the most telling observation is

Canada's reticence to constitutionally occupy the jurisdictional field on matters such as Indian child care and Indian education.

This uninspired legislative agenda for advancing Indian interests predates the constitutional discussions of the 1980s. Curiously, even if a First Nation decides to pass Band bylaws under Section 81 of the *Indian Act* R.S.C. 1985, Chapter 1-5, then in a colonial and paternalistic manner, the Minister may disallow the bylaw within forty days. Surely any proposed power-sharing structure would be an improvement upon this system.

The responsibility of defining our place in Canada's constitution and the functioning of our governments has always fallen upon our shoulders. This challenge is not without constructive possibilities.

Options

At present, aboriginal nations in Canada maintain, justifiably, their inherent right to self-government. Obviously, Canada and the provinces are not about to vacate the current constitutional framework in which all jurisdictional matters are vested in either federal or provincial authority, and admit to exclusive aboriginal jurisdiction within Section 35.

Inherent within the last federal proposal in March of 1987 was a requirement that any right to aboriginal self-government would not derogate from the jurisdiction or legislative powers of Parliament or a provincial legislature, without their consent. Clearly the very foundations of constitutional structures and jurisdictions will not change unless consented to by the relevant government parties. The 1987 federal government proposal would have constitutionally committed the parties to negotiation without any guarantee of concluding the talks in a satisfactory manner.

This format was partially adopted as part of the Yukon *Umbrella Final Agreement* in April of 1990. The Yukon proposal constitutionally commits Canada and the Yukon territorial government to enter into negotiations with any Yukon First Nation which so requests. In addition, the powers of Yukon First Nations may include powers to enact laws for the governing of settlement lands and all matters ancillary to such a general power. Further, the listing of matters which a First Nation may include as a subject for negotiation is comprehensive, yet not exhaustive.

For example, a Yukon First Nation may include any of the following for inclusion on its self-government agreement:

65

- Yukon First Nations constitutions;
- Yukon First Nations community infrastructure, public works, government services and local government services;
- Community development and social programs;
- Education and training;
- Communications;
- Culture and aboriginal languages;
- Spiritual beliefs and practices;
- Health services;
- Personnel administration;
- Civil and family matters;
- The raising of revenue for local purposes, including direct taxation, subject to federal tax laws;
- Economic development;
- The administration of justice and the maintenance of law and order;
- Relations with the Government of Canada, Government of Yukon, or local governments;
- Financial transfer arrangements;
- An implementation plan; and
- All matters ancillary to any of the foregoing or as may be otherwise agreed upon.

Although the foregoing list is fairly comprehensive, nothing in the Settlement Agreements respecting self-government shall preclude any First Nation from acquiring additional constitutional protection for self-government as may be provided in future constitutional conferences. Also, nothing in self-government agreements shall effect the interpretation of aboriginal rights within the meaning of Sections 25 or 35 of the *Constitution Act, 1982*.

In addition to the constitutional commitment to negotiate self-government arrangements and the provision of a "shopping list," the Governments of Canada and the Yukon have also agreed to negotiate financial transfer arrangements. The intent of the negotiations on financial transfer arrangements is to specify a method for determining levels of government fiscal transfers to Yukon First Nations. It is intended to specify the obligations of all parties to the agreement, including the minimum program delivery standards for programs to be delivered by the Yukon First Nation. The financial transfer arrangements also address requirements for contributions from governments respecting the funding of Yukon First Nation institutions and programs, and the provision of funding through a block funding mechanism over five year intervals.

Legislative Authority

Recognizing that every self-government agreement would respond to the differing priorities of First Nations, it is anticipated that no two sets of self-government agreements would be identical in Yukon. The particular format of legislative authority must respond to the specific needs and desires of that First Nation. The foregoing list may indeed be the starting point for First Nations or may be more or less ambitious, due to each First Nation's political, social, and economic aspirations.

It is clear that all First Nations consider that most matters are ones for either exclusive or concurrent jurisdiction. Those matters which are of exclusive jurisdiction can be readily determined. Recognizing that First Nations will not preclude any matter from their constitutional authority, many matters will be the subject of concurrent authority.

For example, there is little doubt that matters such as First Nation constitutions, culture, and aboriginal languages are the exclusive domain of a First Nation. Likewise, child care and education are indeed exclusive matters for a First Nation. Non-aboriginal governments have assumed legislative authority over these matters without the consent of First Nations. To achieve the proper recognition of First Nation authority in these areas, there must be a process to devolve the necessary programs and services from existing governments to successfully give full effect to the exercise of First Nations control.

Therefore, government must not only commit to negotiations but also commit to full recognition of First Nation constitutional responsibility for these matters. Failure to conclude negotiations in this way would needlessly protract the inevitable assumption of these legislative matters by First Nations and would engender an atmosphere of bad faith.

Simply put, governments cannot continue to operate under the old constitutional framework without expecting a continuing degeneration of First Nations participation and trust.

First Nation Lands

Would First Nations' legislative authority be only applicable to First Nation lands? The obvious answer is no. First Nations would own fee simple lands, reserve lands, and other lands. In the case of fee simple lands purchased or obtained within existing municipalities, the prevailing municipal bylaws and regulations would apply. For those First Nation lands that are reserve lands or are acquired by treaty or settlement agreements, when they are in or adjacent to municipalities, I would expect that the First Nation could maintain its exclusive jurisdiction and carry the financial burden of all community infrastructures and public works. Or it could enter into service agreements with the neighbouring local government. Numerous examples of these options exist in Canada in which First Nations maintain their legislative authority over lands in urban settings or through the contractual purchasing of services from local governments.

On rural lands, a First Nation may retain its legislative authority yet enter into various agreements on matters such as land use planning or environmental assessments. These are two rather obvious examples. Compatible land uses on adjacent lands would make eminent sense. So too would an examination of the environmental impacts of development within a region that contains First Nation lands. Assuming resolution of the current transboundary conflicts among First Nations with overlapping territories, these matters could fall within each traditional territory of a First Nation.

In addition, traditional pursuits such as hunting, fishing, and trapping need not be limited to First Nations lands but could extend throughout the First Nation's traditional territory, a much broader area, as presently contemplated in numerous treaties and in all northern land claims settlements. Furthermore, heritage resources of a First Nation need not be confined to its legally retained lands but may extend throughout traditional territories. In other words, the inherent legislative authority of a First Nation would extend beyond its reserve or settlement lands.

These are only a few examples of how First Nations could share in resource management in their traditional territories.

Nonrenewable Resources

All nonrenewable resources under First Nation lands should vest in that First Nation. This would ensure consistent land use practices, as well as provide an economic base in the event of development. In order to prevent "have and have not First Nations" within the Yukon, Yukon First Nations have decided to share in all subsurface resources.

Equally important, First Nations must share in nonrenewable resource development through a royalty scheme which will provide

ongoing access for First Nation financing on all resource development within traditional territories. For example, both the Yukon and
Dene/Métis claims have a guarantee of at least 10 percent royalty
sharing in their respective traditional territories, which would be
equally shared amongst all of their First Nations. The combining of
planning and assessing resource development with that of realizing
and utilizing any monetary gains would assist in the economic and
social growth of First Nation communities.

Financial Arrangements

First Nations must have access to sufficient fiscal resources to effectively manage and run their traditional forms of self-government.
Obviously, First Nations will have power to tax their members
(except for income) and their lands. First Nations will continue to
raise revenue through economic opportunities on First Nation lands
including nonrenewable resources. Governments have agreed to
sharing of royalties derived from traditional land bases particularly
in northern Canada. The immediate financial resourcing must be
acquired through intergovernmental financial transfer arrangements. The success of these arrangements would depend upon the
generosity and creativity required to give full latitude to First Nation
development.

Citizenship

The most important resource of any Nation is its citizens. Every First
Nation constitution and in particular each citizenship code will
necessarily reflect the cultural traits of that First Nation or tribal
group. For example, the Yukon has fourteen distinct First Nations
within seven linguistic and tribal groupings. The resulting overlap of
citizenship must be resolved in the context of historic and time-
honoured tradition.
Agreements on the resolution of conflicts respecting citizenship
codes must be concluded amongst various First Nations. These
principles may be premised upon international law or uniquely
devised by First Nations.

Tribal Courts

First Nations should have the power to administer justice with respect to their citizens or those who have violated First Nation laws within the domain of that First Nation. These "courts" would adjudicate many of the matters that are between First Nations and First Nation citizens. Their structuring may be considered as an item of negotiation respecting self-government.

Summary

The recognition of the entrenchment of aboriginal self-government is fundamental to any negotiating process dealing with self-government. The issues appear to be resolvable, notwithstanding the present constitutional structures that exist in Canada. Although time does not permit a full review of the many options in greater detail, a general summary depicting pragmatic approaches to self-government may remove discussions and debates on this topic from the realm of rhetoric. Clearly there are constructive options that aboriginal people and governments could explore in achieving aboriginal self-government in Canada.

Daniel Bellegarde

First Vice-Chief
Federation of Saskatchewan Indian Nations

Indian Sovereignty

No country has the power to rule its people and territory free from controls exerted by other sovereign Nations. To varying degrees, compromises are made. These affect all those powers of any sovereign Nation that are necessary for self-government. Through such compromises, a Nation can act in a sovereign way to give up part of its sovereignty, and enjoy the protection of another power. That does not make its sovereignty any the less real. The Nation keeps its inherent right of self-government. Sovereignty is retained as long as this right is not given up.

Prior to the Treaties, the Indian Nations of Saskatchewan had

70

thriving political, cultural, economic, and social institutions. We had governments, and exercised all the powers necessary to maintain social and political stability. These governments had clearly defined lines of authority and jurisdiction. Europeans, their immigrant societies and their courts, have applied their term "Nation" to our flourishing governments.

Treaty-Making and the Royal Proclamation

One attribute of a sovereign Nation is the power to make those formal legal agreements which are called Treaties. We made Treaties with the British Crown. These deal with our ongoing political and economic relations, and, as part of international law, define the legal relationship between our Indian Nations and Canada.

The British Crown has a long history of recognizing and acknowledging the inherent and Treaty rights of Indian Nations on this continent.

The *Royal Proclamation of 1763* is a primary constitutional document that protects our rights. In it, King George III confirmed Indian ownership of Indian Lands and stipulated that these could be acquired only by the Crown, and then only with the consent of the Indian tribes affected.

The instruments chosen by the Crown to acquire Indian Lands were designated as "Treaties," rather than as "contracts" or "agreements." The Crown recognized the capacity of Indian Nations to enter Treaties.

Treaty-making based on Indian consent was to be the required and sole procedure for the Crown and its agents in dealing with our Indian Nations over land or political matters. The process of Treaty negotiations was, and is, that of mutually-recognized sovereign Nations coming together to establish an ongoing relationship. That process is bilateral in nature, between the Crown and the Indian Nations, and must be utilized if the Treaties are to be affected in any way.

The Crown's responsibilities now lie with the Government of Canada, which has assumed exclusively all obligations contained in the Treaty relationship. These cannot be delegated to third parties. However, through its policies and agreements the Government of Canada has allowed such delegation to the provinces, to the detriment of our rights.

Furthermore, the Government of Canada bears trusteeship obligations towards Treaty Indian Nations, which the federal govern-

71

ment has the task of fulfilling. These include measures to ensure the maintenance and development of our societies' cultures and resources.

Guarantees Under Treaty

Our Treaties have guaranteed us the following:

1. Lands and Reserves

Our rights in lands and reserves, including mineral and water resources, are guaranteed. These rights were recognized in the *Royal Proclamation of 1763*, the Treaties and the *Constitution Act, 1930*. The Treaties guaranteed these rights to the Indian parties and their descendants. Treaty No. 4, for example, states:

> And Her Majesty the Queen hereby agrees and undertakes to lay aside reserves for farming lands, due respect being had to lands at present cultivated by the said Indians, and other reserves for the benefit of the said Indians . . .

It is not only reserve lands that were set aside under the Treaties; special kinds of lands were guaranteed to the Indians by the Treaties, including additional land for agricultural purposes.

2. Self-Government

The right to Indian self-government exercised by the Chiefs and Councils over their people and territory, according to their own laws and customs, is also assured. Indian Nations have the right to their own institutions, to establish court systems and to administer justice. The guarantees were made in the Treaties, both in the text and orally. Thus:

> [The Indians] promise and engage that they will in all respects obey and abide by the law, and they will maintain peace and good order between each other, and also between themselves and other tribes of Indians . . . they will aid and assist the officers of Her Majesty in bringing to justice and punishment any Indian offending against the stipulations of the treaty . . .

3. Hunting, Fishing, Trapping, and Gathering

Rights to wildlife are guaranteed by the Treaties and the *Constitution Act, 1930*. As an example, Treaty No. 6 states:

72

Her Majesty further agrees with her said Indians that they, the said Indians, shall have the right to pursue their avocations of hunting and fishing throughout the tract surrendered . . .

The Treaties included a conditional surrender of the lands, with a right of access by the settlers to those lands, recognizing the continuing title of Indians in these off-reserve resources.

4. *Education*

This is guaranteed by the Treaties. For instance,

Her Majesty agrees to maintain schools for instruction in such reserves . . .

5. *Health and Medicine*

That a medicine chest shall be kept at the house of each Indian Agent for the use and benefit of the Indians . . .

Interpreted in modern-day terms, this means the availability of health coverage to our people through Canadian programmes.

6. *Socio-Economic Development*

Programmes to achieve these objectives are guaranteed by Treaty.

7. *Taxation and Military Service*

Exemptions from these are guaranteed in the Treaties, as recollected by the Commissioners and the Indian signatories. The Commissioner who negotiated Treaty No. 8 for the Crown reported:

We assured then that the treaty would not lead to any forced interference with their mode of life, that it did not open the way to the imposition of any tax, and that there was no fear of enforced military service.

Canada's Performance

In the past, most of the intended legislative and administrative protection for Indian Nations have proved to be ineffective in addressing our political status, land claims, land entitlements, resource development, property and territorial jurisdiction, Treaty enforcement, and the Crown's trusteeship responsibilities.

In place of protection, we witness Canada's attempts within the United Nations and the International Labour Office to prevent the international community from recognizing, or even studying, the status of our Treaties. With provincial support, the federal government denies any reality to our Aboriginal and Treaty rights, as entrenched in the Canadian constitution.

Canada is campaigning to municipalize our lands and communities under provincial control, and to call this "self-government," when it is really delegated local administration. Canada controls how our Nations define our own citizenships.

Canada unilaterally interpreted the content of the Treaties, and has to engage in bilateral negotiations to ensure that those agreements are fully implemented, our claims fairly settled, and ongoing protection provided. The FSIN and Canada signed a bilateral agreement in June of 1989 to work on issues of an Aboriginal nature. This is the only agreement of its kind in Canada at this time.

The Treaties we made certainly include self-imposed limitations on our sovereign abilities, but they do not provide for the many kinds of domination which Canada continues to impose. Recognition of our inherent sovereignty and Treaty relationship as the bases for Canada's policy towards us is crucial if non-Indian governments are to be kept from interfering in our internal affairs.

The Canadian Constitution and the Proposed Schedule

The Constitution Act, 1982, entrenched our inherent and Treaty rights in the Canadian constitution. Our Nations sought the addition to the Act of a Schedule which would specify these rights and provide for the establishment of a bilateral process to implement them.

These rights include the right to self-government, the rights recognized and confirmed by the *Royal Proclamation of 1763*, and those rights recognized and confirmed by Crown-First Nations Treaties, including those executed outside the present boundaries of Canada.

The Schedule would detail those subjects under which Indian governments might exclusively make laws, these being:
- the form of government;
- conditions for citizenship in the Indian Nations;
- the administration of justice and its enforcement, and adjudication;
- the regulation of domestic relations, including marriage, divorce, illegitimacy, adoption, guardianship, and support of family members;
- the regulation of property use;
- economic development, including trade and commerce;
- social programs, including the health, education, and welfare of members of First Nations.

74

All natural resources, including lands, waters, wildlife, timber, and minerals, which are reserved to us by our Treaty and inherent rights should continue to be vested in the Crown in right of Canada, for the use and benefit of Indian First Nations. We should not be deprived of them except with our full consent, and with settlements or agreements determined through the bilateral process which should be established.

Transfer payments should be allocated directly to the Indian governments of the First Nations, and Canada should be committed to making equalization payments to ensure that the Indian Governments have sufficient revenue to provide levels of public service reasonably comparable to those in non-Indian communities in Canada.

Further, any amendment to the Constitution of Canada in relation to any constitutional matters affecting our rights should only be made with our full consent.

In the four subsequent First Ministers' Conferences on Aboriginal constitutional affairs we received repeated refusals to deal with these rights and their implementation, on the pretext that they are obscure and need definition.

The Treaty position is that our relationship with Canada is a bilateral one between the Indian Nations and the federal government. The province does not have the right to deal with Indian Treaty rights. Therefore, the constitutional conferences were not the appropriate forum for discussion of our inherent and Treaty rights, and the Indian/Canada relationship.

The Meech Lake Accord

Then the federal government denied our First Nations the opportunity of taking part in the federal-provincial meeting on constitutional affairs held at Meech Lake in 1987. The Accord reached there had serious and adverse implications for our inherent and Treaty rights.

It gave constitutional recognition to Quebec's distinctiveness in Canada and speaks of the French and English-speaking peoples as together comprising "a fundamental characteristic of Canada." This could only have worked against Treaty Indian Nations' legal and political rights.

The Government of Canada has extensive Treaty obligations to our Indian Nations, and any shift of political or financial power to the provinces brings with it threats to our existence. Along with all the other attempts to bring us and our land under provincial jurisdiction, the Accord was one more stage in the path to assimilation, with implicit denial of our inherent and Treaty rights.

We are vitally concerned with federal and provincial arrangements in relation to social and economic programmes. Under the Accord, if a province opted out of national programmes in areas of its own jurisdiction, there would be no guarantee that we would continue to have access to federal programmes. This was a major threat to our health, educational, and other rights.

What would have prevented provinces from diverting any of the "reasonable compensation" they would receive from Ottawa away from federally-defined goals?

With "the death of Meech Lake," these threats have been removed and our right must never again be subject to such a federal-provincial conspiracy. At all times, there must be adequate protection of our rights. It is the federal government's responsibility to provide it.

Any discussion of federal-provincial roles in relation to federally-funded programmes must be preceded by a resolution of the issues of Treaty rights to health, education, social services, and economic development. The present federal government has avoided discussion with us of these issues.

A Treaty Commissioner

The results of the Meech Lake meeting clearly show that such conferences have a direct impact on our inherent and Treaty rights, and that protection of our rights in this process is essential.

We recommend therefore that an Office of Treaty Rights Protection be established, and that a Treaty Commissioner be appointed to head it, with meaningful powers.

The Commissioner would report to Parliament, and monitor and evaluate the implementation of the Treaties by both parties. He would have the right to intervene directly in future First Ministers' Conferences if Treaty issues are being affected. An Office of Treaty Commissioner was jointly appointed by the FSIN and the Minister of Indian and Northern Affairs last year, but his scope for action is limited, and must be strengthened. Even so, the value of his present office is being clearly demonstrated through federal and provincial action on his recent report on Treaty land entitlement. Negotiations on some Bands' outstanding lands are already under way, using principles drawn from his recommendation.

Our inclusion within Confederation therefore would be through an entrenched bilateral process and through the Office of the Treaty Commissioner.

Protection of our rights must be guaranteed in the annual Conferences on the Economy and Other Matters, and in the Constitutional Conferences. These are of major significance to us. Senate reform and fisheries are on the agenda for the latter meetings. The two topics are particularly important to the First Nations.

A conference must immediately be convened between the Prime Minister and the Treaty Indian Nations to discuss our inherent and Treaty rights, and their place within the Canadian Constitution, including the *Constitutional Amendment, 1987*.

The conference with the Prime Minister must have on its agenda appointment of the Treaty Commissioner. This officer would have a mandate to hold hearings and report on the federal government's performance on our inherent and Treaty rights, and on what redress should be forthcoming where those rights have not been upheld, whether in constitutional or other areas. This would include a review of the government's claims policies and the development of proposals for their reform in a fair and just fashion.

In addition to the appointment of the Commissioner, other agenda items should include: Treaty rights, constitutional developments, financing Indian government, and an ongoing bilateral process.

An agreement on such an Office would issue from the bilateral Treaty process, an existing process to which the federal government should demonstrate its full commitment.

The Need for an Indian Judicial System

In the matter of Indian Justice, our judicial systems have broken down. They have been replaced by a Euro-Canadian approach, which is foreign to our people. This has led to high incarceration rates, and socioeconomic crises in our communities.

Indian peoples, in exerting their inherent right to self-government, wish to develop and enforce their own laws which will govern themselves. Discussions have been opened with the federal and provincial governments towards achieving this.

Financing Indian Government

It is essential that there be adequate finances to develop and maintain

Indian Government. A major source of such finance should be from resource-revenue sharing, that is, the Indian share from the development of all natural resources retained by the Indian Nations under Treaties and Aboriginal title.

Ian V.B. Johnson

Chief Negotiator
United Indian Council of Chippewas and Mississaugas

Introduction

This presentation will discuss briefly some ways in which First Nation governments can exercise their authority within their own areas of jurisdiction, while being consistent with the Canadian federal model and complementing existing governmental regimes. It is arguable that First Nations have a better grasp of what is possible within the Canadian federal system than the Canadian Government has.

Federalism

Many indigenous nations in North America were members of larger indigenous confederacies long before settlement, and many of these continue to operate today. First Nations citizens know that it is an essential part of life to know that you belong to a family and to a clan and at the same time be a citizen of your First Nation, a citizen of your tribal group, and a citizen of your tribal confederacy. Many Indian people know all of this and still consider themselves to be a citizen of the province in which they live and of the country as a whole. Urban Indians add to this a sense of citizenship to the city they live in.

This is not unusual. Many Canadians understand themselves to be citizens of their city, their province, and their country while also identifying themselves with the nationality and culture of their fore-fathers. Most Canadians take for granted that they have multiple citizenship and that the different governments that they are members of have different powers, authority, and jurisdiction with respect to their lives and activities. In many areas the local or provincial government has exclusive jurisdiction where the federal government cannot interfere directly. This is the federal system.

It requires only the direct application of the federal principles to which Canada adheres to recognize the powers, authority, and jurisdiction of Indian Governments.

Co-jurisdiction

It is entirely possible within the Canadian system to negotiate and implement co-jurisdictional regimes. A co-jurisdictional regime could recognize a joint and equal partnership and/or could recognize exclusive areas of jurisdiction with appropriate linkages and support systems. The United Indian Councils, for example, are negotiating recognition of exclusive First Nation jurisdiction in certain areas and co-jurisdictional regimes with the federal and provincial governments in others. Even in areas of exclusive First Nation jurisdiction, there will be provision for First Nations to utilize existing authorities and regimes to support their jurisdiction.

There are many different kinds of examples that can be cited.

Co-management

It is possible for First Nations to negotiate management control over matters that may exist under the jurisdiction of another government. This route can be advantageous where a First Nation does not want or cannot accommodate the liabilities or responsibilities in a certain area, say regional environment, but is in a position to manage or co-manage that sector. Co-management of matters off-reserve where the jurisdiction is that of another government can provide economic and employment benefits to the First Nation, while providing improved management capabilities.

General

There are many areas within Canada where existing jurisdictional and management regimes cannot meet their responsibilities. To some extent, matters such as Crown lands, park lands, conservation, the environment, justice issues, various service sectors, finance, and many other areas can be better managed under local or regional jurisdiction by the people who are most affected. Recognition of First Nation jurisdiction in these areas will provide direct benefits to the federal and provincial governments and to Canadian citizens. It also will provide the opportunity for the wealth of native and non-native resources that is currently directed at the debilitating debate over jurisdiction to be turned to the more constructive task of developing this country in the best interests of all of its residents and in the spirit of co-existence with which we all started out.

Allen Paul

Former Chief
Alexander First Nation

The Alexander Band signed a research agreement based on the federal government's self-government policy about three years ago. It was an agreement to look at the different models and the different power structures of self-government.

After this work, we want to recommend to the general public and to all levels of government that you have to keep an open mind. You have to take those blinkers off. You can't look at just one side. You have to look at it from all perspectives, if this situation is going to work.

The recognition of our rights in the *Sparrow* decision was important. When there is recognition of rights (and we're thinking in Alexander that treaty as well as aboriginal rights are included in that idea), then the right to self-government is also recognized and affirmed through different pieces of legislation.

Indian government didn't go away. Legislation didn't kill it. But, where is it? We like to use the example of the bear, when we are thinking of Indian government. The bear sleeps for a period of time, but then what happens when it wakes up? That's where we're at in Alexander. We're finally waking up to realize that something has to be done with the components of sovereignty, the recognition of Indian government. We know that it is there. It is alive. It cannot be seen, but it is there. That's where we're coming from.

We want to encourage the people all across Canada to look at this issue with an open mind, in a positive way. Again, back to the sleeping bear. It seems that when this bear wakes up, it has to do a lot of things. It has to start rebuilding its energy, some of its thinking, how it is going to survive. Well, that is how we see it in Alexander—we have to start rebuilding some of those institutions, to start rebuilding our strength.

How we start rebuilding our strength is by looking at ourselves as

Indian people. We have to do a lot of personal growth. We have to start healing our communities, to start rebuilding the institutions. We have to start rebuilding the languages that were destroyed. We have to start rebuilding our cultures, the things that were outlawed, the potlatch, the sundances. These types of things we have to rebuild. While we are doing that, we have to start building the new things. In order to make power-sharing work, we have to start building our schools. We have to start building our education programs. We have to start building new programs to look after the elderly and the children.

We also have to start rebuilding some of our own systems that sometimes governments think that we didn't have. I'm talking, for example, of child welfare. They're saying we didn't have child welfare, and that we have to go with their legislation. In Alexander, we feel differently.

We also have to look at lands. Alexander has looked at lands from a totally different perspective. Our people are saying that it is our land, but yet the federal government tells us, no you are just using it. We are loaning it to you. We're agents of the Crown, so to speak. We are trying to correct this attitude.

We have to take a different approach to land because our people feel it is a very important aspect of self-determination. We're also using the different court decisions on which our rights are recognized. We're looking at 1763, the *Royal Proclamation*, and we're also looking at the different precedents that recognize that Indian government is there. Every time the province comes to the chief and council on any reserve across the country, that means that they are recognizing us, that they have to go to us for approval.

There are different ways that we can probably look at how sharing power can work. We know we have shared power in our band. What about the federal government and the provincial government? Again, we will look at the example of the bear. If you look at the bear from the Indian perspective, that's Indian sovereignty. If you look at the guy that wants to throw the turd, well, that's the federal government. Once they do so, they will go and say the bear took off, but what that guy will do is go get a gun and start shooting those Indians. That's exactly what's happening today. The moment that you oppose any government policy, they're going to get you one way or the other. They'll get you by giving you less funding for housing. They'll find excuses to say we'll give everything to the province, because you can't look after yourself.

In closing, I want to say that we have used the federal self-government policy to do research, but we're changing the perspective of that around. We're using that self-government policy not to look at delegated authority, but to look at different models of Indian government, and to look at sovereignty. So we can change that around. We're not looking at it as Indian Affairs does. We're looking at it as tribal members.

Sharon McIvor

Executive Board Member
Native Women's Association of Canada

I have listened to people talk about the concept of self-government and where the roots of aboriginal self-government or First Nations government comes from, and have come to the conclusion that the terms in which we're speaking are non-aboriginal terms. This is particularly true about the concept of power. As aboriginal women, we don't have power. As aboriginal communities, we don't have power. What we have, and what we have had traditionally, is responsibility. We have responsibility for our people.

I was talking to a friend of mine, and we discussed this symposium and what self-government means and then looked back into the aboriginal language, and there is no term synonymous with self-government. The closest thing that we could come to was "the way we live." As aboriginal women, we have the responsibility for the way we live. We have had it traditionally, and we still have it. We have responsibility for the land. We have the responsibility for the families. We have the responsibility for the health and happiness of our families. That could be translated, I suppose, into self-government.

The problem with responsibility and power is that power gives the connotation that there is something that you can wield at will. We've witnessed it with our Prime Minister wanting to wield his power to get things passed that he would like, and being fair to him, he thinks it is best for everyone concerned. In aboriginal communities, we don't have one person speaking for the community and making decisions for a community without consulting the community. That's the difference between power and responsibility. We don't want the power, because power corrupts. And we don't want to corrupt our communities. We want to have the responsibility to have control over the way we live.

We have talked and played a lot of word games and semantics about where do we get this power, so to speak, to control the way we live.

We have talked about the common law of aboriginal title, when in the 1600s, Spain and Portugal talked about whether the aboriginal people of the New World were human or not, and decided, after much debate, that they were. Once they decided they were human, certain rights were attached to being human, and I believe aboriginal title might have been one of those. We have talked about the *Proclamation of 1763* and how it recognized whatever rights we had. We talked about Section 35 of the Constitution and how it protects aboriginal rights and whatever aboriginal rights holds for us. Again, word games and semantics.

We have the right to have control over the way we live. The debate isn't whether that right is there. The debate is over who recognizes that right, and whether we talk about pigeon-holing it in different kinds of concepts or not. We as aboriginal women know we have that right.

How do we make it work? We have to have the involvement of our communities. We as aboriginal women working in the field of aboriginal women's rights talk to our women, and when we ask, "What do you think about aboriginal self-government?" the answer invariably is, "I want to know how I am going to feed my children today. I don't have time to worry about self-government. I want to have a place to sleep, to protect my children today. I don't have time." Until we get our people into a position where they don't have to worry about the basics of health of our children, and food for our families, and shelter for our families, it is very difficult to talk about representing our communities and self-government for our communities.

It has been mentioned that federal Minister of Justice Kim Campbell said that there would never be a separate justice system for aboriginal people. It is very, very difficult to imagine our people staying in the justice system when the percentages of them actually in the system is proportionately higher than non-aboriginal people. We talk about who do the police pick up? Who do they suspect of crimes? Our people normally fall into that category. When in custody, our people's rights are more often violated than are the rights of non-aboriginal people.

When we go into the court systems, our people tend to receive higher sentences, go to prison more often. When they get into prison, they tend to stay there. They don't get paroled as often. When you try to get into the justice system and educate who is there on the aboriginal concepts, it is really difficult to teach someone who for the last forty-five years has had certain touchstones of values, and tell them there is a whole different set of values out here. Very, very difficult.

In conclusion, our position is that First Nations must be able to have full control over the way we live. To ask for permission or to take legislative permission, which has been suggested at various times, is akin to forfeiting or selling out the right and the duty that we owe to our future generations of First Nations people. When we deal with our non-aboriginal counterparts, and speak about taking control over the way we live, we have to do it on our own principles. To go in and negotiate with deception and make plans for movement is against aboriginal principles. We must deal in our own principles, and those are the principles of integrity and respect. As many of you know, we haven't had a lot of respect, and we haven't been dealt with with integrity for a long period of time, but to give that up for ourselves is buying in to what has brought our destruction.

Dick Martin

Executive Vice-President
Canadian Labour Congress

The concept of power-sharing is an important one and critical to a resolution of the grave problems confronting First Nations. The starting point for discussions about power-sharing arrangements must be premised on mutual respect and good faith. We have witnessed all too clearly that this is not the case in Canada.

The contemporary reality of indigenous peoples is dire and can be understood in terms of the consequences of a process that has involved dispossession from, and physical colonization of, indigenous lands and exploitation of their natural resources. Indigenous social and political institutions have been suppressed and supplanted in varying degrees by legal and administrative systems imposed by the dominant state. Although these practices began in the age of European colonialism, they have been continued through the actions of successor states structurally indistinguishable from those of the colonial era.

Ever since the first Europeans set foot in the so-called "New World," indigenous cultures have been under attack. The Indians, then the Inuit, were systematically taught to believe that their religions, their languages, their ways of raising children, their whole way of life should be discarded. Although the natives' enforced retreat has resulted in shocking casualties, they have refused to assimilate.

European and successor states have consigned indigenous issues to domestic contexts, using racist, paternalistic doctrines and rationales for political advantage in the acquisition of indigenous lands and resources.

It was much easier to deal with indigenous nations if they were deemed to be under the jurisdiction of the colonial power, characterized as a "domestic problem" and thereby removed from international scrutiny and the protections afforded by international legal standards.

This unilateral action was carried out with neither the compliance nor the consent of the affected indigenous nations. States talked more and more of "aboriginal rights" in a domestic context and less of how to justify legally their own territorial and sovereignty claims. Because of this inversion, indigenous nations found themselves on the defensive, having to justify their claims to land and other rights through the dominant colonizing power's courts.

Indigenous peoples enter into negotiations acutely aware that the recent past has been desperate, the present seems hopeless, and the future looks bleak. We must begin to redress basic injustices that still constitute the reality of the indigenous peoples. The Canadian Labour Congress feels we have a particular obligation to provide the support necessary as indigenous nations continue their quest for recognition. It is a role that requires jettisoning the paternalistic baggage we have inherited through centuries of a self-imposed colonial mentality. We have to learn to distinguish between providing support for, as opposed to direction to, indigenous peoples. The latter is a prerogative of the peoples themselves. Failure to do so will perpetuate the mentality that is the root of injustices we seek to redress.

We recognize that the concept of power-sharing must be firmly rooted in the principle of self-determination. Until this is so, First Nations will continue to be viewed as supplicants in their own territories.

Doreen Quirk

President
Federation of Canadian Municipalities

You have asked me to address the topic "Sharing Power: How Can First Nations Government Work." Before I do, I'd like to explain to you what the Federation of Canadian Municipalities is. The Federation of Canadian Municipalities or FCM is an association which represents 575 municipalities across the country as well as fifteen provincial/territorial associations and one Indian District, the District of Sechelt Indian Government in British Columbia. I note that the Sechelt Indian Band is one of two bands that already have a self-government act in place.

FCM was formed fifty-three years ago to represent local government interests and to pursue research and education on matters of concern to municipalities. Our municipal members comprise 75 percent of the Canadian population. Municipalities are the level of government closest to the vast majority of Canadians. Municipal leaders often know first-hand how most people feel about the major issues of the day, whether they be protecting the environment, affordable housing, or new ways of coping with drug addiction and crime prevention in our society. Native rights is also a concern that many municipal politicians share.

Like the First Nations, municipalities are not recognized in Canada's Constitution. The *British North America Act* of 1867 divided powers between the federal and the provincial governments. The federal government kept for itself those powers considered in 1867 to be the most important—the power to levy direct and indirect taxes and the right to make laws on banking, interest and currency, trade and commerce, the military, navigation and fisheries, criminal law, weights and measures, copyright, penitentiaries, the postal service, marriage and divorce, and, as you well know, Indians and land reserved for Indians. In addition, all powers not explicitly enumerated in the *B.N.A. Act* were to be vested in the federal government.

The *B.N.A. Act* gave the provinces powers over issues that in 1867 were considered to be of lesser importance: education, hospitals, municipal institutions, provincial jails, saloons, the "solemnization of marriage," property and civil rights, and the administration of justice.

Thus, in 1867 and in Canada's new Constitution, municipalities are not considered a legitimate level of government, but rather "creatures of the provinces."

The powers and authority of local government in Canada are derived from provincial and territorial statutes such as the *Municipal Act*, the *Planning Act*, the *Line Fences Act*. The broad scope of local government activity arises much more from the services expected by citizens than through any constitutional underpinning. The degree of local autonomy varies among provinces, with the province of Quebec offering the greatest independence to its municipalities.

Although the powers and responsibilities in municipalities vary from province to province, we are generally responsible for providing services to our citizens in the following areas:

- Fire protection and emergency services;
- Community health;
- Environmental protection;
- Policing;
- Building and maintenance of parks;
- Provision of recreational programs and the building of community centres, including ice rinks and swimming pools;
- Building and maintenance of local roads;
- Building and maintenance of sewers and water mains and ensuring our citizens an adequate supply of clean water;
- Garbage collection and waste disposal;
- Local planning;
- Building inspection;
- Enforcement of bylaws;
- Protection of heritage buildings;
- Provision of public transit;
- Industrial development, that is, the attracting of a large number of industrial and commercial enterprises; and
- Libraries (although the latter are generally run by a Library Board, most of their revenue comes from the municipality).

In addition, we have a social assistance role in perhaps half of the Canadian provinces. We administer and partially fund social services such as day care, housing for seniors and others, and longterm welfare. In most, but not all, provinces, education is provided by regional boards of education led by school trustees elected at the same time as municipal councillors.

And how, you may ask, do we pay for all this? In a number of ways:

1. Conditional grants from your provincial governments—these grants are earmarked for specific purposes, such as policing, building roads, maintaining libraries, running a transit system, both regular and for the disabled, or for education. The provinces feel that if they didn't set down conditions, we might "squander" their money on other things.

2. Other provincial grants are called unconditional grants. We may spend them as we wish. These grants tend to fluctuate according to the political philosophy of the provincial government of the day. Under Ontario's former Liberal government, our unconditional grants were drastically reduced, as we were not deemed to be wise enough to choose our own spending priorities. Ontario's new NDP government seems intent on further restricting our powers through even more acts and regulations, although they did raise our unconditional grants for 1991.

3. Grants in lieu of taxes. Most municipalities contain property that is owned by other levels of government. Since both the federal and the provincial governments feel they're superior to municipal governments, they are unwilling to pay us property taxes. However, they have recognized many of the costs we incur in providing service to their property, particularly in areas where there is a military base or a large number of government buildings. Thus, each year both the federal and provincial governments pay every municipality a grant to compensate for our services to their property.

4. Property taxes provide approximately 50 percent of our revenues. As we all know, property taxes are a very regressive form of taxation, as there is no direct correlation between the tax and the ability to pay. In many provinces, the provincial governments are shifting more and more responsibilities onto municipalities and school boards without giving us the money to pay for them, so the average citizen in my municipality, for instance, is now paying approximately $2500.00 a year in property taxes. Seventy-three percent of that goes for education, while Markham and our Regional government split the other 27 percent. You can see why municipalities in Ontario and in many other provinces feel they need other powers of taxation. Maybe other provinces should heed the example of New Brunswick and Quebec and to a lesser extent, British Columbia, who have removed the costs of social services and education from the property tax.

5. Debentures are available to municipalities for longer term financing of ten, twenty, or thirty years. A debenture is similar to a mortgage. They are calculated as a percentage of a municipality's operating budget, and in Ontario, for example, the Ontario Municipal Board has various formulas to ensure that the amount a municipality borrows does not exceed prescribed limits. Again, municipalities generally must get approval from someone else before they can borrow money via a debenture. In Ontario, no local municipality can issue a debenture. We must get approval from our regional government (that is, Metropolitan Toronto as opposed to the City of Toronto), and also from an appointed body called the Ontario Municipal Board.

6. Business taxes, which again are tightly controlled by legislation.

7. Finally, municipalities have resorted, in increasing measure, to user fees. If you want to play hockey, you pay the municipality all or part of the cost of making ice. If you want your child to take swimming lessons or you want to take an exercise class, you pay for the privilege. Developers pay for new sewers and water mains

and make substantial contributions to our capital costs in providing community centres, firehalls, arenas, and libraries. Builders pay through their building permits and taxi drivers through their license fees the cost of inspecting their buildings or their taxis. This helps to ensure that taxpayers who don't use many services (and I'm thinking mainly of seniors) at least don't pay for their total cost.

How are municipal governments structured? There are many models, but all include a mayor who is elected every three or four years by all the eligible voters of the municipality. Councils also have a number of aldermen or councillors. Originally, all elected city representatives were called by the British term "alderman." Lately, many councils have chosen to call themselves "councillors" to recognize that some of the aldermen are women! There is no such word as "alderwoman."

Councillors or aldermen may be elected at large across the municipality with everyone entitled to vote for four or five or however many are to be elected. Or they may be elected by wards. Some municipalities (like mine) use a combination of the two. My town has four councillors elected by voters from across the municipality and eight who represent one individual ward. The benefit of individual ward councillors is one of accountability. When all are responsible, sometimes no one accepts the responsibility.

In fast growing areas of British Columbia, Ontario, and Quebec, the provinces have created regional governments and have delegated a few of their powers to the region—the power to approve subdivisions for example. Each region operates under its own provincial act, and each one (even in the same province) appears to differ in at least some respects from its fellows.

Who may vote in a municipal election? Anyone who owns property or is a tenant in that municipality. But you may only vote once in a municipality. If you have time, you could vote in Markham (where your home is located), in Gravenhurst (where you own a cottage), and in North York (where you own a business and lease a property for that business).

How do councils run their municipalities? The most effective councils act as a Board of Directors who set policy and make periodic checks to ensure that their policies are being carried out. They hire staff to manage the corporation on a day to day basis. For example, Council will make a policy decision to snowplow the streets whenever there is a snowfall of two inches. Staff will hire the snowplow operators and will tell them which streets to plow first and how many

89

times a street should be plowed to achieve Council's desired standard. Occasionally, individual councillors start trying to manage their corporation. That's when problems arise and costs escalate.

Whether or not the model of local government in Canada will be useful in the quest of Canada's aboriginal peoples for self-government and their proper place in Confederation is not for me to decide. I recognize that you want far greater jurisdiction than we municipalities can exercise. I can give assurance, however, that FCM and its members would be more than happy to assist by way of expertise and advice should structures similar to local governments be created.

I thank you again for inviting us to take part in this panel discussion. The FCM hopes that you can learn from us and that we can keep on learning from you—in so doing, we will all better be able to make decisions that will lead to the best kind of coexistence and sharing so that all Canadians can lead worthwhile and richly creative lives free from want and discrimination—in a genuine spirit of mutual respect and harmony.

George Da Pont

Director General
Community Negotiations and Implementation Branch
Department of Indian Affairs and Northern Development

First Nations want a new relationship with the Government of Canada. The Department of Indian Affairs and Northern Development (DIAND) supports that goal.

The purpose of this paper is to elaborate briefly on a few of the steps that DIAND is taking to bring that goal closer to reality.

Constitutional Recognition of Aboriginal Self-Government

First Nations' preferred option to enhance their governmental powers lies in an amendment to the Constitution of Canada. The federal government remains committed to pursuing constitutional recognition of aboriginal self-government.

In the post-Meech climate, however, the constitutional schedule is not clear. In the meantime, the Government will continue to work with aboriginal peoples—within the existing constitutional framework—to realize their aspirations.

A number of options are open now to First Nations to enhance their governmental powers. These options include initiatives both beyond the *Indian Act*, and within its confines.

Beyond the Indian Act

Progress has been made to move beyond the *Indian Act*. The most significant steps in this process are community self-government negotiations and a major joint review of the lands, revenues, and trusts (LRT) aspects of the *Indian Act*.

The objective of the federal government's community self-government process is to negotiate practical new arrangements for First Nations' government at the community level. These arrangements are given effect through legislation. If a community decides to take this route, most aspects of the *Indian Act* can be replaced with legislatively sanctioned new arrangements, designed specifically for that community.

It must be stressed here that the community self-government process does not replace the constitutional process. The negotiation process and any agreements and legislation that result will not interfere with treaty and aboriginal rights, or the eventual outcome of any constitutional deliberations. However, working self-government arrangements will no doubt play a useful role in shedding light on certain aspects of the constitutional process.

Community self-government negotiations are based upon three principles.

- First, the negotiated arrangements will substantially increase local control and decision-making.
- Second, the process is flexible in order to accommodate the social, cultural, and political diversity of Indian communities across Canada.
- Third, the new governing arrangements will lead to greater accountability by Indian governments to their own electorate rather than to federal authorities.

A broad range of topics can be discussed within the community negotiations process.

Some of these are basic to the foundations of community-based self-government, and must be included in a self-government agreement. These topics include:

- institutions and procedures of government;
- membership;
- land and resources management;

91

- legal status and capacity;
- financial arrangements;
- application of the *Indian Act*;
- negotiation of an implementation plan; and
- the negotiation of an environmental impact review regime.

Self-government agreements can also include a wide variety of other subject matters, such as: education, culture, health, child welfare, social services, environmental management, and the administration of justice.

In these areas, the nature and extent of community control depends on negotiation with other levels of government. The aim here is to make as much room as possible for the exercise of authority by the community government and to create workable practical arrangements, tailored to the circumstances of each community.

At this time, the Government of Canada is in substantive negotiation with some thirty bands, and a further twenty-nine bands are at the framework negotiations stage. About 170 additional bands are undertaking developmental work on self-government. In our experience, communities that have been working for some years to enhance their own administrative and financial skills may find this a useful preparation for community self-government negotiations.

Community self-government negotiations work best when they are community driven. The Government of Canada works closely with the community to provide advice on constructing contemporary forms of public administration. That is ultimately the challenge, to design structures of public administration to suit the needs of communities in Canada today.

The Government considers community self-government arrangements an important adjunct to the comprehensive land claims process.

Community self-government negotiations are open to those communities involved in comprehensive land claims negotiations. For example, in Yukon, as provided for in the *Umbrella Final Agreement* between Canada and the Council for Yukon Indians, the Government can work towards self-government arrangements with the bands. Under a land claims framework agreement, the Government is also working towards self-government arrangements with the Nisga'a in British Columbia.

Presently, there are two self-government acts in place, the *Cree-Naskapi (of Quebec) Act*, and the *Sechelt Indian Band Self-Government Act*. It is anticipated that in the next three to four years we will see more First Nations' self-government legislation.

Perhaps one of the most important initiatives in enhancing First Nations' governmental powers is the Government and First Nations joint review of the LRT aspects of the *Indian Act*. While many First Nations agree that self-government is their ultimate goal, the *Indian Act* will likely continue to play a large role for many Indian communities.

The review of the *Indian Act* is providing the forum for the discussion of a broad range of issues that directly affect First Nations government, including the kind of powers First Nations need to exercise control over lands, monies, membership, and the governmental structures that best suit First Nations' goals.

It is important to note that any changes to the *Act* would be optional: First Nations will determine what options best meet their needs. A number of communities feel that there should be an incremental process to move from the *Indian Act* to self-government.

With the current review, and with First Nations involvement, the *Act* can be transformed into a more flexible document aimed at enabling Indian communities to take greater control of their affairs.

Within the Indian Act

Many tools for greater autonomy, many tools to make First Nations government work, exist now.

First Nations can exercise a measure of local control under the current *Indian Act*. The Government is currently involved with First Nations in supporting increased local control through the exercise of these authorities. While the Government recognizes that there are limitations to the amount of local control that can be achieved by these means, the Government is fully committed to establishing the capacity of communities to take on increased powers.

First Nations can, for instance, make use of their bylaw powers under Sections 81, 83 and 85 of the *Indian Act* in order to enhance local authority. The Department of Indian Affairs and Northern Development has undertaken a number of activities in order to support First Nations in the development of bylaws. For example, trained professional staff are available to advise First Nations on bylaws and to ensure better performance of departmental responsibilities in relation to bylaws; a bylaw handbook has been published and distributed to First Nations; training courses are being conducted; and discussions are occurring between First Nations and local law enforcement agencies in order to secure better enforcement of bylaws.

First Nations' desire for increased local control will continue to be supported in other areas as well, such as the management of lands and monies, the conduct of elections, membership control, and on an individual level, estate planning.

Under the *Indian Act* as it is presently structured, bands may assume a role in managing their own lands by exercising delegated authorities under sections 53 and 60 of the *Act*. Under section 53 a band may sign leases and permits for its designated lands on behalf of the Crown. Under section 60 a band may approve allotments, set aside land for community purposes, sign permits, and sign locatee leases on behalf of the Crown.

There are limitations inherent in these delegations, however, and they derive from the fact that under sections 53 and 60 of the *Act* the band is acting as an agent of the Crown. As such, the band is subject to departmental policies and procedures, and may not take any actions which would put the Crown at risk. Bands exercising section 53 and 60 authorities may not therefore institute legal actions on behalf of the Crown, and may not take any actions, such as cancelling leases or permits, which might lead to legal action against the Crown.

In the area of elections, a First Nation may choose to select its chief and council either under custom or under the electoral provisions of the *Indian Act*. Some First Nations, having held their elections under the *Indian Act* in the past, have requested the Minister to remove the application of the *Indian Act* from their elections so that they can return to a custom procedure. The department has developed a policy to deal with these requests, and a number of bands have returned to selecting their leadership under their custom.

Bands now have the option of establishing their own band membership rules and assuming control of their membership. This option enables First Nations to have local control over this very fundamental matter.

Financial/Program Initiatives

Devolution has enabled First Nation governments to assume greater control over the administration and delivery of federally-sponsored community programs. As a result of devolution, some 70 percent of DIAND's *Indian and Inuit Affairs* budget of nearly $2.4 billion is now transferred to First Nations for the delivery of programs such as education, child welfare and social services, and housing and community infrastructure.

94

Rather than the Government administering and delivering these programs, Indian community officials—who are in closer touch with the needs and desires of the community—manage community programs in the most appropriate manner. For instance, the number of band-operated schools increased from 53 in 1975/76 to 280 in 1988/89, a fivefold increase.

Alternative funding arrangements with DIAND is another avenue to work towards placing greater control in the hands of First Nations government. AFAs provide for much more flexible financial and administrative agreements between First Nations and the federal government. AFAs permit communities to budget more efficiently and deliver services more effectively.

Long-term planning is greatly improved because the community knows at the start of each fiscal year what its budget will be, and exactly when monies will be paid. Under AFA, the community can reallocate funds among various programs once an agreed level of service has been delivered. This allows *community* leaders to place resources where, in their judgement, they are most needed.

To date, some 73 AFA agreements have been signed involving 136 bands, for a value of $1.1 billion over five years. By the end of the fiscal year 1990/91, we anticipate that fully 25 percent of DIAND contribution funds will be under the AFA process.

First Nations also can participate in tripartite agreements. Through these, First Nations can play a greater role in the development and delivery of social programs and economic development activities.

One example of a tripartite agreement is the *Canada-Nova Scotia-Indian Child and Family Services Agreement* recently signed between the Micmac Family and Children's Services Agency, the federal government, and the Nova Scotia government. The Agreement transfers authority and funding for delivery of child and family services on reserve in Nova Scotia to the Micmac Family and Children's Services Agency.

Since 1981 in Ontario, to give another example, tripartite agreements have provided for the delivery of band police services to some sixty-five bands.

The Government is also working to strengthen the economic base of First Nations communities, a fundamental source of local autonomy. This is being done via the promotion of viable community-based economic development through a series of coordinated policies, including an improved Indian taxation regime, the Indian business development program, and assistance to communities

95

through the Resource Development Program to identify and help them exploit mineral, oil, and gas holdings.

Conclusion

When discussing the issue of how First Nations government can be enhanced, it is important to bear in mind that there are a variety of ways already available to First Nations who wish to increase their decision-making powers and autonomy. Whether a community wishes to pursue its goals through the means available within current policies—the provisions of the *Indian Act* or the provisions of a revised *Indian Act* that provides for more local control—or through the community-based self-government negotiations process, the tools for such change are available to First Nations today.

The Government of Canada is committed to moving on all fronts to achieve greater autonomy and self-sufficiency for First Nations. The initiatives above are those we are working on now, in close cooperation with the First Nations. These, however, are not necessarily the only avenues towards a better future. The Government remains open to creative ideas and plans to suit the needs of the First Nations. The impetus for the increased autonomy the First Nations seek must come from the First Nations themselves. The ultimate goal of the federal government is to put decision-making power where it belongs—in the hands of the First Nations communities.

Charles Wilkinson

Moses Lasky Professor of Law
University of Colorado at Boulder

It is an honour and a pleasure to have the chance to learn more about the important events in First Nations' policy in Canada. I am going to briefly give one person's perspective on developments and tribal strategies which have occurred in the United States, and will suggest some avenues that might be taken as well as some others that might best not be taken in Canada. American Indian leaders and their supporters are looking up to Canada with genuine respect for the persistence and courage you have displayed and for the progress that you have managed to make in spite of difficult times.

As you know, one of the cornerstones of United States' federal Indian policy and law is embodied within three opinions penned by

Chief Justice John Marshall. Commonly known as the Marshall trilogy, these case opinions were handed down by the Supreme Court between the years 1823 to 1832. These three opinions laid out most of the comprehensive principles that even today govern the relations between American Indians and the federal government over land, political power, and natural resources issues.

The Marshall trilogy is something of a "mixed bag." The doctrine of discovery was announced; yet, on the other hand, there was a square recognition of aboriginal land rights. Additionally, the trust relationship was acknowledged as well as Congress' broad power over Indian affairs. Perhaps the greatest statement made on this subject was written in 1832 in the *Worcester v. Georgia* opinion. I really believe that this is one of the most significant statements on human rights that a nation has ever made: the recognition of the tribal sovereignty of American Indian tribes. It was announced with true respect by our greatest jurist, John Marshall, and had such great potential that it has been relied upon in Canada, Australia, and elsewhere.

Over the next century and a quarter, the Marshall decisions remained on the books, but the government did not act in accordance with them much at all. From the 1850s through the early 1960s, tribes suffered great land losses. There was warfare, assimilation, and other policies that took American Indians into a deep trough. The truth is, they are still trying to dig themselves out of the results of that era's government policies.

Beginning in the late 50s and early 60s, Indians in the United States began what is one of the greatest social movements that has ever taken place in the country during the post-World War II era. The tribes developed a rough consensus on what needed to be achieved and on how to go about making the necessary changes, and they began their difficult work. One of the main tactics of that consensus was a litigation strategy that resulted in nearly one hundred cases being handed down from the United States Supreme Court alone. Furthermore, well over one thousand tribal rights cases were decided in the lower courts.

For the most part, the tribes prevailed during that historic litigation offensive. The rights of tribal courts became and are now, I think, quite extensive. They have misdemeanour jurisdiction, including serious misdemeanour jurisdiction, over their own members, and have broad civil jurisdiction over non-tribal-members. The right to tax and to regulate tribal affairs was recognized, including the right to tax and regulate, in some circumstances, non-Indians. The litigation offensive also included natural resources issues, and the tribes established extensive water, hunting, and fishing rights. One of the more important decisions regarding tribal rights to natural resources use was a 1979 decision in the Pacific Northwest, the Boldt decision, which recognized the broad off-reservation fishing rights of tribes.

The tribes also were active in Congress and developed their own legislative agenda. Again, it was an informal agenda, one recognizing that just as Congress has plenary power to deny tribal rights, so too does Congress have broad power to recognize tribal rights. Tribes obtained, with varying degrees of success, legislation dealing with reform of the Bureau of Indian Affairs, with economic development, and with natural resources issues, including major settlements in water development disputes.

Perhaps most importantly, the Indian Child Welfare Act was passed in 1978, legislation many of you are familiar with and which might be of real use to you in Canada in upcoming years. This Act gives tribes not only complete jurisdiction over adoptions of children who live on the reservation, but also provides strict rules for judges to follow when an Indian child's custody is adjudicated in state courts.

Since about 1989, we have seen a turn in a Supreme Court that had developed a very powerful tradition of recognizing the minority rights and the sovereignty of tribes. While there have been a couple of decisions favourable to the tribes, it is clear that this Court will no longer see itself as the Court of last resort for American Indians and other dispossessed people. There have been a number of decisions that, by their results and also by their language, have cut into tribal sovereignty, or at least indicate that it is not at all likely that tribal sovereignty will be expanded.

Most recently, tribes in the United States have undergone a reassessment. They will continue to litigate in the courts. They have to do that. Yet, although they will continue to win some cases, there is a recognition that the "real action" from now on will take place in Indian country itself. As a result, tribes are now working hard to enhance their economic development and are increasingly providing more services. For example, there are now twenty-eight Indian colleges operating on the reservations. Additionally, there are an increasing number of elementary schools and clinics as well. I believe that these are very important developments. Tribes are also engaging in more extensive natural resource management, trying to buttress the actual exercise of sovereignty in Indian country.

I continue to believe that there is much for both Canadian natives and tribes in the United States to learn from each other. Admittedly, I am not as conversant with the issues in Canada as I would like to be, but I do have one impression, that, in spite of the extraordinarily difficult context in which you are operating, the Canadian natives may have a real advantage due to the knowledge and sophistication that your leadership possesses. A person can reasonably expect that after five, ten, or fifteen years, you will look back upon the ferment that is occurring now as a very historic time of accomplishment.

Richard Simeon

Professor of Political Science
University of Toronto

I cannot in any sense be considered an expert on the profound questions that the country, and this conference, must deal with, as we consider how to define and implement aboriginal self-government in Canada. My reading in preparation for this presentation only confirmed that fact to me, as I saw the bewildering complexity of issues, the vast variety of interests and positions, the huge range of possible alternatives for constitutionalizing self-government, the complex, and still not fully resolved, questions about process, and so on.

So, I will speak simply as one concerned non-aboriginal Canadian citizen, one whose chief interest is in the operation of our federal system. I will speak not of the interests of aboriginal groups, but of what the Macdonald Commission calls the "Canadian constitutional order." I want to offer some very tentative observations on some of the issues that are raised in the debate about the character of the Canadian political system, the quality of our democracy, the meaning and nature of the multiple political communities within which we live, and the evolution of our constitutional system with its three existing "pillars" of parliamentary government, federalism, and a constitutional charter of rights.

I start with a number of premises that guide my own thinking. First, that whatever the difficulties in defining, entrenching, and implementing it, I am fundamentally in agreement with the legitimacy and desirability of autonomy and self-government for aboriginal communities in Canada. I agree with Mr. Penner that this is part of the completion of the circle of Confederation.

Second, that while the larger Canadian community has legitimate interests at stake, and legitimate values to preserve, the presumption must be that it is the aboriginal peoples' conception of their needs and interests which must be the starting point. This, it seems to me is the real importance of the term "self-determination."

Third, that it is vital that the concept be explicitly recognized in the Constitution, more directly than it is at the moment. But having said that, I also think we need to get the discussion of the real, practical concrete moves towards self-government off the constitutional table as soon as possible. Indeed, the constitutional framework is essential: to underline the legitimacy of the fundamental claim, to create a genuine obligation to make progress, and to provide a means whereby agreements can be given permanence.

The constitutional process also has large costs. It puts a premium on the symbolic, the abstract, the issues around which compromise is most difficult. It seems to create, partly for that reason, an incentive for all sides to keep the debate going on and on, with no resolution. All parties seem to have an incentive to avoid bringing the debate to a conclusion.

Keeping the debate at the constitutional level means that we devote an inordinate amount of time to crossing the t's and dotting the i's in order to anticipate every possible eventuality which might end up before the courts. Moreover, the language of the debate seems to have become mired in mind-numbing, legalistic detail conducted among a group of arcane specialists. This threatens to lose sight of the great principles and purposes, and to make it very hard to build public support for the goal of aboriginal self-government. There is a drastic need to simplify.

All this means that the constitutional process diverts an enormous amount of skill, talent, money, and time—both of governments and native leaders—to these negotiations and away from the even more enormous task of the social, economic, and cultural development of the aboriginal peoples, and the education of Canadians in support of greater economic and political justice for them.

Fourth, no doubt a great many non-aboriginal Canadians regard these discussions with a mixture of boredom, frustration, and hostility. My own view is, rather, that we should—just as with the earlier debate over Quebec in the federation—regard them as a great privilege.

The issues raised here go to the very heart of the most fundamental questions about our political life—about the meaning and nature of democracy, community, rights; about our sense of justice and fairness; about coming to terms with our own past. They pose, in stark terms, profound questions about the relationship between the individual and the community. That relationship, as the recent American book *Habits of the Heart* so well demonstrates, is one that most North American societies are unable to deal with effectively. Few countries are asked to rethink these kinds of questions very often: the debate on aboriginal rights and self-government gives us that opportunity, for which we should be grateful.

I want to focus on the tensions between aboriginal self-government and some of the other basic values in our political culture. At one level, they are indeed profound; for some perhaps even irreconcilable. Stated as absolutes, as stark choices between either/or, that may be quite correct.

In the real political life of countries—and especially of Canada—there are very few absolutes. We are for parliamentary government with its assumption of majority rule. But we are also prepared to temper that first with federalism—since it limits the scope of authority for majorities at both the federal and provincial level—and more recently with the Charter of Rights and Freedoms. We are for provincial autonomy, but are willing to temper that with certain national norms in the area of individual rights, and we have a national, constitutional commitment to using the authority of the federal government to transfer wealth from richer to poorer regions. We are for individual rights, but have tempered them with constitutional procedures which allow at least some of them to be overridden in the name of majority rule.

And so on and on. In the real world, political values are seldom pure. They are a collection of "oughts" which continually get in each others way. The political process is all about how they are reconciled in practice. Absolutism in the defence of these kinds of values, despite Barry Goldwater's statement that "extremism in the defence of liberty is no vice," is untenable.

Moreover, all of Canadian history, perhaps especially its recent constitution-making process, demonstrates our ability to make these somewhat awkward compromises. They are awkward, in the sense that they seem to introduce inconsistencies and contradictions into our constitutional life. But when we realize that they represent attempts to balance different "goods" rather than unconscionable derogations from some pure value, we see them not as awkward and illegitimate, but rather as the simple conditions of a life together in a country like Canada.

It is this accommodating, indeed capacious character of what Alan Cairns calls the "living constitution," and especially the precedents federalism provides, that makes me optimistic about an accommodation with respect to aboriginal self-government. I realize that given aboriginal leaders' frustrations with executive federalism, it is perhaps foolhardy to set federalism up as a helpful model.

101

My defence of federalist ideas here should not be seen as a defence of our current practices, but rather of the lessons implicit in the values that federalism represents—the legitimacy of multiple communities, the virtues of shared and divided authority, the hostility to homogeneous models, the advantages of small communities and decentralized power, and perhaps especially important in the present context, the stress on the idea of a "covenant" among communities. The central point I want to make is that in this complex of ideas we can find a rationale for aboriginal self-government consistent with, rather than hostile to, many forms of aboriginal self-government.

Let us look at some of the tensions in more detail. Despite what I have just said, they are real, and difficult; and even if we could all agree on the need for balancing, we would still probably end up drawing the lines in different places. In its largely unsympathetic discussion of aboriginal self-government, the Macdonald Commission raised a large number of practical issues concerning membership, financing, and the like, but its real concern was the potential effect on "the overall structure of Canadian government," on the "rights and obligations of Canadian citizenship." It stressed that any agreement must conform broadly with the institutional and constitutional structure of Canada, particularly with "Parliament, federalism and the Charter of Rights."

Liberalism: Individual Rights

The first, and most important tension is between individual rights and the rights of the community or collectivity. The overwhelming thrust of the Charter of Rights is to give primacy to the rights of individuals; and to see citizenship as an abstract, universal concept, in which each individual is the same as every other, taken out of an historical or social context. The Charter is hostile to any subordination of the individual to the collective interest; it is hostile to any differentiation of rights; it is hostile to the maintenance of distinctive cultural values.

Some see the growth of these liberal, individualist ideas as characteristic of the age. The American authors of *Habits of the Heart* see a kind of pathological dominance of the language of liberal individualism as denying us even the language or words with which to talk meaningfully about communities. Thus, the Charter has been seen not only as a *reflection* of the growth of such ideas, but also as a powerful stimulus to their extension—perhaps signalling a profound

102

change in our view of the world, sweeping more community based ideas before it, including those embodied in aboriginal self-government.

This is a very partial view—and most regrettable if it were to happen. In fact, the Charter itself contains many group rights even in its own text—for religious and linguistic groups, for aboriginal peoples, for some newly recognized groups, as well. It is not only about individual rights. Moreover, the Charter embodies explicit provisions whereby individual rights may be overridden in the interests of the larger whole.

Nor is there much, if any, evidence that our Canadian tendency to place a high value on group rights and the preservation of communities is fading. We have seen recently, just to mention a few examples: the expansion of Roman Catholic education in Ontario; the approaching division of the Northwest Territories largely on ethnic lines; and the continued support of regional development. With respect to aboriginal peoples, I don't think anyone holds anymore to the individualist model, which asserted that aboriginal peoples were to be treated no differently from other Canadians, and which was reflected in the 1969 White Paper.

More generally, it is clear that the assertion that there is a fundamental dichotomy between individual and group rights is false. In fact, it is by virtue of our membership in a larger community, and through the protection of its institutions, that we have rights at all. Community is implicit in rights. Conversely, the only justification for community is that its strength and vitality is essential to the well-being, indeed the rights, of each of its members.

Communitarian ideas remain strong in this country, and aboriginal self-government, reflecting one crucial conception of community and a profound sociological reality, therefore, retains a broad legitimacy. Canadians do indeed bristle at "special status"—the idea that some have special rights and privileges denied to others—but, it seems to me, that Canadian culture also places a very high value on community preservation, self-development and the like. The point is strongly reinforced by Rick Ponting's data. As he shows, it is entirely possible to define and justify self-government in terms which would be rejected by the vast majority of non-aboriginal Canadians. But it is equally clear that in our political culture we have an ample repertoire of terms and concepts to define and justify it in ways likely to receive very wide support. Strategic considerations alone suggest the importance of emphasizing these supportive values and symbols.

Perhaps more importantly in the Canadian context, it is not so

103

much the legitimacy of community identities per se, but rather the question of which communities are most important, and which claim primacy, that have most deeply divided us. During the constitutional debate, Prime Minister Trudeau asserted the primacy of the single national community, embodied in the federal government, over all the provincial communities. This of course clashed with the basic assumption of federalism, which asserts the equal legitimacy of provincial and national communities for different purposes. Some provinces, on the other hand, asserted an equally exclusive view of the primacy of the provincial community. These two views both clashed with the idea of Canada made up of two basic communities, based on language. The constitutional debate revolved around these conceptions, each becoming defined in more and more mutually exclusive terms.

Of course, the essential message of federalism is that it is a regime of multiple loyalties, each of which is legitimate; and its central political task is to balance, accommodate, and compromise them. Indeed, federalism itself would not survive if one image was to predominate.

Moreover, federalism assumes that there is no necessary conflict among these identities; they are complementary, indeed mutually supportive. The Canadian national community is itself defined in large part by the existence of vibrant regional communities. These provincial and regional communities, in turn, derive much of their strength and vitality from their membership in the wider Canadian community.

No policy better expresses this sense of the complementarity of regional and national communities than equalization: it is a program of the national government using its authority to tax and spend for all Canadians, whose sole purpose is to ensure the effective autonomy of the poorer provinces. It is thus *both* an expression of centralization and decentralization. It shows that the country defines as a primary purpose the strengthening of provincial communities, and that one *condition* of strong provincial self-government lies in participation in the wider community.

So federalism gives us the key to reconciling multiple communities. Moreover, while it is federal and provincial communities that are built into our political structure, we have ample precedents for recognizing many other kinds of communities and identities, both in law and in the constitution, such as language and religious groups.

The key lesson, for me, is that we are indeed in a prison so long as we tend to see identities and communities as somehow in conflict

104

with one another, when we see identities as exclusive or when we worry about *fragmented* identities. We are on much more fruitful ground when our starting point is the legitimacy, in fact desirability, of multiple loyalties, multiple communities, coexisting and strengthening each other. I think this is the lens through which we must look at aboriginal communities and their relationship with other Canadian communities, both provincial and national.

Majority Rule

Another fundamental political value in Canada with which aboriginal self-government may clash is the idea of majority rule. To the extent that aboriginal governments have real powers, not just delegated ones, they do indeed reduce the authority of the majorities represented by federal and provincial governments. Power is placed in the hands of a different majority—that of the aboriginal communities themselves.

True, this may create all sorts of practical difficulties: decisions by aboriginal governments may contradict or undermine those of other governments. As in the federal system, all sorts of intergovernmental agreements will be necessary. To the extent that there remain, as there must, extensive transfer payments to aboriginal governments, the same kinds of problems with accountability inherent in federal transfers to the provinces will arise. But again, I do not see the fundamental conflict. Or, more precisely, we must remember just how much we already temper and constrain majority rule in this country. We do so simply by the fact that we are federal: the constitution restrains both provincial and national majorities.

We now do so through the Charter. And we do so in other ways as well, such as the overrepresentation of the smallest provinces in the House of Commons and Senate. The most important current proposal for Senate reform would have a Senate with real power representing each province equally. We have not made majoritarianism, any more than our other central values, an absolute.

More generally, I think it is a truism that we cannot operate Canada successfully on the simple majority, 50 percent plus one, winner-take-all model. That is a recipe for national breakup. We must always seek the largest possible coalitions.

Again, the relevant model is federalism. I am not suggesting that aboriginal governments would be in all respects like provinces; much less that aboriginal governments automatically participate in the whole range of intergovernmental relationships. It is simply that federalism, through the division of powers, gives us the right lens. It allows us to ask: For what purposes and ends is it that the aboriginal majorities in each of their communities make policy and rule; and for what purposes is it that aboriginal peoples are part of the wider whole, with their interests represented through provincial and federal legislatures as all other citizens? What is the most appropriate division of labour?

Federalism also provides us with a rich array of instruments—equalization, unconditional grants, Economic and Regional Development Agreements, etcetera, through which assistance can flow between orders of government. Finally, federalism legitimates the ideas of decentralized, small-scale government, of a locally based democracy as that which provides the most opportunities for citizen participation, for government responsiveness, for variety and experiment—again, lessons easily extended to aboriginal self-government.

In arguing this way, I do not mean to say that there are not real difficulties here. Parliamentary sovereignty will be undermined a bit more than it already is. Federalism will be further complicated. The Charter's homogenizing, individualizing effect is likely to be tempered.

There remain massive uncertainties about the powers to be exercised by aboriginal governments; about the ambit of federal and provincial laws as they apply to aboriginal peoples; about the division of governmental authority with respect to those many aboriginals living in cities; about accountability, given continued (albeit hopefully diminished) fiscal dependency, and so on. Similarly, I do not mean to minimize the real, concrete conflicts of interest over land ownership, resources, the environment, and the like, which are bound to remain.

My point is simply that I do not see anything in the debate about aboriginal self-government that undermines my own sense of the fundamental values of Canada as a political community. On the contrary, my own conception of federalism, which welcomes and embraces cultural diversity and the positive contribution of multiple communities, combined with a strong sense of the need for sharing and redistribution, is enhanced rather than diminished by aboriginal self-government.

So to return to the Macdonald Commission's assertion that self-government must conform broadly to the institutional and constitutional structure of Canada, I would argue that it does; or, put differently, that nothing in the argument for self-government undermines my sense of the essential character of the Canadian political community, or of its already highly decentralized political structure.

We must put aside the either/or mentality, which sees only the tensions, and look for the larger complementarities. For non-aboriginal citizens and politicians, the debate will go far more easily once we put aside the fear that self-government is somehow fundamentally un-Canadian, and instead recognize that our constitutional order has been remarkably open to new conceptions, and provides a rich repertoire of instruments for making the accommodations.

We must realize that despite fears of complicating our federal system through creating a "third order of government," aboriginal self-government is fundamentally consistent with the larger values of community and democracy. Certainly it is easy to see threats to central values. But success will be found when we exercise the political will to see in aboriginal self-government not threat, but opportunity.

Implementation:
How Will First Nations Government
Happen?

Dan Christmas

Directory of Advisory Services
Union of Nova Scotia Indians

We are in a very critical period of time during which we *must* come to grips with some very pressing questions, which if left unaddressed, may consume and disrupt Canadian political life for the remainder of this decade. In the spirit of cooperation, the Union of Nova Scotia Indians is pleased to be invited to contribute its Mi'kmaq perspective to constructive dialogue. The questions that I am prepared to address are: "How do the Mi'kmaq foresee the development of their governments?" and "How do we envision their operations and functions?"

Mi'kmaq government finds its basis on aboriginal and treaty law not on parliamentary or legislative authority. The source of its power and its right to govern is, therefore, an inherent one—not deriving from any settler institution. Its relationship to settler governments is a government-to-government arrangement based upon British-Mi'kmaq treaties concluded at the time of settlement. The covenant chain of treaties is the key that defines the nature of the relationship that our ancestors sought and that we, as contemporary Mi'kmaq, wish to continue and to maintain.

It is our opinion that our ancestors sought a nation-to-nation alliance with the British Crown and strove to enter into the British Commonwealth as one of its protected states. Our ancestors' treaties clearly demonstrate the recognition of the Crown's "dominion" with the Crown's assurance of protection for the Mi'kmaq tribes.

We, therefore, believe that our modern day relationship must adhere to the very same pattern. Mi'kmaq government must be *within* the Canadian federation and continue to maintain its unique relationship to the Crown, based on the treaties. Although the Mi'kmaq did not participate in the constitutional amendment process of the mid-eighties, we had proposed that the Mi'kmaq nation be recognized as an equivalent to the provinces and that it exercise Section 92 powers as a third order of government.

With this as a background, the structure and the development of Mi'kmaq governments can now be addressed. Again, the old and the new come together. Our history tells us that the Mi'kmaq Grand Council, called "Sante Mawi'omi," conducted the nation's overall political interests. The nation was then subdivided into seven distinct districts or regions. Smaller still, individual bands or villages also exercised their own level of leadership.

Today, we still have a similar three-tiered level of Mi'kmaq

111

government. We have proposed that the pattern be expanded and developed even further. We envision our Grand Council as "the Crown in right of the Mi'kmaq" in whom is vested Mi'kmaq sovereignty and statehood. The council will continue to conduct the foreign affairs of the nation and direct church relations but have no budget and no power to make laws on its own. Political associations or tribal councils, which we have termed as Mi'kmaq regional authorities (MRAs), will perform an advisory and technical function for the Grand Council and for the bands. They would act as regional secretariats.

The bands will become autonomous, self-governing parts of the Mi'kmaq nation. They will exercise the necessary decision-making and legislative powers for their individual communities as well as jurisdiction over lands, law enforcement, education, economic development, revenues, social development, health, and other program areas. The following chart, developed in 1987, outlines the three levels of Mi'kmaq government.

The fiscal capacity of the Mi'kmaq government will derive from its aboriginal title to its traditional territory. It is clear from our history that the Mi'kmaq have never ceded any land, and, it is our strong contention, that Mi'kmaq aboriginal title remains. We firmly believe that, by virtue of the 1763 *Royal Proclamation*, Mi'kmaq territory was "reserved" until it was ceded or purchased by the Crown. This was never done.

Therefore, there still remains a Mi'kmaq interest in our traditional territory. We do not seek a lump sum cash settlement or an extinguishment of our title, but rather a recognition of our Mi'kmaq interest as defined by the *Royal Proclamation*. We have proposed that the recognition of aboriginal title become the basis of the establishment of a special Mi'kmaq property tax to be assessed against existing land users. The revenue generated from this tax levy will become the fiscal basis for the support of Mi'kmaq governments—who will enjoy full and unencumbered power to administer the resulting revenue according to its own priorities.

One further item is worth expanding on at this point. It is all but inevitable that the larger political institutions will affect Mi'kmaq governments indirectly or directly. To alleviate confrontations, we have proposed that the heads of the MRAs become automatic members of the House of Commons. Mi'kmaq aboriginal and treaty rights interests can then be represented directly within the Canadian federation. It has also been suggested that Chiefs may wish to have seats in the legislative assemblies to assure that Mi'kmaq interests are not infringed upon by provincial governments.

112

In summary, then, the Mi'kmaq perspective brings forward several direct challenges to existing policies of settler governments. The full and meaningful recognition of aboriginal and treaty rights is first and foremost. Secondly, Mi'kmaq governments must be recognized as a third order of government within the Canadian context based on those aboriginal and treaty rights. Lastly, the existing federal lands claims policy must be revised to accommodate Mi'kmaq options for resolution. We believe that these are practical, workable options that are worthy of serious debate and consideration.

Reorganization of Mi'kmaq Government

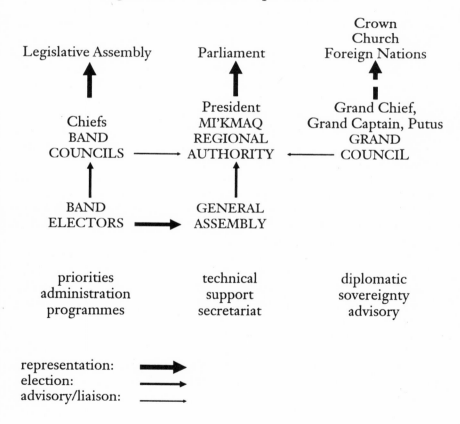

Matthew Coon-Come

Grand Chief
Grand Council of the Crees (of Quebec)

My name is Matthew Coon-Come; I am the Grand Chief of the Cree
Nation of Northern Quebec. I come to you directly from a Cree
hunting camp. This is where I go to put myself in touch with the land
and with our Cree traditions. After a few weeks in a Cree hunting
camp you get the impression that the rest of the world is not
important. Everything is there—food, shelter, friends—and once in
a while there is a certain feeling of pride in recognizing that this was
the way of our ancestors, and it is also our way. No, I didn't bring
you any moose meat. Maybe next time.

Otsimaw, that is what my people call the leader of a Cree hunting
camp. He is the one who decides where the group will go. He presides
over feasts and, following our traditions, determines the way the camp
will operate. *Otsimawin* is Cree leadership and authority. It surpasses
government, *Tibeytachewin*, because it sets the rules for good government. It is with our term *otsimaw* that we translate European concepts
referring to leadership and sovereignty.

Most of the debate in Canada about what is sometimes referred to
as "Indian self-government" takes place in the English or French
languages. This is a result of the vast linguistic and cultural differences
which characterize indigenous peoples in Canada. However, the
debate in many indigenous communities, including the Cree communities of James Bay in Quebec, is usually in the Cree language.

I raise this fact because in Cree, the concept of sovereignty,
otsimawin, has to do precisely with the issue of resource distribution
and use, and with the interpretation of our laws, that is, our traditions.

When the Cree people on the prairies signed—I might add,
without the benefit of legal counsel—the numbered treaties, they
did so with the knowledge of their traditions and with the understanding that they would be able to continue their ways of life. The
extinguishment of native title contained in those documents was a
foreign concept. This policy of extinguishment of native title
unleashed radical changes in land use and land resources use and
made the exercise of the right to continue the indigenous way of
life illusory. From the indigenous point of view—I think from the
point of view of the reasonable person—these treaties were a tragic
deception on the part of the federal government. The new factors
which intervened subsequent to the signing of the treaties and
which often made the continuation of their ways of life impossible

114

must today be considered as cause to return to the fundamental question of native rights.

In 1970 Robert Bourassa announced the construction of the James Bay Project. He proceeded with Phase I, the La Grande Project, without consulting the Cree people. We challenged and, after six months of testimony, stopped this project in the courts. One week later, the Quebec Court of Appeal overturned this decision and stated that the damages to Cree rights could be compensated. While we believe that you cannot buy a way of life, we had also lost confidence in the judiciary. We had grave concerns about the independence of the judiciary in this case; however, we knew that we would lose the La Grande River even if we appealed the main case to the Supreme Court.

We also saw that our self-appointed trustee, the federal government, was caught in a dilemma. It could not act at the same time as an advocate of our rights, when we had named it as a defendant in our suit for our rights.

We negotiated the *James Bay and Northern Quebec Agreement* because we did not have a choice. Through the agreement, which we signed under the duress of losing our lands and our way of life, we thought that we had managed to regain control of the education of our children under the Cree School Board, and of Cree health under the Cree Board of Health and Social Services, and of police, justice and local government, etcetera. We thought that we had gained a foothold in environmental protection and in the economic development of the Cree territory.

In fact, we did make some progress under the agreement, but everything that we have done has required continued court actions and confrontation. In 1982 the federal government realized that it had a shortfall of at least $62 million in implementation of the agreement. With the $32 million of this money accorded to the Crees, we renovated nursing stations and built basic sanitation facilities and water supplies in the Cree communities.

By 1986, the Auditor General of Canada reported a $190 million shortfall in implementation. The Cree communities lacked one hundred houses, promised access roads were not built, and the economic development section of the agreement had fallen flat. Cree education was not properly implemented. The Ouje-Bougoumou people lived in shacks by the side of the road; victims of mining and forestry companies, they had been relocated seven times. Nothing had been done to implement the federal obligations for environmental protection.

115

We learned through our experience with the agreement that the non-implementation by government is systemic. Not only is government unwilling to live up to its obligations, but it is often unable to do so because of the way the agreement is interpreted and twisted by bureaucrats. We call these deliberate patterns of distortion "white collar terrorism."

Now, fifteen years after signing the agreement, we find Quebec once again at our door, wanting to proceed with James Bay II. This proposal is comprised of two hydroelectric projects; the Great Whale River Project and the Nottaway-Broadback Ruperts Project.

Combined, these two projects will destroy the last eight remaining large natural rivers on the Cree territory. They are multi-basin diversion projects which will flood seven thousand square kilometres. It is equivalent to flooding the area from Toronto to Guelph and the whole Niagara Peninsula.

These projects threaten caribou calving grounds, wildfowl nesting and staging areas. They threaten rare species of birds (Eskimow Curlew), fishing, and freshwater seals, which inhabit the whole Great Whale River system. They cause mercury contamination of fish, which ultimately threaten the osprey, eagles, and man, high on the food chain. They also cause the vegetation to rot and over fifty years will send one hundred million tons of carbon emissions into the atmosphere.

History repeats itself. The James Bay II project, if it goes ahead, will make the Cree way of life impossible for all but a fraction of the present Cree population. Will the treaty, the *James Bay and Northern Quebec Agreement*, afford us the protection necessary? The record to date is not good. We pursue our case in the courts, and here today with you.

Forestry operations are also destroying our lands. In spite of guarantees in the agreement that forestry be done in accordance with the requirements for Cree land use, Quebec has illegally sold the Cree forest to multinational companies. The clearcut of six hundred square kilometres of land per year, equivalent to one Cree hunting territory, is not being done either in accordance with the principle of sustained yield or in accordance with basic principles of environmental protection. From satellite imagery, you can see the deterioration in water quality caused by these practices in the Cree territory.

What did we have in mind when we signed the James Bay and Northern Quebec Agreement? We certainly thought that the Cree way of life would continue. We had in mind something like what is contained in the international covenant on civil and political rights, to which Canada is a signatory. It states:

116

Part I, Article I:

1. All peoples have the right to self-determination, by virtue of that right they freely determine their political status and freely pursue their economic, social and cultural development.

2. All peoples may, for their own ends, freely dispose of their natural wealth and resources without prejudice to any obligations arising out of international economic cooperation, based upon the principle of mutual benefit, and international law. In no case may a people be deprived of its own means of subsistence.

3. The states parties to the present covenant, including those having responsibility for the administration of non self-governing and trust territories, shall promote the realization of the right of self-determination, and shall respect that right, in conformity with the provisions of the Charter of the United Nations.

The Canadian Constitution states under Part II, entitled "Rights of the Aboriginal Peoples Canada": 35.

1. The existing aboriginal and treaty rights of the aboriginal peoples of Canada are hereby recognized and affirmed.

2. In the Act, "aboriginal peoples of Canada" includes the Indian, Inuit and Métis peoples of Canada.

In defiance of the Constitution of Canada, officials from the Canadian Government have been aggressively arguing before the United Nations for the past several years that the "aboriginal peoples" of Canada are not "peoples" in the sense of the "international covenant on civil and political rights."

Something is rotten in the state of Canada. Some say that if our rights to continue to pursue our way of life and to freely dispose of our resources were recognized and upheld by Canada, development would stop. This is clearly untrue. It is in fact a scare tactic used by proponents of the status quo. In the first place, most Canadian development takes place in southern industry. Secondly, we are interested in development to the extent that it does not rape the land. Modest in-basin hydroelectric projects could be built so as to benefit the people and environment in an area. Mining can be done, if it does not contaminate whole river systems. Forestry can be done so as to protect ecological diversity and indigenous land use. None of this, however, can be accomplished by removing aboriginal peoples from the land.

If you examine a map of Canada today, you will see that the full Cree nation extends from northern Quebec to British Columbia. You will see that the Dene and Inuit peoples also inhabit areas that are crossed by artificial provincial and territories boundaries. In the talks on the Canadian Constitution which must surely come, the fact that we, the indigenous peoples in Canada, are the majority resident population and our language and culture are dominant in this area must be considered. We are not at present adequately represented in the House of Commons or in the provincial Legislatures. We have been disenfranchised, yet we are the majority, original, and permanent residents of Canada's hidden province. We will not be silent.

Victor Mitander

Chief Negotiator
Council for Yukon Indians

As you might know, Yukon Indian people have been involved with the Government of Canada in land claim negotiations since 1973, some seventeen years. The Umbrella Final Agreement was initialled by the federal, territorial, and Yukon Indian negotiators on March 31st of this year. It has now been provided to our people for their consideration. We have a chapter in our Agreement which addresses the matter of self-government. What we've got in that chapter is not really self-government, or even a guarantee of self-government, but an affirmation that both the federal government and the government of Yukon will negotiate self-government with Yukon First Nations. Within the general terms set out in the Umbrella Final Agreement, each Yukon First Nation will negotiate its own self-government agreements. Because it does not make sense to separate the two, we expect that self-government arrangements will be negotiated at the same time as First Nation land settlement agreements.

Yukon First Nations will address self-government with respect to the broad range of subjects, such as committed infrastructure; education; training; aboriginal languages; revenues for local purposes, including direct taxation; justice; relations with governments; and financial transfer arrangements, to mention a few. We will negotiate the devolution of programs from the federal and territorial governments in fields such as native languages, culture, tribal justice, and child welfare, as well as policing, law enforcement, and other matters which are vital to our people.

We will not start from scratch in creating the development of institutions needed to run these various services. Out of our own history and experience in operating programs, we have acknowledged what governments should do and should not do. What our governments will do will be based on our own traditions and culture.

118

As one example, one Yukon First Nation, the Teslin Tlingit Council, already has a traditional form of government in place. It operates via the clan system. Under the Teslin constitution, five elders, who are the clan leaders, give direction to the Board of Directors. Discussions are now underway with other Tlingit communities such as Atlin and Carcross in the development of a broader tribal government.

We worry about taking over government powers without being given sufficient opportunities to acquire the skills to exercise these powers or sufficient funds to operate effective self-government in perpetuity. We will need a comprehensive and sustained training program to prevent the perpetration of a situation in which we are forced to hire much of our personnel and expertise from outside of our communities. The federal government has been keen to devolve programs to Indians, but less keen to devolve the resources needed to run those programs.

We have already experienced a great deal of frustration in trying to develop a training program. Our frustration is part of the larger situation currently facing Indian people across Canada. As noted in a report by the Cree-Naskapi Commission, the full cost of self-government has not been given sufficient recognition by the government. The Commission has expressed concerns about a government misconception that after settling their claim, the Crees are rich and that the public funding of their activities should be curtailed. It observed that the Cree financial statements clearly demonstrated that land claims compensation monies had been used to meet other government obligations. That is not the kind of situation we want to get into.

We have to judge the federal government's seriousness about Indian self-government by its willingness to put its money where its mouth is.

Resources for self-government must not merely come from the old style federal contribution agreements or alternative funding arrangements in another form. As we interpret the government view from discussions we have had to date, the funding of self-governing Indian nations would be based on historical levels of funding to particular bands. In other words, the Sechelt model. In our view, this would probably not take into account the much wider powers self-governing Indian nations will exercise, nor the fact that historical funding to Indian bands has proceeded at about the most wretched, sub-poverty levels imaginable in Canada.

We propose that the funding of self-government should take

119

several elements into account. First, that it recognize the full actual cost of running a modern government. The federal government should treat self-governing First Nations as it would treat its own departments in terms of providing for adequate salaries, benefits, supplies and other costs. It should bear in mind that the programs and services that a First Nation will take on in perpetuity are constitutionally, legitimately, and by long-standing practices the responsibilities of the Minister of Indian Affairs. The Minister has a continuing role to ensure that sufficient resources are provided, in perpetuity, to enable those programs to be carried out properly.

Second, additional funds should be provided for a period of time to enable First Nations to develop the human resource base that will be needed for effective self-government. We do not know how long this period will be, but given the complex issues that modern governments have to deal with, it is unlikely that it will be less than ten years. Probably much longer.

Like other native people, and like so many developing peoples throughout the world, we are faced with the task of devising an educational system that blends elements of our culture and language with necessary and worthwhile elements of non-native culture. Whatever we do by way of an initial push to enable our people to run our own governments, it must be compatible with the educational objectives we see for the long run.

Third, in Yukon First Nations, and I am sure in First Nations everywhere, the quality of community infrastructure, services and housing is far below acceptable national standards. For example, a study undertaken in Yukon communities in 1982 indicated that to bring the community infrastructure and other utilities in those communities up to an acceptable standard would cost about $32 million. That would be in the order of $50 million in 1990 dollars.

Self-government, with a very limited, almost nonexistent tax base, should not be expected to begin life behind so large an eight-ball. This suggests—again for a limited period of time, and again this would have to be negotiated—that funds should be made available to enable First Nations to develop and manage community infrastructure to an acceptable standard. Again, this would have to include all First Nation people, whether they be status or non-status people.

Fourth, to enable us to undertake both short- and long-term planning, we need guaranteed funding levels. This could best be done through a five-year agreement, similar to the formula financing arrangements that are in place between the federal and territorial and provincial governments.

120

Fifth, ensuring that governments meet their commitments towards native people has been a major problem in the history of Canada. We want to ensure that governments are compelled to meet the commitments that they have made to our First Nations when self-governing negotiations have been completed. One approach which warrants serious consideration is the establishment of an outside monitoring agency, like the Cree and Naskapi Commission.

Owing to the strange logic that prevails around such matters in Canada, our claims settlements will be constitutionally entrenched, whereas the self-government institutions that are needed to operate those settlement operations will not be. The federal government is unwilling to consider constitutional protection for native self-government when we negotiate our Umbrella Final Agreement. It has been the position of the Council of Yukon Indians from day one that self-government agreements must be entrenched agreements in Section 35 of the Constitution.

Our relations with the Government of Yukon are good, and have been cooperative, but there is a lot of room for improvement. There is every reason to think that we could support Yukon's constitutional ambition if they support ours. Today, Canada is going through a period of high constitutional tension. The relationship between Canada and the aboriginal peoples is at its lowest point in history. For too long the governments of Canada, and generally Canadians, have avoided confronting our issues.

There has been a long history in which the federal Department of Indian Affairs bureaucrats have never produced any good for our people, nothing but suffering. We have looked at the reserves where there is the highest unemployment anywhere—between 70 percent and 90 percent. Anywhere else in this country, that would be called a depression. The time has come to stop talking and studying Indian problems and issues. The time has come for concrete action, positive action.

Aboriginal peoples and Canadians across Canada are very concerned that something be done that is positive. Here is an opportunity to show Canadians, and for that matter the rest of the world, that we have a vision and wisdom about what can be done to resolve these most important questions. These issues must be addressed now in a fair and honest way, as they will never go away.

Bill Erasmus

President
Dene Nation

Similar to the Yukon, we've been working at trying to spell out a relationship with Canada since the early 70s, since 1973. To date, we have very little to report of any good standing. I have been wrestling with this question of how to make known to you the problems of implementation, because for many years we have been gearing up for it. For many years we have been trying to outline a process for ourselves, so that we could in fact implement something. But really—because of the way negotiations are run in this country, because negotiations are based on extinguishment, on asking us to detach ourselves from our lands, detach ourselves from our being—in the final analysis there is very little to implement.

On the part of the federal government, on the part of the territorial government, I imagine they would have a lot to implement because if you are talking of authority and if you are talking of power, they're the ones that are getting it. And they are coercing us over a long period of time to put into black and white that they ought to be the party that has the ultimate authority.

There's no degree of meaningful dialogue on sovereignty, because in their view it doesn't exist. And that's the state of the art. Charles Wilkinson says that sovereignty isn't a thing to be afraid of. It's working in the American context and the United States is still there.

I don't think this government is serious. I don't think they want to sit down with us, and I don't think they want to correct any kind of wrongdoings that have happened. Or they don't want to spell out a relationship with us. And I don't know what it is, I don't know if they're afraid of us. Or they're too preoccupied with being colonists, but it certainly has to change.

When we talk of sovereignty, the Dene have talked about it for a long time. We've talked about implementing what we feel is applicable in our situation. That's very, very simple. What we mean is that we have a home in the North, that's where we're from. It belongs to us, it's always been ours, it's our place, our place of being. We're willing to share it, and all we ask, basically, is that anything that happens in our home happens with our consent. It's a very, very fundamental question. If government would put that on paper, if they would agree to that, that it is our home, then we wouldn't have any problem. But that's what they are denying us through this process. They are denying the fact that it is our home. They're denying our

122

history as Dene, and they're trying to coerce us to become something else.

It's a whole denial process, and they're continuing to do it even though we have the Supreme Court of Canada's *Sioui* and *Sparrow* judgements that say otherwise. Because we initiated an agreement in April to bring to our people for ratification, we are unable now to even look at *Sparrow*, which was announced in June, and see how that might change an agreement we initialed a couple of months before it came out. That's how dead this government is.

It is very difficult for me to express my feeling to you. We're at the table, we've been there for a long time. I hear the government saying, and I heard the Prime Minister saying, they're going to make changes. They're going to allow more people to come to the land claims negotiations table. At the same time I get a letter in which Minister Siddon says: "It's not my intention to recommend to Cabinet a further review of our comprehensive claims policy." So the status quo is going to remain. They might allow more people to come to the table. They might put a few more dollars into it, but the status quo is going to be there.

So people with innovative programs or initiatives like the Micmac are going to run into the same situation as our people. Beautiful ideas. Wonderful thoughts from your people, but you can't implement them. And it's not because the Constitution denies it. Because everything is there in Section 35.(1). It's because the government does not want to implement self-determination. And what they want to implement is not something for which we are asking.

So I have very little to offer, very little to tell you, about what we as Dene are going to implement. And we're at the final stage of negotiations. We've initialled a final agreement, and they're asking our people to ratify it by March of this year. That's the reality out there.

Michael Whittington

Chief Negotiator, CYI Land Claims
Department of Indian and Northern Affairs

I'm not going to address the broad issues, which I recognize are of great importance. Rather, I want to talk about five "nuts and bolts" problems in the implemention of land claims agreements and self-government agreements, with particular reference to Yukon.

My first point is that the relationship between the implementation of self-government and a corresponding land claims agreement has to be closely integrated. In Yukon, where I have taken part in the negotiations as the federal negotiator, they clearly have been tied together. We've been negotiating these agreements at the same table, even though because of current federal policy one agreement won't be constitutionally protected and the other agreement will be. Nevertheless, we've dealt with the process as a single process and with the support of the Department of Indian and Northern Affairs in Ottawa. In fact, the commitment to negotiate self-government agreements is entrenched in the Yukon land claims agreement.

This is good news because what it means really is that the process of implementation of self-government, the process whereby Yukon First Nations will acquire various legislative powers, can be phased in. It can be spread over a long time period because the commitment to negotiate, which is constitutionally protected, remains in place. It remains in place in perpetuity with a very long menu or list of items to be negotiated. This menu remains constitutionally protected, allowing time for the First Nations to get themselves up to speed and to take over programs and legislative responsibilities, as they feel capable of doing so. The bad news, from the aboriginal perspective, is that the self-government agreements themselves are not to be constitutionally protected at this time. I think probably that the jury is still out on that in terms of political negotiations, but it is really not an implementation question. It's a much broader question.

The other point I want to make with regard to the relationship between self-government negotiations and claim negotiations is that the land claims in the Yukon can't be implemented until the self-government infrastructure at least is in place. We've always anticipated that the various powers and responsibilities that are given to the Yukon First Nations in their land claims will be carried out by their governments, rather than by a corporate entity as in other agreements.

The plan is that the First Nation governments will go into place at the same time that the agreement is ratified and that these governments will be the operative agencies taking over responsibility for managing the land and things such as that. It's interesting to note that there are a number of self-government powers in the Yukon land claims agreement itself. These might have slipped in through the back door, but there definitely are legislative responsibilities granted to the Yukon First Nations through the claims agreement. Thus while the self-government agreements themselves are not to be constitutionally protected at this time, there definitely are a lot of constitutionally protected self-government type powers lurking in the

124

Umbrella Final Agreement that will appear in the Yukon First Nation final agreements as well.

My second overall point has to do with the relationship of the territorial government to the process. I think the unique thing in both territories is that most of the bread and butter issues—bread and butter programs and legislative powers—most of these have already been devolved to the territorial government. It's not like the Indian Affairs branch is transferring programs directly to Indian bands. Most of these responsibilities are now being borne by the territorial government, so that the territorial government has to be intimately involved when negotiations of the transfer of legislative authority to Yukon First Nations occur. Both territorial governments are sympathetic to this. I don't think it's going to be a problem. I feel optimistic about the outcome.

There has to be some caution so that, in transferring legislative authority and transferring, more importantly perhaps, financial powers from the Yukon territorial government to the Yukon First Nations, nothing gets lost between the cracks. There must not be any interruption in the delivery of services to non-native Yukoners and to native Yukoners whose First Nations have not yet taken over those legislative responsibilities.

The third overall issue has to do with financing self-government. There's never enough money, I think we all agree with that. But there are four major problems that we will have to deal with on the financial side of the implementation process.

First, is the problem of diseconomies of scale. Most of the communities in the Yukon are so small that they are not going to be able to afford to deliver all of the programs at the community level. I think of acute care health programs, for instance. Every community with 350-400 people can't have a hospital. We're going to have to encourage the Yukon First Nations to combine into regional groupings or even into some kind of a confederation of Yukon First Nations that will allow them to deliver the big expensive programs to the various communities.

Again, respecting financing, there's a need to integrate new legislative transfers of authority with existing Alternate Funding Arrangements (AFA). Alternate Funding Arrangements are just transfers of funding for existing programs. What we're doing in self-government is transferring the legislative authority, along with some funding. I would expect when the transfer of legislative authority is over, that the programs may turn out to be quite different, as the Yukon Indian people start asserting their priorities. It is important that we recognize that the new legislative powers have to be integrated with the existing AFA responsibilities so, again, there is no loss in the continuity of the delivery of these important programs.

There's also the problem of calculating how much a program is worth. It's difficult to say, for instance, what percentage of the Department of Indian Affairs' budget in the Yukon is affected by the fact that the Public Service Commission in Ottawa provides some services to the Department. You have to figure out some way of disaggregating the overall administration and service costs of programs way up in the Yukon by perhaps working out a formula that says it costs so much to deliver a program. Hard to calculate, but we've got to figure out ways of doing it, if the transfers of financial responsibility are going to reflect the true demands on resources.

And finally, I think it should be clear that the ultimate goal of self-government should be that the First Nation governments are financially independent. Ultimately what we want to happen is for the Yukon First Nations to pay their own bills, to have the revenue gathering authority and the economic base to be able to do that. Because as long as the federal government or territorial government is paying the bills, First Nations can't really be truly independent. Governments can always get at First Nations through fiddling with their budget. The financial independence, the self-sufficiency of Yukon First Nations, has to be an ultimate goal.

The fourth point is that self-government agreements have to be phased in. The institutions must be in place to start with. We have to agree on how we share responsibilities between governments and First Nations. Basically, we would like to see First Nations develop their constitutions and develop their own ways of making decisions internally.

Next, there's the question of money, again. The responsibilities that the Yukon Indian people get in their land claims agreement have to be paid for. The funding for this probably will come through land claims agreement implementation funding, but clearly this has to be built into the process.

The third phase involves not just taking over existing programs, but taking over legislative powers. As responsibility for health care and education programs is transferred, the money that is being spent now has to be transferred along with it. You get the legislative power. You get an increase in the formula of funding for the Yukon First Nation. Then, with that lump of money, you change your program legislatively and do anything you want. That's the kind of model we're looking at—a genuine third order of government.

From then on, as each program or area of responsibility is transferred to a Yukon First Nation, an increase in the amount of financial help is negotiated, and that gets built into the financing formula. This isn't firm policy that I am speaking of, it's the kind of process we have been developing in the course of negotiations in the Yukon.

Tribal justice, policing, and similar issues are particularly important ones and will require much working out because they intimately involve the relationship of the non-native justice system with the native justice system—a conflict of basic values, in many cases. Because they are so important, these issues probably will have to be negotiated, on a broader scale, over a longer period of time than many other issues, but we should get on with it, because they are some of the most important items on the menu for the Yukon First Nations. All of the Yukon First Nations have expressed an interest in getting justice powers transferred to them very quickly.

And, finally, training is my fifth overall problem area. I think there is no question that the political skills are already there in the Yukon. There's no question that the political leadership is there. We don't have to train the Yukon Indian people to be politicians. I've been snookered by them too many times. They are smart. They are competent. They know how to use the media. They know how to play one government against another government. I have a great deal of respect for their political acumen.

Where there is going to be a gap is at the level that all Indian people across the country, not just the Yukon Indians, like to malign, and that's the bureaucratic level. It is the administrators and managers who have to get down into the bowels of the government and actually make things work. It is at this level where I think the skills of the aboriginal people, the skills that are there among the aboriginal people in the Yukon, have to be developed, because self-government is not going to work if Yukon First Nation governments have in the jobs Indian people who aren't adequately trained. Nor is it going to work if they have to go to Toronto, Vancouver, or Whitehorse and hire a bunch of non-natives to do the jobs.

Training has to focus on management and administrative skills, and then, of course, there has to be training in all sorts of technical and vocational areas, so that the various operational responsibilities of the Yukon First Nation departments can get carried out. The sooner we can start the process of training and start flowing funds for this purpose to the Yukon First Nations, the better. That's the key to effective self-government implementation.

Adam H. Zimmerman

Chairman and CEO
Noranda Forest Products

As you would expect, as a businessman, I want to understand clearly what a problem is before attempting any solution. Furthermore, the definition of any problem requires a clear definition, understanding, and acceptance of the surrounding circumstances. So, what is aboriginal self-government? Does the native person understand the same notion of it as does the bureaucrat, the elected official, and the ordinary non-status person?

Given the fact that we live in an advanced industrial society with a fast growing world population of five billion persons, 75 percent of whom live a lot less well than Canadians do, native people can't expect their circumstances of three and four hundred years ago to be recreated, maintained, or reasonably appropriate. Even if a majority wanted a return to the traditional way of living, they would find it impossible in all but a few isolated pockets of geography. There are just too many people. The world is shrunken by fast travel and instant communication. Very few people can live in isolation. These factors are basic to any future arrangements in any society.

It is clear that Canada's native people are restive. The events at Oka are strong evidence of something not working. Have the Oka Indians been taken over by some kind of power faction? Do they all get a fair opportunity? Do they all understand the same thing relative to their rights, their obligations, and their options?

One could speculate that the Canadian native person must face two considerable hurdles beyond those facing many others. The first of these is language, and while I'm no expert on that, it is a fact that there are probably hundreds of dialects in use by our native people. We, the other Canadians, would normally expect all people in the country to understand either French or English. In fact, some of our native people may understand neither, and for that matter they may not clearly understand one another.

There are those who will argue that the destruction and failure of transmission of language is at the root of all native problems. Native languages are disappearing as fast as elder speakers are dying, thus cutting off the present-day native from his past and his heritage and leaving him exposed to a myriad of misunderstandings in our very complicated society.

The second hurdle after the language hurdle is lack of capital. The concept of capital was originally foreign to most native people. I suppose simply because they didn't need it. With the boundless riches of a huge country teeming with fish and wildlife, once he could keep himself warm and dry, the native could provide for all his needs. Specialization was not a factor. The fact that these conditions no longer exist has been recognized by society, although the response has to be questioned because it doesn't seem to be working.

Canada currently spends something approaching $2.5 billion annually on 550,000 native persons through over one hundred programs. This works out to about $24,000 for a six-person family per year, which by most standards is a fair start in a rural setting. Regrettably, what it seems to have done is lock an awful lot of people into a cycle of welfare dependency. Obviously this charity does nothing other than ease middle class consciences.

I have mentioned two factors I believe to be hurdles in the matter of native self-government. These are language and capital. A third element is that of education, which although presently and widely available, is often considered as useless in that it equips a native person for jobs that are not there on the reserve when he comes out the other side.

Probably the last question I would like to raise is: "Could someone please define native self-government?" What behaviour or organization is to be governed, and what present level of government does it replace or enhance? In Canada, now, we all endure three and sometimes four levels of government.
1. The federal government is responsible for trade, currency, general welfare systems, foreign relations, and defence.
2. The provincial governments are responsible for education, health, highways, and natural resource management.
3. The municipal governments (which often have two levels—cities and towns plus county and metro) provide the basic infrastructure, roads, fire protection, schools, police, and welfare.
All of them have taxing authority.

All of the foregoing are background considerations to the notion of native self-government. It is possible these and others no doubt could be discussed, understood, and focused on in an assembly such as we enjoy here. Clearly to do so requires a firm, well-defined, and comprehensive agenda. Properly chaired, such a group can develop a consensus and come to a reasoned written conclusion. An example of such a process was the Canadian task force on the environment and the economy, which, by including all interested parties, developed a constructive response to the environmental imperatives brought forward by the Brundtland Report.

Such a process by itself would be strong evidence in favour of native self-government. It would spike the guns of the vocal special-interest groups; it would ventilate all reasonable points of view and synthesize an agenda for action. It would, or it could. If people held to some of the more extreme forms of tribal individuality, it might be a lot harder. If the demand were for a form of governance that superseded that of the rest of Canadians, if it sought to enshrine unreasonable or impossible special privileges, it might fail.

Probably the best tactic is incrementalism. A little bit at a time. Above all, that would demonstrate compromise, cooperation, and accountability. That, of course, always has been a hallmark of the leading native groups in Canada.

However much any of us might yearn for the old days, they are not going to come back, they cannot be recreated, and the best any of us can hope for is a gradual change from whatever is our present culture to whatever is to be the case in future.

Frank Cassidy

Director, Administration of Aboriginal Governments Program
University of Victoria

Federal policy in relation to First Nations has clearly come to an impasse. At best, the Government of Canada is paralyzed as it reels from crisis to crisis, from non-response to non-response. At worst, the Mulroney government has adopted a repressive stance towards First Nations. In this sense, the use of the army at Kanesatake and Kahnawake was more than a unique response to a particularly perplexing problem. It was a symptom of the fundamental failure of Canada's Indian policy.

Nothing has happened since summer to indicate that any real changes in this policy are contemplated. Prime Minister Mulroney called for "a new relationship between aboriginal and non-aboriginal Canadians based upon human dignity, trust, and respect . . . ." In the Commons, he admitted that "what I would want most of all in Canada would be equality, fairness, and justice for the native peoples of this country. Their denial and the denial of these fundamentals are something that one sees on a daily basis." This denial continues. There has been no real progress in building the "new relationship." In fact, Mr. Mulroney's view of a "new" relationship sounds much like the old relationship, as glittering generalities are substituted for a recognition of aboriginal rights and, in particular, the reality of aboriginal self-government.

To date, Federal Indian policy has been posited upon an assimilative approach, which purports to adhere to a goal of bringing aboriginal peoples into the mainstream of Canadian society, while, in actuality, it features the gradual imposition of a bureaucratic welfare state on Indian reserves, a welfare state which Indians are to administer for themselves and which ignores the need for a real land base and significant autonomy. Assimilation has not worked, and the last refuge of any government—military and police power—has now come into play. The Oka crisis may be over, but, unfortunately, we may see more Okas. Is this the Canada that Canadians want?

The Government of Canada can improve its relations with First Nations and restore its national and international reputation as one of the great centres of freedom and progress in the world. To do so, it must move from denial to recognition. First Nations can no longer be rebuffed. Much as French Canada is, First Nations are a fact of life in Canada, a fact of which all Canadians should be proud.

Non-aboriginal Canadians and our governments should not try to make aboriginal peoples over so they are more like us. Rather, First Nations in Canada should be recognized as a distinct force, as the original founding peoples of this country. And this recognition should be made not on the basis of race, but rather, on the basis of historical, political, and legal realities.

It might justly be asked: "How can this change take place? Is it practical?" The real sadness is that not only is a move from denial to recognition possible, but the elements of the kind of transformation required have been well articulated by the leaders of many First Nations and by several federal task forces. The vast majority of the 1983 recommendations of the Penner Committee, a special committee of Parliament, are still awaiting acceptance, despite the fact that they were widely applauded both inside and outside of the federal government.

Calls on the part of organizations such as that of the Canadian Human Rights Commission for "a new commitment" by Canada to justice and recognition have gone unheeded. Government silence on the real issues and on the necessary solutions to these issues remains, only to be broken when there is a pressing need to *appear* to be responsive because of an upsurge in public opinion such as the one that took place in the aftermath of Elijah Harper's brave stand and the Oka crisis.

There are several measures Canada can and should take to better its relations with First Nations. Before outlining these measures, it is important to note that, ultimately, the most realistic and just approach to the presence of First Nations in Canada can be found in a recognition of their status as *the* founding peoples of this country and a specific enumeration and affirmation of their inherent powers—including the power to govern themselves and other aboriginal rights—in the Constitution. In the long run, a constitutional approach is the only one that can provide certainty and the kind of just foundation upon which this country can build and flourish.

In addition, it also needs to be noted that any measures the Government of Canada takes in relation to the challenges presented by the realities of First Nations governments should be taken within the context of serious and extensive consultation with First Nations. Canada should not make unilateral policy decisions in relation to the aboriginal peoples of this country. This is truer today than it has been in recent history, for First Nations governments are much stronger than they have been in many years. Paternalism and assimilation have not worked in the past. They certainly are not going to work in the future.

If its relations with First Nations are to improve, there are many steps Canada needs to take. The following nine would provide a good starting point for a reconcilation that would create national unity and restore respect for Canada on the part of aboriginal peoples, the international community, and the many citizens of this country who have become ashamed of official insensitivity and frustrated with political intrangience.

1. Reaffirmation of Aboriginal and Treaty Rights

Aboriginal and treaty rights are recognized and affirmed in the *Constitution Act, 1982*. The Government of Canada should stop challenging aboriginal peoples in the courts as they attempt to protect these rights, and it should cease acting as if the sections of the Constitution that affirm aboriginal rights are an "empty box." Instead, the government should issue a clear policy statement that it recognizes and respects aboriginal rights, including the inherent right to self-government as well as other rights that relate to matters such as culture and land and resource use. Moreover, it should begin actively to encourage provincial governments to do the same.

The recognition and affirmation of aboriginal rights are part of the law of the land. As the Prime Minister and other Ministers of the Crown have so frequently pointed out, no one is above the law nor can anyone unilaterally dismiss the law. It is time for the Government of Canada to realize that it, too, must adhere to the Constitution, that it must affirm and protect aboriginal rights, as embedded in the law of the land.

2. Establishment of a Modern Treaty Process

The *Royal Proclamation of 1763* provides the basis for a more appropriate approach on the part of Canada to its basic arrangements with First Nations. This approach should be based on the notion that nation-to-nation treaties are the foundation for lasting relationships. Such treaties must respect the views of aboriginal peoples concerning land and its spiritual significance. They must also respect the need for a protected and extensive land and resource base to preserve and enhance a distinct way of life. Where prior treaties are considered just by aboriginal peoples, they should be honoured by Canada. Where they are not, treaties should be renegotiated.

A modern treaty-making process should be designed in a fundamental departure from the federal comprehensive claims policy of the last twenty years. An appropriate policy cannot be based on the idea of the extinguishment of aboriginal rights or title. It cannot force a detachment of aboriginal self-government arrangements from matters that relate to lands and resources. Nor can it be administered through a cumbersome and restrictive regime that allows only a few negotiations at any one time and attempts to force settlements with threats that a failure to comply with federal timelines will result in a discontinuance of negotiations until time immemorial. A modern treaty-making process must be based on respect, fairness, and equity.

3. Acceptance of Canada's Special Trust Responsibility

Constitutional expert Brian Slattery has noted that: "The Crown has a general fiduciary (i.e. trust) duty toward native people to protect them in the enjoyment of their aboriginal rights and in particular in the possession and use of their lands." As the Supreme Court of Canada stated in the recent *Sparrow* decision on aboriginal fishing rights: " . . . the honour of the Crown is at stake in dealing with aboriginal peoples."

Affirming aboriginal rights and working to enhance the possibilities for the enjoyment of these rights are not merely policy preferences. The Government of Canada has a special responsibility to elevate matters relating to the rights of aboriginal peoples to the top of the national agenda. The federal government should be in court supporting and standing alongside aboriginal peoples as they defend their rights. It should not be a party to their denial by provincial authorities or others. First Nations are not the adversaries of the federal government. They are, constitutionally, its partners.

4.   Accommodation within the Federal-Provincial Arena

Provinces have nearly independent powers in areas over which they have constitutional jurisdiction. Ontario does not tell Alberta what to do about education. Nova Scotia does not make health policy for Manitoba. These are areas of provincial sovereignty. In light of the inherent jurisdiction of First Nations governments, the Government of Canada might adopt a policy that assumes the jurisdictional powers of First Nations to be somewhat similar to provincial powers. Why should other Canadian governments tell First Nations what to do about education or social services or land use planning or similar matters? The sovereignty of First Nations must be respected.

When there are matters that reflect differences requiring federal-provincial agreements, those matters are settled at First Ministers' Conferences. First Nations should be included in all such conferences. They should be guaranteed a vote on all matters that directly affect them. The Government of Canada should work to see this happen, to recognize First Nations as full partners in Confederation and honoured members of the federal-provincial system.

5.   Repeal of the Indian Act

There is no avoiding the truth: the *Indian Act* is colonialist legislation. Originally proclaimed in 1876, this act of Parliament denies the right of First Nations to define who is and who is not an Indian in Canada. It provides the basis for the federal government to control nearly every activity on reserve lands. Indeed, it imposes a single framework of governance upon First Nations that are classified as Indian bands, a framework that, even after well over one hundred years, is alien to all but a few First Nations. The *Indian Act* ignores First Nations' laws and institutions. In fact, it treats First Nations as if they never existed. It is the ultimate act of denial.

What should replace the *Indian Act*? Here is one matter that will deserve intense negotiation between First Nations and Canada. Something will have to replace the *Act*, since it is currently the legislative basis for setting the guidelines concerning which members of First Nations receive social benefits from the federal government and which do not. Such a measure may be necessary, but it is neither necessary nor appropriate to have new federal legislation that defines the scope, powers, and institutions of First Nations' governments. Never again should a piece of federal legislation be allowed to define the nature of aboriginal governments. The powers of First Nations should be enumerated in the Constitution and not within the context of federal jurisdiction.

Rather than circumscribing First Nations governments, in coming years, as the Government of Canada commences to recognize the governments of First Nations, it will face an old challenge which will require new responses. That challenge revolves around the traditional laws, political institutions, and leadership of First Nations. Over one hundred years of repressive legislation has not been able to terminate these manifestations of aboriginal sovereignty. In an era of recognition, the traditional dimension of aboriginal governments will become all the stronger. So, too, will be the need to recognize and honour this aspect of aboriginal Canada.

6. Creation of a Federal Department of First Nations Relations

The Department of Indian Affairs has a long and deep history. It is set in its patterns. It was established to accomplish two goals: to govern Indians and to support their assimilation into Canadian society. From time to time, it has tried to do other things. Currently, it even has self-government programs. The Department will never be able to surmount its history, nor will it be able to assume the kind of new and innovative mandate that an arm of the federal government must have, as that government moves from denial to recognition.

As the Special Committee to Parliament on Indian Self-Government, the Penner Committee, recommended in 1983, Indian Affairs should be shut down and replaced with a much smaller bureaucracy that has the mandate to support and advocate for First Nations as they establish their true role in Confederation and seek to enjoy their aboriginal rights. The exact nature of this new department should be determined by negotiations between First Nations and the Government of Canada.

135

This measure is not as fundamental as those that have been described previously. Taken in isolation, it might not be very meaningful. In fact, it could be a misleading, or perhaps even a negative, measure, as it might be used to reduce Canada's financial commitment to First Nations. Given the devastated nature of most First Nations economies, such a development would spell doom for many aboriginal peoples; but in the context of a policy based upon recognition and respect, it would be a necessary and inevitable step.

7. Achievement of Economic Self-Sufficiency

The power of money cannot be ignored. Between Canada and the First Nations there must be a new fiscal relationship that reflects the new political relationship. The two must go hand-in-hand. The level of the financial commitment of Canada to First Nations should not be reduced until economic health is restored within aboriginal communities and territories. To help First Nations governments realize the goal of economic self-sufficiency, the federal government should transfer to them the resources that will enable appropriate economic activities to flourish once again.

Because of the condition of most First Nations economies, it is going to be some time before their governments establish an adequate fiscal base. The Government of Canada needs to develop a new financing formula similar to the current equalization arrangements that exist between the federal and provincial governments. Program funding should not be allowed to drive the standards for and design of programs in First Nation communities. Moreover, so there is stability in the relationship, the global amount of federal funding for First Nations should be established over a term longer than one year.

8. Establishment of Innovative Intergovernmental Institutions

When the autonomy of First Nations political institutions is recognized, many matters of concern to First Nations will continue to require the cooperation of the federal and provincial governments. The on-going necessity for intergovernmental coordination will be one important reason for the establishment of innovative institutions of governance between various jurisdictions. Another will be the need for ways in which to monitor agreements between governments and

136

the implementation of relevant legislation. Still another reason for new institutions will revolve around the strong likelihood of difficult-to-reconcile disputes between First Nations and other governments.

Even with the most just and appropriate federal policy, there will be times when there are disputes between the provinces and First Nations governments or between various third parties—business, union, or other nongovernmental interests—and those governments. There will be instances in which the federal government is accused of not living up to its special trust responsibility. There will also be occasions upon which citizens of First Nations believe that their rights as Canadian citizens are being violated by their governments. The courts should not be constantly brought into play in such circumstances. Independent mediation and dispute resolution arrangements should provide an avenue for avoiding a good measure of the costly and adversarial litigation that is currently taking place and, indeed, mounting.

Institutions that provide opportunities for conflict resolution, the monitoring of agreements and legislation, and cooperation between First Nations and other governments are already developing. The Cree-Naskapi Commission in Quebec and the Indian Commission of Ontario are but two examples. There will be many more after the proper recognition of First Nations governments.

9. Restructuring of the Justice System

The current justice system has resulted in a great deal of injustice for aboriginal people. A thorough-going reform of the prison system is needed so that those members of First Nations who are currently incarcerated can have a better chance of returning to their communities and families. Moreover, there needs to be a further development and recognition of tribal courts and policing systems. This is one area where Canada has lagged sadly behind the United States in its relations with First Nations.

Many of the methods of social control present in aboriginal communities are disrupted by a court and prison system that takes accused offenders out of the very communities where effective measures to right wrongs and alter unacceptable behaviours can take place. There can be no reconciliation between First Nations and other Canadians without a restructured justice system, and there cannot be a properly restructured justice system without the recognition of First Nations' governments in terms of their own laws and conventions. Given the costs and some of the more frequent and deplorable outcomes of the current justice system, a change would benefit many Canadians.

On the basis of the Government of Canada's expressed policy preferences over the past several years, it may not be very likely that the current federal government will look favourably upon a program such as the one that has been outlined here. The impetus for change may have to come from the outside. In the 1980s, it looked as if a series of First Ministers' Conferences might be a catalyst for change, but, in the end, the FMC process was unable to result in agreement on the nature or existence of the aboriginal right to self-government. After the events surrounding the demise of the Meech Lake Accord, in the near future the FMC process seems to be a dead end in any case.

One means for spurring the needed changes in federal government policy might be a Royal Commission, or, in the phrases of the Canadian Human Rights Commission, a commission of inquiry on aboriginal affairs. Such a Commission would be able to hold hearings across Canada and to conduct research on key matters such as fiscal arrangements and conflict resolution mechanisms. These might be worthwhile initiatives, but the Penner Committee engaged in similar activities, and a new Commission's findings may be not much different from that Committee's. More to the point, even if a Royal Commission were able to identify a cogent approach to the matter, its' recommendations might face the same fate as many similar task forces: they might turn yellow on the shelf, for such groupings are often organized as a substitute for, rather than a prelude to, decisive action.

Other approaches such as a special task force of the federal Cabinet might be considered, but such a grouping might be *too close* to the centre of power to accomplish any real change. It may well be that a Royal Commission is the best chance for initiating a process of change. If so, the creation of the Commission should be accompanied by some immediate measures that would clearly and genuinely signal that a significant change in federal policy was taking place. Such measures might include a more aggressive opening up of the land claims negotiation process; direct funding, without strings, to First Nations for research on self-government; and pro-active federal support of the efforts of First Nations governments to assert their powers in various jurisdictional areas that, under current Constitutional arrangements, are normally seen to be under provincial jurisdiction.

Measures such as these pale in comparison to those that have been outlined in this brief paper, and in the long run, they will not be adequate. Soon it may dawn upon the Ministers of the Crown that they can no longer talk of *giving* aboriginal peoples the right or powers to govern themselves or of sharing the Canadian land base with these peoples. "Our native people" were never *our* native people, they are their own people, they are First Nations. They belong to no one else, and no one, not Canada nor any provincial government, needs to, or can, give them what they already have—the right to self-determination, in the fullest sense of the phrase.

The movement from denial to recognition will not be an easy one. There are many reasons for a lack of optimism, but the costs of failing to create a more just and appropriate policy on the part of the Government of Canada would be high. Indeed, they might include the formation of a police state that no one, aboriginal or non-aboriginal, wants. Can Canada afford not to act?

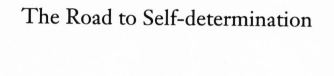

The Road to Self-determination

Tony Penikett

Premier
Government of Yukon

I want to talk about aboriginal rights, aboriginal title, and aboriginal self-government. I will come right to the point. I represent a government that *is* committed to aboriginal rights, aboriginal title, and aboriginal self-government, in principle and in practice, because they are right and because they work.

Our commitment is concretely expressed in the Council for Yukon Indians Land Claim Final Agreement, to which the Yukon Government is a party.

In the Yukon we are engaged in the difficult, complex, often frustrating work of defining a new place for First Nations in Yukon society, of grounding it in historical traditions and adapting it to the modern world in which we find ourselves, of setting forth fair principles and then defining what they mean in our institutions and in our daily lives.

I speak only for one region of Canada, but I believe all regions can come to grips with aboriginal self-government in principle and practice. And more than ever, I think we *must* do so. Because the one overriding lesson of Oka is that there is no good alternative to negotiating seriously and in good faith.

How?

- By agreeing on fair principles, as the government and First Nations of the Yukon have done;
- By finding processes that give practical expression to self-government agreements, again as we have worked hard to do in the Yukon; and
- By making these principles and practices of self-government into a national policy, which I want to propose.

Principles

Our principles are few but fundamental:
1. Aboriginal self-government is a right that must be included in the Constitution of Canada;
2. Canada must be obligated to negotiate self-government agreements with each First Nation;

143

3. Canada must be obligated to provide adequate resources for First Nations to carry out their agreements, whether through exclusive or shared institutions; and
4. Aboriginal title must be recognized and entrenched, not extinguished, on lands retained by First Nations.

These principles have guided our negotiations in the Yukon, and I believe they can serve Canadian governments and First Nations well, as we work to come to grips with aboriginal self-government in the months and years ahead.

Let me describe each of them briefly, including our experience in the Yukon, and how they may be applied in other parts of Canada.

Principle #1: Aboriginal self-government is a right that must be included in the Constitution of Canada.

Aboriginal self-government must be recognized as a *right*, to be exercised by First Nations at a time of their own choosing. This is the position of the Yukon Government, and I strongly urge other governments to accept it as well.

I know that many non-aboriginal people argue against recognizing self-government as a right. Included are a number of leading political figures, including First Ministers.

I urge them to re-think their positions. The relationship between First Nations and governments today in Canada is abysmal. A new relationship founded on respect is essential. In my view, there will be no progress on aboriginal political, social, and economic development until First Nations are recognized as nations—within Canada and the Canadian Constitution—for whom self-government is a right.

Externally-imposed non-aboriginal values and solutions have failed miserably. If the right to self-government is recognized, a lot of time and energy wasted on unproductive conflict will be eliminated.

The right to self-government, and the exercise of that right, must take place *within* the Canadian constitutional framework. This means not only that First Nations must recognize and accept that they are part of Canada, but also that Canada must recognize that aboriginal self-government agreements must be part of the Constitution of Canada.

Principle #2: Canada must be obligated to negotiate self-government agreements with each First Nation.

There must be a constitutionally entrenched obligation on the part of Canada and the provinces to *negotiate* self-government agreements. Far too many provincial premiers and other Canadian political leaders have simply refused even to negotiate self-government, thereby making it impossible for self-government ever to become a reality.

I think Yukon First Nations can take some satisfaction from their Yukon Land Claim Agreement, which will constitutionally entrench the obligation to negotiate self-government. I believe this comes very close to confirming that self-government is, in fact, a right available to Yukon First Nations.

Furthermore, self-government agreements must be negotiated with *each* First Nation. It is futile to try to make one set of rules for all First Nations across the country, and to try to define First Nations as having federal, provincial, or municipal-type powers. In fact, they will have different combinations of powers in each region of Canada, shaped to meet local needs.

And I do not think these powers need to be seen as threats to other governments, because they can be reached by mutual agreement. In fact, as a survivor of many federal-provincial conferences and of Meech Lake, I don't feel threatened at all by the prospect of negotiating aboriginal self-government. It couldn't possibly be worse than the Meech process.

Principle #3: Canada should be committed to provide adequate resources for First Nations to carry out their agreements, whether through exclusive or shared institutions.

Self-government will only be possible if First Nations have an adequate land and resource base and adequate financial and fiscal arrangements. Again, in the Yukon, we have through our claims agreement recognized that land and resources are essential.

Fiscal arrangements have not been addressed to any substantial degree in the Yukon agreement. But it is self-evident, I believe, that Canada will not meet its fiduciary responsibility if it does not guarantee First Nations adequate financial resources through equalization and other fiscal arrangements.

More about this later. First I would like to address the complex issue of exclusive and shared jurisdiction and institutions.

All sides must recognize that First Nations must and will have exclusive jurisdiction over some matters, such as internal political processes and structures, the use and management of aboriginal lands and activities on such lands, and other matters agreed upon in negotiations.

145

This area of exclusive jurisdiction must be constitutionally protected, so that governments cannot arbitrarily interfere in the internal affairs of First Nations. In other words, self-government agreements must be constitutionally entrenched.

This is something the Council for Yukon Indians has demanded, and we have joined them in this demand. But to date the federal government has refused to agree.

Areas of joint or shared jurisdiction must also be identified, and the principles for such sharing stated clearly.

I think these powers can be shared in practical ways, just as existing governments work together in areas such as revenue collection, environmental standards, or social services.

I would expect that the areas of exclusive and shared jurisdiction will, to some degree, vary according to the views and wishes of individual First Nations. It will be important that these differences be accommodated and that agreements on self-government reflect local community and regional differences in First Nations.

There must be recognition as well that many self-government powers will be most effectively exercised through joint or shared institutions. This means that such institutions will need to be subject to cooperative management, under power-sharing arrangements.

This will be particularly important at the community level. We in the Yukon, for instance, have many small communities, populated by both aboriginal and non-aboriginal people. In many cases, it would make no sense and, in fact, would be wasteful of our limited resources, to develop separate parallel institutions.

The way forward will involve an agreement that power must be shared. And the way to do so will be through First Nations exercising their powers and through community institutions recognizing these powers. We have already gone some way to ensuring this will happen, by requiring under our new Education Act, for example, that the government role for First Nations must be recognized and implemented through self-government negotiations and agreements.

In the case of the Yukon agreement, it goes well beyond the community level in defining a role for First Nations. First Nations will be partners in a number of territory-wide public institutions, including resource management, land use planning, and development assessment and approval institutions, to name but three.

Principle #4: Aboriginal title must be recognized and entrenched, not extinguished, on lands retained by First Nations.

Aboriginal title must be recognized and continued on lands retained

146

by First Nations, and there should be no demand for the extinguishment of aboriginal rights on these lands. An insistence on such extinguishment is neither fair nor realistic.

I think the Yukon Land Claim Agreement breaks important ground in this respect, in that Yukon First Nations and Yukon aboriginal people are not required to surrender aboriginal claims, rights, and titles in and to lands retained by First Nations.

Processes

Assuming we all have the determination to seek principles, practical solutions—and again, I think the lesson of Oka is that there is no good alternative—what is the way forward?

Let me divide the questions of process into two parts: negotiations and money.

On the subject of negotiations, many Canadians of goodwill this summer no doubt felt governments and First Nations should sit down, sort out, and resolve the issues between them—preferably over the summer in the post-Meech vacuum . . . and before Labour Day.

I wish it were that easy. So do you, I'm sure. Our experience, of course, is quite the opposite.

All sides must bring to the table some fundamental prerequisites:
- First, a commitment to the negotiating process, as the preferred and most productive route to results.
- Beyond that, the patience and strength and courage to stay at the table when the going gets rough. The Yukon has seen land claim negotiations for seventeen years, which, in my mind, is too long. But our current agreement took five years to reach, and we still have to negotiate concrete settlements with individual First Nations.
- Equally, understanding the empathy for quite different cultures and difficult concepts. It is not helpful either for negotiations or for public education, for example, for leaders to say they do not understand aboriginal title or self-government. I would argue that it is our responsibility to learn.
- Finally, the vision to see that defining aboriginal self-government will be an ongoing process, that there is no magic moment when it is all done and can be taken for granted. Like Confederation itself, these issues will be debated and re-formed as long as there is a Canada.

All these qualities—commitment, patience, understanding, and vision—are fundamental to successful negotiations. But, as I said before, it can be done: in the North, in B.C., in Quebec, anywhere in Canada.

Just let me add that it is helpful if negotiations can take place in a context of meaningful consultation about many issues, in and out of the aboriginal rights arena. In our case, it is becoming an established tradition to consult actively and thoroughly and, when needed, repeatedly on major issues.

In the past few years, communities have had a strong hand in shaping economic policy, education reform, the health system, wildlife and environmental acts . . . all of great interest and importance to aboriginal people.

Now, let's talk about money, which I raised earlier as an important point.

I have two things to say about money. One, that the federal government is already spending a lot of it, not very effectively. And, two, that First Nations must have access to resources to develop their economies.

The first point, of course, will surprise no one in the room today. Billions have been spent in the past, billions more are being spent now, and still more billions will be spent in the future. Quite simply, this money should be turned over to First Nations to meet their own needs and set their own priorities. They could not do a worse job than government has done for them.

Beyond this, though, Canada has a very long-standing "fiduciary" relationship with aboriginal people, just as a lawyer has with his client. Now I'm not a lawyer—and I am one of the minority of politicians who isn't—but it seems to me that Canada has not fully carried out its trust responsibility to aboriginal people, that if Canada were a lawyer hauled before the bar to explain its handling of a client's trust fund, it might well be found wanting.

My point is that Canada in its Charter inherited the responsibility for the well-being of aboriginal people within its borders. I think the federal government's pleading that it has spent the money elsewhere has no validity. The money must be found. It is Canada's duty.

Similarly, my second point, on the need to develop aboriginal economies, reflects a duty by Canada to ensure that aboriginal people have the land and resources needed. Again, because it is right and because it works.

I think the rightness of this, the historical justification, is self-evident. Aboriginal economic development is also a way out of the century-long spiral of aboriginal poverty and powerlessness.

148

This must change, if First Nations are going to be meaningful entities at all. They must have strong economic bases made up of taxes, royalties, profits, contracts, and jobs if they are to compete on an equal footing in a modern industrial world.

I am not overlooking the importance of subsistence economies and traditional cultural values, which are also protected and advanced in the Yukon Land Claim Agreement. But in this context, I want to focus on the importance of creating a financial and economic base for First Nations. I think it is irresponsible and, in the end, will not be successful to define and confirm responsibilities to First Nations without ensuring adequate resources to carry out those responsibilities.

Conclusions

Let me conclude by telling you what lessons I see in all this for Canada.

As a government deeply involved in and committed to aboriginal issues, we have worked long and hard and reflected often on what is happening—and what can happen—in our society. We think it makes a difference. And after this summer, I am sure many Canadians agree.

The federal government should make a fresh start in relations with First Nations by:
- Recognizing aboriginal title;
- Entrenching the right to aboriginal self-government in the Constitution; and
- Making a commitment to negotiate and fund self-government agreements throughout Canada.

In particular, I today call upon the Government of Canada to embark on a deliberate and concerted effort to define and entrench aboriginal rights in the Constitution. They can do it, and they should do it.

The constitutional entrenchment of self-government agreements has been controversial. Both the Yukon First Nations and the Yukon Government have asked Ottawa to constitutionally entrench self-government agreements arising from the Yukon land claim. The federal government has so far refused.

There is no legal impediment to federal entrenchment of self-government agreements, such as the Yukon's, in the Constitution. To do so would be tangible evidence of the new relationship with First Nations which the Prime Minister promoted last week.

There is no need to convene more First Ministers' Conferences and wrangle endlessly and futilely in search of unanimity. As a First

Minister, I now believe this form of unilateral federal entrenchment of negotiated self-government agreements will be more successful than further First Ministers' Conferences.

The First Nations of Canada were sadly and almost completely overlooked in the writing of the Constitution. Almost, but not quite. Section 35 gives the federal government and First Nations a useful tool to create and protect aboriginal self-government in Canada, one area at a time. I strongly urge them to do so.

Bob Rae

Premier
Province of Ontario

I want to speak to you very directly about some directions—and I want to make it very clear that I'm not using this opportunity as a chance to make a totally novel and bold statement, though it may be interpreted that way by some.

But I'm going to simply state, as clearly as I can, the approach of my government, and what we hope to accomplish in the time that the electors have given us for the first time. As Leader of the Opposition, and Leader of the New Democratic Party for over eight years, I spent just about every summer and several winters travelling north of the 50th parallel. I had an opportunity to go places and visit people and see communities that I had never seen, prior to becoming Leader. I've spent a great deal of time discussing and talking and learning—and I'd like to share with you some thoughts on what I've seen.

The first, which is so obvious that it needs to be said over and over again, is that native people were here first. And that has profound implications for the relationship between and among us, as fellow citizens of this country.

The notion that somehow this land was given to us by the people who were here first is not, I think, a perspective that is really going to advance us very far in understanding what the current conflicts are all about.

I think it's extremely important for us to understand what some of the political and, yes, legal arguments are all about. And many of the hangups that we have—and I don't think they are only linguistic; I think they are very real and that they have to do with power, and with our understanding of power—have to do with our use of the word "sovereignty." I want to talk about that.

The Calder case was, I suppose in the modern context, one of the

150

first breakthroughs. The Supreme Court of Canada at least gave a hint of there being a possibility of our dealing with these issues in a more understanding way. Mr. Justice Hall made a very fundamental point which needs to be made, and I'm quoting:

> When the settlers came, the Indians were there, organized in societies and occupying the land as their forefathers had done for centuries.

First came the land, then came the people, and the people exercised power and, yes, sovereignty in a system of law over that land. We now begin to realize—I say "we," I mean non-native people—that there was a very sophisticated, a very highly developed culture, civilization, and system of law.

That was true for Canada. It's true of the United States. It's true all through Central and Latin America. Some of the most articulate, sophisticated cultures and civilizations ever known developed long before European settlers came to this part of the world.

The hangup about sovereignty is something we have to deal with. And, ironically, it is the very notion of federalism that has, in fact, allowed Canadians to deal with this issue in a very significant way for a long time.

The Government of Ontario has sovereignty over some areas and some jurisdictions and some subjects. That's a fact. So does the Government of Canada. With respect to the signing of international treaties, the Government of Ontario doesn't have complete autonomy. On the other hand, we are perfectly able to have negotiations and discussions with other countries, which we do. We have commercial and other relationships with other governments, and we do this within the context of a federal state.

It seems to me that the great potential strength of our approach to this issue lies in starting from the premise, the basic understanding, that before European settlers came, before, if you like, the treaties were signed in 1763, before Confederation in 1867, and before the Constitution of 1982, there existed north of the 49th parallel societies which had a system of law in place, which had a system of power and values in place, which negotiated with British and French governments as they arrived.

What we have seen since that time is that those powers and those values have steadily been eroded, taken away, whittled away, and redefined under laws asserted by, if you will, the conquering power. There's no other way to describe it: a classic colonial situation.

The *Indian Act* is a classic expression of Victorian colonialism. While they were passing an *Indian Act* here, they were passing similar

151

legislation in other parts of the world where the British Empire had been extended—including South Africa.

It's important for us to understand that this is the nature of the history we are trying to overcome, the burden of the history we must overcome. It's important for us to understand its origins and its implications.

I say to you that when I go north of 50, I see communities that have been left in the same colonial status, with all of those implications. Powerlessness, mistrust, people forced to speak English, destruction of native customs, destruction of native language, destruction of a native economy—destruction of a way of life that is no different from the destruction that is taking place everywhere where imperial power has been extended.

And so, as a leader of the Province of Ontario, I tell you that in the time that is given to us, I am determined to do what I can, and our government is determined to do what it can, to see that we come to terms with this history.

Quite specifically I say to you this: We believe that there is an inherent right to self-government, that that inherent right stems from powers, and if you will, sovereignty, which existed prior to 1763, certainly existed prior to 1867, and certainly existed prior to 1982.

Now, let me also say this—that I'm not talking about a demand for national independence, because I don't think that's what's being discussed. I don't think that's what's at stake. I think that's a classic red herring.

I think what's at stake is how we negotiate and come to terms with what these powers actually mean, what impact we can have in a process of negotiation, in creating a common understanding and constitutional framework where self-government will have some meaning—and mean something to the people who are living in communities, in our case, across Ontario.

The second thing that I want to say is that we are prepared, as a province, to discuss this constitutional question, and to play as much of a leadership role as we can in making progress on this constitutional question. But I also say to you that we do not want to allow the fact of a constitutional impasse to dictate the progress that we can make in the Province of Ontario.

You know what I mean. I mean the game that has been played for a very long time. You all know what happens in these discussions. The negotiators go to the table, and we've had instances of this for years. Federal and provincial negotiators go to the table and they say, "Well, we'll get back to you on this one." One level of government

152

says to the other, "We haven't got any money." And the other one says, "We haven't got any money either. It's not a very high priority."

None of us can disagree with the statement that we don't want to see arms used, that we don't condone the use of arms. I certainly don't; I don't want there to be any misunderstanding about that, none at all. But the tragedy is, that it is Oka which drove everyone to understand that something has to give, and something has to move.

For those of us who are opposed to the use of arms, I say we have a special obligation, an obligation to set out a framework for negotiation, to set out a timetable for negotiation, and to say that at the conclusion of this timetable, some things will be settled, and some things will be done!

The process cannot be a Never-Never Land process. Look at the roadblocks we've created for ourselves. We've got a constitutional problem that can't be solved because we can't get agreement. We have a land claim process that is totally stymied at the moment because federal and provincial negotiators have no authority to ever reach any agreements. That's been the frustration, and that frustration grows, it grows tremendously. We've seen the extent of that frustration.

Finally, we have the fact that there are reserves across the country where conditions are—as I have seen them, and as I have tried to describe them and write about them at various times—a classic expression of colonialism. And one of the main features of that kind of system is that people are literally powerless.

I mean, let's be blunt about it: What kind of leverage do the people living in Fort Severn really have?

Unless we, together, resolve to change the status quo, and change this position of powerlessness, and work together to try to change that system of powerlessness, and endeavour to empower people and recognize certain rights as being inherent—as part of people having been here and having had a society long before European settlement came—we'll change nothing.

So there has to be a commitment financially to transfer resources, and that commitment has to come from the federal government, and it has to come from the provincial government.

On behalf of the Government of Ontario, I say we are prepared to transfer some resources, and we hope and pray that the federal government is prepared to transfer some resources. Because, unless we are both prepared to do it, I think everybody here knows that change won't happen quickly enough.

We're not going to play constitutional ping-pong for the next five years, I can assure you. I have no interest in getting into jurisdictional battles with the federal government, in terms of "You go first, Alphonse," and "No, after you, Gaston." We are not going to play that game any more.

It's like people asked in the 1960s: What does Quebec really want? A similar question is implicit in what many politicians are saying: What do the native people really want?

I think native people are entitled to ask politicians who are elected in Ontario and in Manitoba and in Quebec and in the federal government: What do you really want? What are you really prepared to do?

I say to you that, insofar as any one jurisdiction can help to drive the agenda, we are going to drive the agenda in this province for the next five years, and make some progress in this area, and achieve some serious results, which will mean that self-government has a meaning.

Now, people say to me, well, what exactly does it mean? Is it like a provincial government or is it like a municipal government—what does it exactly mean? I say to you, that's what negotiation is all about. This is to be negotiated, this is to be created. This is a creative process.

You know, it's very interesting if you look at the situation in the United States or in other jurisdictions which are wrestling with relationships between settlers and aboriginal communities.

We're not unique. This is an international phenomena. It's the culmination of the great explosion of exploration and international conquest that took place over two or three hundred years. We're all the survivors of this process.

Surely to goodness there's enough creativity—we've got enough lawyers, professors, and anthropologists, and all sorts of people here who have all kinds of ideas—for us to draw on what's happened in other cultures and civilizations and to learn that our concepts are not fixed in stone. Surely, it's not beyond us to find a system of law in this country that is sufficiently flexible to recognize that what's unique about Canada is that we are not like England or France or the European countries.

We are not simply like them. We are a new country. We represent something new in the world. And yes, we share the land. But we sure as hell haven't shared it very fairly, have we?

And that is what is at stake here. I am not going to pretend that the issues are easy. We know the tensions that exist within communities. We know, bluntly put—and let's call it what it is—we know the racism that is still there, still a fact of our society. It is an ugly fact of our society.

154

But we cannot fail to make this progress, and we must not get hung up in old concepts, and fail to come to terms with the issues of power, and of how we share jurisdiction, of how we share responsibility, or how we recognize that responsibility and sovereignty as being there.

No sovereignty in the world is absolute today. It is all relative. We are looking for a Constitution in which every Canadian can look into the constitutional mirror and see his or her reflection.

I really believe that has to be our objective—to create a Canada, a Constitution, a system of power and values and of law, where an elder, sitting in a one-room shack in Fort Severn, can look into the Canadian Constitution and see himself there.

Yes, and where a woman living in Thunder Bay—raising her family very differently from the way her ancestors raised their families, but raising it in Canada—can look into the Constitution and see her reflection, as well.

I don't think that is beyond our creativity, or our power, if we have the political will to do it. And I am here to tell you that we are determined to try.

The Hon. Tom Siddon, P.C., M.P.

Minister of Indian Affairs and Northern Development

I am extremely pleased that my department was able to join the Assembly of First Nations, the University of Toronto, and the Ontario Attorney General's office in sponsoring this important symposium. The events of recent weeks have undeniably focused the eyes of Canada on the very real concerns that face Indian people in this country. Canadians are more aware of these issues today than ever before—and we can be certain that aboriginal people, governments, the business community, the labour movement, and individual Canadians from coast to coast will be giving much attention to our deliberations.

If non-native Canadians are more sensitized to native problems today, I believe they are probably also confused and troubled—perhaps even frightened—by declarations of sovereignty and demands for Indian self-determination.

The timing of this symposium is therefore appropriate, as it provides us with an excellent opportunity to begin to address this issue, which has come to the forefront of public debate in Canada. In my own mind, self-determination means giving native people the capacity to develop and implement their own solutions to their special political, social, and economic problems. It means giving them greater control over their lives, so that their children and successive generations can live in dignity, with honour and respect. This is the concept of self-determination that the Government of Canada supports.

It is towards this end that Prime Minister Mulroney announced a four point agenda for dealing with Indian concerns. Under this agenda, the government will:

- accelerate the settlement of specific and comprehensive land claims and treaty land entitlements;
- work to improve economic and social conditions on reserves;
- address the concerns of aboriginal peoples in contemporary Canadian life; and
- address the relationship between aboriginal peoples and governments.

Each of these initiatives is important, but given the theme of this symposium, I would like to focus my remarks today on the final point—our relationship with First Nations.

If the events and images of this past summer accomplished anything, it was to reaffirm that First Nations want a new relationship with the Government of Canada. I have been saying for some time—and the Prime Minister reaffirmed last week—that the Government of Canada also wants a new relationship with First Nations. And self-government can help us achieve that.

Over the past six years, my department's efforts have ultimately been directed at providing Indians with greater control over their lives. Whether we are talking about land claim settlements, economic development initiatives, social services, education programs, or band administration, we have worked hard to place decision-making and accountability where it should be—with Indians.

And we have made progress, as Georges Erasmus acknowledged in the eleventh annual report of the Assembly of First Nations. Georges wrote, and I quote: "In the past twenty years the landscape has changed a lot for us. I can sum it up by saying that we have taken a good deal of control over our lives and affairs as First Nations persons."

It was gratifying to see such an acknowledgement by a national Indian leader. Nevertheless, I believe we have only just begun the journey to Indian self-determination. We still have a very long way to go, but the important thing is that we have set out—we have established the political will to take on this task. This political will is based on the recognition that Canadians—native and non-native

156

alike—want to plan a better future for themselves, their children, and their fellow citizens.

Over the past few weeks, however, we have reached a fork in this symbolic road to self-determination. On one side lies the path of negotiation, consultation, and cooperation. While this path will by no means be entirely smooth and without obstacles, it is the route I believe we must take, together.

On the other side lies the path of confrontation, acrimony, and distrust. We cannot begin to know where it would lead us, or the repercussions it might have for our children and grandchildren. Perhaps we saw glimpses of where this path could lead us this past summer. It is clearly not an option at all, but rather a road to bitterness, anger, violence, and hatred.

My message today is that the federal government can only build a new relationship with First Nations in a spirit of openness and cooperation.

Since coming to power in 1984, this government has pursued a three-pronged approach to building a new relationship with Indian people, focusing on constitutional change, legislative change, and administrative change.

When it was patriated in 1982, the Canadian Constitution recognized and affirmed existing aboriginal and treaty rights. The Supreme Court's recent decision on the *Sparrow* case has provided significant guidance on this matter. The Constitution also established a process to further define aboriginal rights—including the right to self-government.

Unfortunately, while self-government has been the subject of a series of First Ministers' Conferences (and even though it has been endorsed by the Prime Minister), we have not been able to reach a broad consensus on this vital issue.

I recognize that full constitutional recognition of the right to self-government remains a major goal of many Indian leaders.

This is also a goal of the Government of Canada. But the debate over the Meech Lake Accord showed us that changing the constitution of a nation is never easy. The reality is that we cannot unilaterally amend the Constitution—we require the support, cooperation, and agreement of other levels of government. Until that is forthcoming, we will not achieve constitutional recognition of Indian self-government.

While it appears that it will take some time to sort out the constitutional path of change, this does not prevent us from moving forward in other areas.

I believe Indian peoples' best short-term hope for a new relationship with the federal government lies in the option of legislative change. Right now, we are pursuing two initiatives on this front.

The first is negotiation of community-based self-government arrangements, most of which will require new legislation to remove these communities from the constraints of the *Indian Act*. These negotiations are aimed directly at recognizing the traditional institutions of Indian communities as the appropriate governing authorities. They are without prejudice to any aboriginal or treaty rights which may be established in the future. But let me emphasize that within these restraints, the government is prepared to negotiate *any* change that First Nations will decide to put forward.

The overriding consideration in all negotiations is that they arrive at practical arrangements tailored to the specific circumstances of the community involved. The approach and process must be community driven and at a pace acceptable to all involved.

We know that this process works—we have proof of that in the *Sechelt Indian Band Self-Government Act*. This legislation has removed the Sechelt Band of British Columbia from the shackles of the paternalistic *Indian Act* and allowed it to assume control over band lands, resources, health and social services, education, and local taxation. The *Cree-Naskapi Act* is another example of community self-government through legislation.

Indian bands have expressed strong support for this community-based approach. As of December 1989, a total of 134 self-government proposals had been received by my department. At least five of these have advanced to the level of substantive negotiations. These communities are now just steps away from taking control of their own affairs.

What does all of this mean? Clearly that we are committed to negotiating self-government arrangements with Indian communities as we work toward our long-term objective of constitutional change.

The second legislative initiative is a major review of the *Indian Act*, which has been under way for some time and in which the Assembly of First Nations has been an active participant.

I agree with Indian people, as does the Prime Minister, that the *Indian Act* is paternalistic and obsolete, and that an improved legislative framework is long overdue. In conjunction with Indian leadership, we are now working toward that objective. A number of options for change have been identified by Indian people, and these are now being further explored. As the Prime Minister indicated last week, we will introduce the first of many changes to the *Indian Act* in the New Year.

158

In addition to these legislative initiatives, we can and will continue to pursue administrative changes that place greater responsibility and accountability in the hands of Indian people.

One means of doing this is through alternative funding arrangements, which permit band governments and tribal councils to take on increased responsibility for program delivery. In turn, the band governments are responsible for maintaining an adequate standard of service to their people and for financial accountability. To date, the government has signed seventy-six alternative funding arrangements with a value of well over one billion dollars.

We are also committed to continuing the process of devolution. Indian people now control more than 70 percent of the budget of my department's Indian and Inuit Affairs Program—a budget that has increased by some 60 percent since 1984-85. My department's administration costs have been reduced to only about 4 percent of total program spending—in other words, 96 percent of our funding is going directly to native communities and organizations.

Getting back to self-government, we are learning through the community-based negotiation process that the perception of what self-government is or should be can vary significantly, both between Indian communities and between Indians and governments. In this regard, we are clearly lacking a solid base of information and knowledge from which to work.

I am therefore pleased to announce today that my department has entered into an agreement with the Social Sciences and Humanities Research Council of Canada to support a program of research in the field of aboriginal affairs.

One of the two principal areas to be studied will be Indian governments, including such matters as their organization, financing, responsibilities, and relationships to other governments in Canada. The second area of research will be aboriginal economic development.

Under this initiative, the Social Sciences and Humanities Research Council will administer a program of research grants and offer support for strategic research networks, workshops, and partnerships. In addition to providing us with objective information and analyses, this program should enhance cooperation between all parties with an interest in aboriginal issues. I am hopeful that the research results, which will be available to both native and non-native decision makers, will provide a solid foundation from which we can develop responsive and effective policies.

As you know, one of the objectives of this symposium is to

"establish a common understanding of the issues involved with the recognition and implementation of aboriginal self-government." In fact, the title for today's session is "Sources of Power: What is First Nations Self-Government?"

This is a difficult question to answer, because there is no single model for self-government, and there are clearly varying degrees of control and responsibility that bands wish to assume. Nevertheless, I think this symposium can serve to clear up some misconceptions and establish some basic parameters for negotiations.

While the Government of Canada is committed to helping aboriginal communities take more control over their own affairs and determine their own futures, this must be achieved through a concept and a process that is within the laws and Constitution of Canada.

Nevertheless, we have acknowledged that First Nations should exercise jurisdiction over matters such as culture, education, social programs, certain aspects of the administration of justice, and any other program presently administered by the Department of Indian and Northern Affairs. Let me address briefly the concept of a separate Indian justice system.

In his speech to the House of Commons last week, Prime Minister Mulroney committed the government to finding practical ways to ensure that aboriginal communities can exercise greater control over the administration of justice. However, we must keep in mind that there will clearly be some limitations on this control.

Like all citizens, Indians live within the wider laws and rules set out for this nation. In regard to civil matters, it may be possible to develop a system whereby civil disputes involving aboriginal people could be settled at the local level. Appeals of local rulings could be heard at some other level.

Criminal matters are more difficult to deal with. In Canada, we have one system of criminal law—and it must be applied equally to all our citizens. Nevertheless, it may be possible for some areas of criminal law to be adjudicated in the first instance at the local level. This issue will clearly require a great deal more discussion and negotiation. Above all, we will need imagination, creativity, and open minds. However, the Marshall Inquiry has shown that the administration of justice is a key area that governments must address.

I believe First Nations have noble goals and objectives, and that the vast majority of Indians want to continue to live within the Canadian nation. But by pursuing their goals, Indians must respect the laws of this country and the rights of its non-native citizens. They must recognize that the path of negotiation, consultation, and cooperation remains the only viable means of achieving meaningful and lasting progress.

As the Minister of Indian Affairs and Northern Development, my job is to safeguard the interests of Canada's aboriginal people. But as a Minister of the Crown, I also have an obligation to uphold the laws of Canada—laws that cannot be ignored by any group or individual in society. The past summer's events have demonstrated our resolve on this particular issue.

Fortunately, we live in a democratic society where laws don't have to be broken to make a point. A range of legitimate political and judicial processes are in place whereby First Nations can effect change. I would encourage everyone who seeks change to work within these processes, to consult openly and publicly so that we can continue to live in this country in a spirit of harmony and mutual respect.

When I addressed the House of Commons last week, I indicated that since becoming Minister of Indian Affairs, I have heard the voices of discontent and mistrust; I have sensed Indian peoples' frustration and anger; and I have heard the earnest and sincere call for changes in the policies and actions of governments.

I also said—as I have said to the Assembly of First Nations on previous occasions—that I am determined to earn the trust and confidence of native leaders. I have great respect for the peaceful way in which native people have approached many of the problems in their communities. And I am confident that this will continue to be the Indian way.

The bottom line is that the Government of Canada, First Nations, and other interested and concerned parties can work together, or we can work apart. But I think we must all recognize that we will only be successful when we reach mutually acceptable solutions to Indian concerns—solutions that are good for all Canadians—native and non-native alike. And we will arrive at such solutions more quickly, justly, and painlessly if we work together.

George Watts

Chairman
Nuu-chah-nulth Tribal Council

Last year I was at a symposium on self-government, and I was trying to relieve the fear of Canadian people about what Indian people wanted. And I said just for starters, to show you Nuu-chah-nulth's generosity, you guys can keep the post office, we don't want it. And I also said, we are really not interested in starting up an army or an airforce or a navy, but I have to say to you publicly, that after watching Oka I want to re-think that. I want to re-think that statement, so we'll put that one down for a maybe.

This symposium was called in light of two things. One was the failure of Meech Lake and the low calibre of discussion that took place around the table at the constitutional meetings with the aboriginal people. And it was felt by many people that we had to start talking to Canadian people, who in turn have to start forcing their politicians to rise above the scum that they generally presented at the constitutional table. And the only possible way to do that is to have people in the same room.

We want to talk to the people who own the big corporations. We want to talk to the people in universities who are teaching young Canadian people about their thinking, ten or fifteen years down the road. We want to talk to labour unions who on many occasions are across the barricades from our people. And we want to talk to deputy ministers who ultimately sign off a briefing paper to the Minister about what they're going to say. And I do have to say I think that the Minister of Indian Affairs needs a new person advising him. We need to talk to those people and they need to talk to us.

I have been involved in an education process for fifteen years now in talking to people in British Columbia. The people are there. There are many, many citizens now that understand and support what we're talking about. Our biggest obstacle is the governments who supposedly represent them. And I was really glad some people got up and said that governments can't represent them. Because it is true. How could Mr. Siddon's statement represent what Canadian people are thinking? It is outright colonialism. It can't be seen in any other vein.

I am optimistic and I am pessimistic. I am pessimistic in terms of the Department of Indian Affairs being involved in our lives, and I'll tell you a couple of reasons. One is that they have this section called Indian Self-Government. To me it is one of the biggest contradictions in life. Having a department within the Department of Indian Affairs called Indian Self-Government. They are two very opposites. You can't have white bureaucrats in a department and at the same time over here you have Indian people who are looking for their inherent right to self-government. Those things are on a collision course.

I believe that the Minister of Indian Affairs represents that collision course. I hope Canadian people are going to challenge him. He is

162

ensuring that violence is going to come to this country. I can read nothing else from that, and I consider myself to be one of the most pragmatic, calm Indian leaders in this country. And I am starting to see that. That this government, I believe, is even at the point of actually desiring to see blood flow in this country over Indian issues. I do not believe that this government represents the people of this country, because I believe the majority of the people in this country don't want to see it.

The other issue that I get tired of is this whole issue of money. When are they going to tell the truth to this country about the money. If you take the money that they're talking about—it's in every one of his speeches, two and a half billion dollars—and divide it by the Indian people that they're responsible for, it comes out to $4,554 per Indian person. Well, I can tell you that our tribal council gets more money than any other Indian group in this country, and we get $1,280 per person. Where has the rest disappeared to? And every time the Minister goes to the public, what does he say? He brags about the money that we're getting. Somewhere along the line 50 percent of that money is disappearing.

I think it's time for the journalists in this country to start doing some reasonable journalism and investigating some of these things that are being put across to Canadians in terms of a new approach to Indian people.

I'm optimistic in terms of the other part of self-government. There are two words there. There's "government" and "self." I come from a strong culture. When one of our oldtimers in a conference says: "You know what self-government is? Self-government is teaching your children to survive." Well, I want to tell the Canadian people we're going to survive. We're going to survive and teach our kids to be tougher than us. That's what we're doing now. We really don't see any visible movement on behalf of governments in terms of finding our place in this country. What alternative do we have? I am not going to bring my kid up with hate in him. But my kid's going to survive. My little two boys and my daughter are going to survive, and they're going to survive as Nuu-chah-nulth. And I don't want to get personal with the people at the Department of Indian Affairs, but you better not be around when my kids grow up because they're not going to put up with you. They're not going to put up with the colonialistic government running our lives.

Unfortunately, I think that's the one failure we have had as aboriginal people. We somehow gave the white people the impression that we were going to put up with it. That's the big mistake that

163

we have made through our generation. Well, I can assure you the next generation is not going to make any bones about it. They are not going to put up with it. And they're going to be fighters.

So whoever is writing the notes here for Mr. Siddon, you tell him. You tell Mr. Siddon he had better change his speeches in the near future because if he doesn't, he's going to guarantee that we're going to have a fight in the street over Indian issues in this country. And I am the last person to ever want to bring harm to anybody else. But you have to realize you're bringing harm to my grandchildren. And violence isn't just out of the end of a gun. Violence happens on our reserve every time somebody commits suicide. So I don't want to listen to his gobbledegook about violence and everything else. They are the ones that have created the violence against our people for 120 years. It's not our people with a gun in their hand that are creating the violence. So whoever is writing the notes for him, put it in your notes.

I want to just say two last things. I'm not running for national chief. And the other thing I want to say is that the next symposium we have, I think we better invite Santa Claus. Because even Santa Claus has got to understand that he cannot give self-government to Georges Erasmus. He can only respect his inherent right to self-government.

Elijah Harper

Member
Manitoba Legislative Assembly

We are here to talk about our future as aboriginal people in this country, our destiny, and the relationship we have with the Canadian people and Canadian governments. I listened to Mr. Siddon's speech and what he had to say with respect to self-government. What he said, as I understood it, was that he was ready to give us self-government. Throughout the summer, with the events of Meech Lake and Oka, I don't think the federal government has listened at all. They have not heard us. We have said to the Canadian people and the Canadian governments: "We want recognition. We want the Canadian Constitution to recognize our inherent right to self-government."

The right to self-government is not something that is given, it is something that should be recognized in the supreme law of Canada. Even in the Canadian Constitution, we are not recognized for the positive developments we have made in this country. We are not even recognized as the founding people. Only two nations are recognized, the French and the English. And yet we are the people that welcomed these people to our shores, to our homeland. And we don't get any recognition at all from the two nations that supposedly are the founding nations in this country.

It is sad in this country not to have the aboriginal people placed and recognized in the Canadian Constitution. As aboriginal people we have to be more determined than ever to fight for our rights and our rightful place in Canada, because I feel that governments are not doing it for us. Every right that we have gained has not been at the initiative of governments, but rather at the initiative of aboriginal people themselves.

People wonder why aboriginal people didn't support Meech Lake. I think there is a lesson to be learned from that. For aboriginal people, certainly it provided a forum and a focus for unity. It provided solidarity for all aboriginal people across this country. It was the first time we, as aboriginal people, stood united. As I often say, we can be a very powerful voice as aboriginal people, if we are united. We can speak with one voice, and certainly we demonstrated that in opposing Meech Lake. The failure of Meech Lake was because government had not listened to us.

For many years, aboriginal people have been frustrated in trying to advance their rights and self-government. Because of the failure of Meech Lake, people have asked me: "Is this situation developing at Oka as a result of the failure of Meech Lake?" And I said: "I certainly hope not; I hope it is not a result of the failure of Meech Lake." And that is one of the reasons why, as an aboriginal leader, I tried to facilitate some discussions with the federal government and the Mohawk nations, because I felt that I had an obligation to provide some way of ending the situation peacefully.

What Oka proved is that aboriginal people are still united and concentrated on specific issues such as land claims and sovereignty. It also showed to the Canadian public and the Canadian government that aboriginal people are more determined than ever to stand up for their rights. We found that the feelings of mistrust, the feelings of neglect, had run deeper.

The onus has to be placed on the Canadian government to provide leadership, and certainly there have been some announcements made by the Minister of Indian Affairs. But they did not address the fundamental issue of the inherent right to self-government. What they addressed was more talk, more study. The Minister addressed the constitutional issue of the legislative process and the administrative process in terms of trying to solve aboriginal self-determination,

165

self-government. It really frustrates me to listen to that kind of statement coming from the federal government because we want to address the real fundamental issue of self-government.

Self-government isn't something that is taken lightly by aboriginal leaders. It is so fundamental because it gives us the recognition to control our lives, to control our destiny. It isn't something that is developed by legislation given to aboriginal people.

I believe self-government or self-determination is already there in the Constitution under Section 35. You wonder why the federal government cannot recognize self-government for aboriginal people. If the Canadian government can incorporate the fundamental laws of common law of Great Britain, then what is more Canadian than to embrace and incorporate the laws, customs, and traditional democracies of aboriginal people in this country?

The real issue is about power and control. I have sat through constitutional conferences and that is why constitutional conferences failed, because they wanted us to define what self-government is, what powers they should give us and what powers they might lose. It is interesting to note that Mr. Bob Rae said the same things we said during the first constitutional conference when we, in our preamble to discussions of self-government, said that aboriginal people were here since time immemorial. We practised our own self-government. We had our own practices of management. And we as a government then tried to form a foundation from which we would negotiate self-government. Even then I was very surprised that many of the premiers at that time didn't even want to admit that aboriginal people were here. They didn't even want to express that kind of recognition.

We still have a long way to go, and, hopefully, with governments changing and some enlightened leadership in this country, we will eventually get recognition, instead of just being given more money to administer our own misery. Throwing money at the problem is not going to solve the issue. We have to have the right to self-government, so we can make our own laws. People shouldn't be scared when we talk about self-government. We are not going to take the country back, or develop our own armies or currencies or anything like that. I don't think that's what we are talking about.

Certainly if you look at other jurisdictions in this world, they have concurrent jurisdiction. When they develop the laws they are able to draw from the three levels of governments. In the United States, the Indian people are recognized as domestic nations, but here in Canada, we only have two jurisdictions. The right to legislate only rests with Parliament and with the legislatures. There is no recognition that aboriginal people can make their own laws. If we can somehow achieve that sort of constitutional process at some point, I think we will have achieved some headway for aboriginal people.

It is going to take hard work, more public pressure, to get the governments to act. I know the Prime Minister has made some statements with regard to the current situation. We have been made so many promises before, and just to speak from experience and to speak from history, the promises don't hold much water. I don't know whether we are going to get anywhere. I'm not sure whether governments are sincere. When I say that, I say it not with hate but because we have been made so many promises before that it is hard to believe that government is going to act. I know there might be some movement in certain areas, maybe claims agreements made here and there, but the whole question of land claims has to be addressed. The whole question of policies has to be addressed. It is going to take some time to do that; it's not going to be done immediately.

There is now more public awareness throughout Canada, and there has been much more support for aboriginal people from other Canadians. We have that support now, and people expect action. We must continue to build upon that support, build bridges, because we need allies in order to achieve our goals.

We have a lot of work to do in terms of trying to get the governments to address our issues. If the government was prepared to restore some of its credibility on land claims and accelerate the process generally, they should immediately restore the funding that they have cut back, particularly for education. They should restore some funding for communication—funding that aboriginal people lost—because it is very important to provide news to aboriginal people in their own languages. They should also restore some funding to many of the Indian organizations that lost it. I know in Manitoba two of the political organizations in my constituencies were cut 100 percent. And you expect people to have dialogue with governments. If you want cooperation and to have native people participate, people must have the resources to do so.

So if the government is really sincere in trying to make some movement, they should look at the funding arrangements that they have, the cutbacks that they made, and restore those funding arrangements so that we can get on with many of the activities that were going on before.

Certainly I will keep on fighting for aboriginal people, keep on my fight wherever I can, and keep on the movement that we have going for aboriginal people. Because we need to be strong. We need to be united. We need to work together. We have so many common issues across the country. Hopefully, in our time, we will be able to achieve self-government and also build a better future for our children and for the generations to come.

Towards a National Agenda

Georges Erasmus

National Chief
Assembly of First Nations

The intention of this symposium was to have a dialogue, to try and deal with some complicated subject matter. We thought it would be appropriate to try and get representatives from as many different sectors of the Canadian population as we could bring into one forum. We wanted to do this because we wanted to get a mixture of opinions. We wanted allies we had in the past. We also wanted to bring in different sectors of Canadian society, that we may not have had a lot of contact with previously.

In particular, I would like to thank Adam Zimmerman for having the courage to come. We invited many presenters from many corporations, and we did not get many takers. As Mr. Zimmerman said, he was "not sure if he was an authority to be at this conference." We, in fact, wanted him here precisely because he felt he was not an authority. We felt that he represents a fairly powerful influence, not only in Canada but in the world, and we would like to have that interest he represents realize that First Nations can do business in the same way in which it is done all around the world, with different nations and different governments.

When we can sort out the land base and get proper recognition of First Nations' right to govern, we still will be able to have development. Obviously, if we are true to our values, our traditions, and our history, we will respect the environment more than we have seen in certain instances in Canada and elsewhere. That will not mean that we will be so anti-development that the resources on our territories will be untouchable. That is not the case at all. We would be much more cautious. We would have very tough environmental regulations. We would monitor development to make sure that environmental damage did not occur. We would definitely do business, no question about it.

We started off our dialogue by taking a look at the sources of First Nations' jurisdiction or power. We compared visions of sovereignty.

We reviewed the whole idea that a flag can be hoisted by someone on a piece of settled land with a vision that there are no people living there. What a myth: there is wildlife, plenty of resources, its a new world, and there are no people there—even when there are. And so "discovery" occurs. Whatever European state has put the flag in first, it just claims the land as far as it can posibly see in all directions!

We reviewed how in the modern day, nearly five hundred years

171

after discovery, these states are still living with that myth or misconception. In fact, the indigenous people were a complicated, holistic, and very advanced society. We were not materialistic, but believe me, we were very advanced in our sensitivity to each other, and virtually all of our institutions focused on why people were alive at all. The reason, we believed, was to become as whole as possible, to fulfil their potential, to become more spiritual with every passing minute and every passing day, to see life in everything, and to be positive. Everything we had in our way of life absolutely demanded and required that every action we took had to have a spiritual aspect to it.

So we compared different ways of viewing First Nations' powers. We looked at historical development. We compared histories. What came out—from native people, academics, and lawyers—was that the indigenous view was that our original responsibility, our original sovereignty, was not diminished to the point that it does not exist any more.

It might certainly have been affected on an international basis, but internally it was never extinguished. In our conscious minds, the First Nations never surrendered that responsibility regardless of the fraudulent documents that have stated that we gave up all responsibilities over ourselves or that we gave up all our self-determination and sovereignty. This is not in our history. We do not teach our children that, and we do not teach children a lie.

The Canadian government put the old model before us. Once again, Siddon reminded us that he thinks we have an empty vessel. Dave Joe's stew pot is empty. Someone has eaten it all. For the ingredients to go back in again, the Minister told us, whether they are going to be moose meat or caribou or beef, or what have you, they have to be something given as a gift by either a provincial or federal government, because the pot is completely dry. There is not even residue of a former stew there at all. Even the pot does not belong to indigenous people. There is nothing there at all. And those are the so called modern constraints that Siddon reminds us of every time he has an opportunity to talk to Canadians and the indigenous citizens of Canada.

So, then, we see the two visions of the world that come in contact and conflict every time an indigenous society comes into play with Canada. We have the problem at a regional level and the national level. It's the same problem. I think we have heard fairly reasonable ideas about how we could get around it.

One of the things that people like myself and others have tried to deal with is the possibility of Canadians misunderstanding what First

Nations are about. We are not trying to dismember Canada. The process of Confederation has never been completed, so in reality, the truth of the matter is, we have never truly been properly included in Confederation. Moreover, if we are talking about the land base that we now have south of the 60th parallel, it is not sufficient. We need more land.

The argument can be made—and we make it with regard to Section 35—that the Constitution already recognizes all aboriginal people and treaty rights, because the treaties were a nation-to-nation, government-to-government, sovereign act.

We have examples in the United States of that point of recognition. We have spent some time talking about how we could borrow that model in Canada. We do not want that model in every aspect. We want the principle of the model to be brought here. The principle of the model is that Canada will operate on a nation-to-nation basis with Indigenous First Nations. Canada will operate on a government-to-government basis with Indigenous Nations. The source of power, or the source of responsibility, for indigenous people would be our own inherent right that our people have always retained. If there is any source that it came from, it is that of the Creator, certainly not out of some sovereign state in Europe.

Some of our discussion centered on how well Canada lends itself to that kind of model. I think a fairly credible argument can be made that because of the very fact that we have federal jurisdiction and provincial jurisdiction, we can have yet another order of jurisdiction. As Bob Rae stated, the province of Ontario is sovereign in many areas. Why can't we be?

Some of the provincial areas of jurisdiction are concurrent with and also governed by the federal government, so we have already a divided sovereignty in Canada. If we can put in place a process that would allow for peaceful negotiations, we could fully recognize that First Nations can continue to enjoy their original responsibility and sovereignty. If so, we could end up in a situation where Canada would have a number of sources of sovereignty and it could be practical—it could work.

I think we have had virtually a stepping back from the federal position to some extent because none of the representatives really have argued very much for the delegated authority to First Nations governments. There was some dialogue, not as much as we originally had hoped, but there were some ideas exchanged.

I think if anything, the federal government walked away thinking that they now realize these guys—aboriginal people—are not separatist. They now realize that we are not talking about separate nation-states. They now realize that we are talking about trying to work out, within one nation-state, the recognition of Aboriginal Nations. We have tried to tell them that in the First Ministers' meetings. Perhaps they did not understand it then. Certainly I got the impression people walking away from here will be walking away with a bit more awareness than they had during the First Ministers' meetings a few years ago.

Next we went through the whole thing of the sharing of responsibility or powers. We went into the U.S. model, because we had people like Charles Wilkinson with us. Dan Bellegarde went through the aspirations of Saskatchewan First Nations and their vision of the world, that we have to have law-making power, executive powers and so forth, and how we must have a judicial system, based on First Nations values.

We had some interesting imagery. We had David Joe's stew pot and Allan Paul's sleeping bear, I thought they were wonderful ways of describing what this is all about. We also had the Federation of Canadian Municipalities, which described the kinds of responsibilities they have. It was very useful information, and it was wonderful to hear, that they are prepared to be involved and assist First Nations either at the negotiating table or otherwise. I thought their attendance, their presentations, and their offer of later participation were very worthwhile.

What was also interesting was that we had two representatives, Allan Paul and Ian Johnson, representing areas of Canada where First Nations are participating in the federal government's community based self-government negotiations. In both cases, we heard the First Nations representatives say that the reason why they were participating was to get the money so they could do the research, have internal discussions and workshops, develop models of self-government, and do the work necessary to plan for the future.

For those people that are non-native, it is important to understand that the federal program is often the only game in town. There is no other way to get money. If you are a First Nation that is insisting that the only model is one based upon a recognition of inherent powers or inherent responsibilities, and this is what you want to look at in preparation for negotiations with Canada, you are not even going to be talked to. There will be no resources.

One of the most useful parts of our discussion was provided by the Native Women's Association, as Sharon McIvor described how we were starting to use terminology that seems to mean we are accepting power relations as they exist in Canadian society generally. She

174

reminded us about how power corrupts. The last thing we want is the same thing to happen to us. I thought this was very relevant.

Now, for Tom Siddon's presentation. It is unfortunate, but sometimes I do get the impression that the government does not really listen to what we say. The presentation that was made by the Minister—he still may be wondering why he did not get a standing ovation, and why he did not get a thunderous applause. What went wrong? It is, I believe, partly the advice he gets and maybe just that he feels that the limitations are very real.

One final comment on that part of the proceedings. I think the initiative of the new government in Ontario, as described by Bob Rae, really lends itself to some possibilities. Ontario is the most populated province in Canada. It has in the range of ten million people, and has over a third of the people in Canada. It is the province in which we might make some serious inroads or advancements, in recognizing and putting in place some very real models of self-government.

I know the Nishnawbe-Aski Nation and the other Nations in Ontario would be very excited to sit down and look at how we could do that very quickly. If we have a willing federal government and we have a willing provincial government, we can deal with both land and jurisdiction in a very real way.

I would like to comment on how we might be able to implement some of the these ideas. It does not look like the First Ministers' meetings are going to resume quickly. That's the only place we have been able to deal with changes to the Constitution, and some would say it is the only place that can happen. I think we have been able to put that argument to rest, hopefully. It is not the only way to implement the inherent right to self-government. We have the treaty-making process, and, in Section 35, we have a constitutional vehicle for the recognition of any treaties that will be derived between Canada and First Nations.

So if Ontario, the federal government, and First Nations decide to move quickly, and the model is based on recognition of our inherent responsibility or jurisdiction and is associated with an expanded land base, you could have, before the end of Bob Rae's term, actual models of First Nations self-determination in Ontario, based on the kind of policy that we are after. This would be good, because the federal government's current policies for implementing First Nations government are based on a denial of history, a denial of reality. They are based on extinguishment, on removing many of the victories in the Supreme Court of Canada.

One of the things the Government of Canada has tried to do in its comprehensive claims policy is to take away the ability for First Nations to have the benefit of the doubt. One of the principles that has been developed at the Supreme Court level is that when a treaty is taken to court and you are looking at a section of the treaty—let's say the concept that indigenous people have that education is one of our rights—if there is any doubt and the language is not explicit, oral arguments can be presented on the indigenous side, and if there is any shadow of doubt what the principle is supposed to be, it goes to the benefit of the aboriginal peoples.

This holds for treaties in the past, but the federal government has tried to forestall this reasoning as far as current treaties are concerned. One of the little tricks that the federal government has learned in modern day treaties is that they put right in the fine print that our inherent rights are gone. So the vision of Canada continuing to come forth from the federal government is one of extinguishment. One representing all kinds of negatives. In contrast, the visions of the indigenous people are based on caring, recognition, affirmation, two sovereignties, two sources of responsibility, and a proper sharing of the land base.

Look what happened in the James Bay situation, where, virtually before the ink was dry, Matthew Coon-Come and his people were starting to have problems implementing their treaties, new treaties. You know the federal government even has a different version from the Cree about whether or not Matthew and his peoples' self-government agreements are actually protected by the Constitution. The Cree insist and we insist they are. It was very clear that the policy they. originally negotiated under included the ability to negotiate self-government with municipal powers as part of the treaty negotiations.

It was part of the policy. We can find those old books, if the federal government ever takes this issue to court, but the federal government still insists that the only parts of the James Bay Agreement that have been entrenched in the Canadian Constitution, the only parts of their modern treaty that are protected by the Canadian Constitution, are the sections dealing with land and so forth. And that's where the differences start.

So we talked about that, and we talked about experiences the Dene had, the Yukon First Nations have had, and the present problems with the federal policy on modern treaties or comprehensive claims.

We could make big changes solely on the basis of a decision about policy. The government could base a revised comprehensive claims policy on the spirit and intent of Section 35, without further constitutional change. Recognition, affirmation, and the question of inherent self-government could then be negotiated at the land claims table. The interesting thing is you can't even negotiate delegated authority at the comprehensive claims table and get it enshrined in the Constitution, so that's how far we are on that issue.

We think we have had a fairly reasonable symposium. We have accomplished most of the things that we had originally intended. I want to deal with a few other items that have come up, items that will affect our self-determination strategies in the near future. One is the role of women and the advancement of their involvement, their responsibilities, their sharing of 50 percent of the load for our struggle.

We are having more women being elected to leadership positions throughout the country. It will take some time. We are obviously having far more women being elected, and then they will have to go through that horrendous process of convincing people that they can do a reasonable job.

On another issue, the suggestion that all of our organizations work at the national level together to develop a national strategy is common sense. I, as an individual, am certainly prepared to start to do what I can, to put that into motion.

For a long time in the Northwest Territories, I worked to create a single organization for all of the descendants of the Dene. We had a Métis organization. We had the Dene organization. The concept that the Dene had was that any descendants of the Dene would be a member of the Dene Nation. And, if a person wanted to call themselves Métis they could go ahead. We opened up the membership to everyone. We never ever did that before. At one point we had virtually 90 to 95 percent of the people actively participating and signed up in the same organization.

It wasn't easy. I am not as unrealistic as I was in my twenties when I was the president of the Dene Nation and wanted to create a single national organization for every citizen of the Dene, so I won't put out the concept of creating one organization at the federal level to represent all the aboriginal people in Canada. It would be a false organization right now, because we don't have the basis to do it at the community or regional level.

In the Yukon, and I have to applaud them for all the years they have been able to accomplish it, we have a single organization representing all of the citizens of the first people in the Yukon. We don't have very many models like that. What I could see as being realistic at the national level is a program that is acceptable to all the national organizations, a program that we jointly agree upon, a

177

program on sovereignty and land rights. If we do have a joint vision of where we are going, perhaps we can even get to the point of sharing or dividing the work load. We could do very simple things, like informing each other of certain meetings and of the work of important committees.

We are strongest when we are united. We are strongest when we have a single agenda. It is obvious that we need a national agenda. We need to work out a better working relationship. I, for one, am very prepared to convince people that this is necessary.

You have to go out and have your people involved. We have a tremendous amount of work to do internally. We can even be stronger than we are, if we have our people far more informed. We have work to do publicly with the Canadian public at large and we have work internally. I think that we are responsible enough to know what needs to be done.

We are strongest when we are using our own institutions, the traditional institutions for implementing responsibly. If we are going to make our own laws, let's not use the *Indian Act* system. Let's not use the Chief and Council and the Band Council Resolutions model. We must use the traditional forms of government we had in the past.

We want to continue on that route, because we expect governments are not going to be moving as quickly as we feel they should. We must have a multi-pronged strategy. We must be internally looking at new constitutions, new institutions we might use in the future. We must be putting our models in place as quickly has possible. We must start practising what we are talking about.

Finally, we must consider what our allies can do. We have had a working relationship with church organizations since the early 70s. It started out as an effort to support the Dene, as they defended themselves against a very large pipeline that was being expanded. Eventually we started to have a working relationship with the larger labour organizations in this country. More recently, we have been working with women's organizations. We are working with students' organizations and so forth, including the environmental network.

This work has never been really fully incorporated into a single strategy and a single alliance. We need to map out a strategy that will take us to the year 2000 and beyond, to ensure that regardless of what governments do, we will move quickly so that we never have to have George Watts's daughters and sons involved in violent confrontations. This is what we must do, if we want to guarantee the kind of recognition and the kind of Canada that we all should have.

Background Papers

Now We Talk—You Listen

(excerpt from *Rotunda Magazine* (Vol. 23, No. 2—Fall 1990),
a publication of the Royal Ontario Museum)

Donald Smith
Professor of History
University of Calgary

In 1939 Dr. Tom McIlwraith, an anthropologist at the University of Toronto and curator of the ethnological collections of the Royal Ontario Museum of Archaeology, and Professor Charles Loram of Yale University organized a two-week conference on the North American Indian hosted by the University of Toronto. Over 70 Canadian and American government officials, missionaries, and academics were invited to attend this important event, which was held at the Museum. More importantly 12 North American Indians were also invited. This was the first conference ever held to discuss Indian welfare and the first Canadian scholarly conference to invite Indian delegates. In the words of the organizers the purpose was "to reveal the actual conditions today of the white man's Indian wards, and in a scientific, objective and sympathetic spirit, plan with them for their future." The conference concluded in a most unexpected way.

Fifty years ago, most Canadians rarely gave any thought to native issues because it was commonly believed that the Indians were a vanishing people. In fact, the famous Canadian anthropologist Diamond Jenness wrote in his book *The Indians of Canada (1932)*: "It is not possible now to determine what will be the final influence of the aborigines on the generations of Canadian people still to come. Doubtless all the tribes will disappear. Some will endure only a few years longer, others like the Eskimo, may last several centuries." Through intermarriage with non-natives, and cultural assimilation into the larger society, it was assumed that Indians would become extinct.

Perhaps it was most appropriate for the conference to be held in Toronto, one of Canada's most populated cities. Indians in the 1930s were a more distant and foreign people to the citizens of Toronto than to Canadians in other urban centres. Unlike Montreal, which had the large Iroquois reserve at Kahnawake (Caughnawaga), or Vancouver with its neighbouring Squamish and Musqueam reserves, or Calgary, with the Sarcee reservation on the city's southwestern border, Toronto had no neighbouring Indian reserve. Once the local Mississauga Indians had held reserve land along the Credit River just west of the city, but the pressure of white settlement had forced them to leave. In 1847 the Mississauga of the Credit had relocated westwards to the Grand River, next to the Six Nations (Iroquois) near Brantford. By the 1930s Toronto had so forgotten the Mississauga Indians that the Indian shown in the city's coat-of-arms was a warbonneted Plains Indian. (The error was only corrected in 1961 when the Indian was given the costume of an 18th-century Mississauga.)

Few Torontonians even knew the meaning of the Iroquois name for their city. The Mississauga had always been told by the Iroquois that "Toronto" meant "looming of trees" or trees growing out of the water. As late as the 1860s one could still look from Queen Street south to Ashbridge's Bay to see trees that appeared to grow from the water.

From 1936 to 1938 Grey Owl was the best-known North American Indian to Torontonians. The famous writer and lecturer, who lived and worked at his cabin in Saskatchewan's Prince Albert National Park, made two important public appearances in the city. He came to Toronto in November 1936 to attend the first Toronto Book Fair. The tall, dark, hawk-faced man, clad in moccasins and buckskins, with a single eagle feather in his hair, had just returned from his triumphant lecture tour of Britain the previous spring. The British press had responded warmly. Shortly after his arrival the London *Times* wrote: "A picturesque figure in Indian dress, with the thoughtful face of a philosopher, Grey Owl comes as the friend of nature." The *Manchester Guardian* reported that Grey Owl spoke in a concerned, earnest way about the wilderness and talked "with the true nasal twang of the Canadian Indian." Just before Grey Owl left London, the *Sunday Express* commented: "There never came a Redder Red Indian to Britain."

The Toronto organizers estimated that 800 people would come to hear Grey Owl in the King Edward Hotel's Crystal Ballroom. Instead nearly 1700 crowded into the room, and another 500 were turned away. He was preceded by his reputation as a skilled writer and lecturer on the land, the animals, and the people of Canada's North.

During his visit, Grey Owl discussed his racial background with Sir Charles G.D. Roberts, one of Canada's most distinguished men of letters. Sir Charles included the details in *The Canadian Who's Who, 1936-1937*. The entry reads, "born encampment, State of Sonora, Mexico; son of George, a native of Scotland, and Kathrine (Cochise)

Belaney; a half-breed Apache Indian . . . adopted as blood-brother by Ojibway tribe, 1920 . . . speaks Ojibway but has forgotten Apache."

Grey Owl also visited the Museum and met with its director, Dr. Charles Trick Currelly. Ken Kidd, then a young assistant to Dr. McIlwraith, took Grey Owl through the exhibit of artifacts from Indians of the southwest United States. More than a half-century later, Kidd recalled, "I did not suspect that he was not an Indian, but in those days I was not familiar with the real thing. The main impression he left with me was his saying that he had been born in Northern Mexico—I think in the State of Chihuahua—as his mother happened to be visiting there at the time. He was quite emphatic about this."

On 26 March 1938, only a year before Dr. McIlwraith's conference, Grey Owl came to Toronto again, addressing an audience of about 3000 in Massey Hall. This was to be his last visit to the city. Grey Owl had returned to Canada three months earlier from a second highly successful tour of the British Isles, in which he delivered nearly 150 lectures, including a royal command performance at Buckingham Palace. After his Toronto address, which was part of a seven-month tour of lectures on the importance of conservation in Britain, Canada, and the United States, Grey Owl returned totally exhausted to his cabin in Saskatchewan. He died in Prince Albert on 13 April 1938. Shortly after his death, the truth about his life was exposed.

By the time of the University of Toronto's conference in the fall of 1939, it was common knowledge that the most popular North American Indian was really one Archie Belaney, born and raised in Hastings, England, who had left home at the age of 17 to live in northern Canada. Belaney had so admired the Indians for their ability to adapt to their natural surroundings that in Canada he created a new identity for himself as an Indian. It was time that Torontonians and North Americans in general learned the facts about the Indian people.

From 4 to 16 September 1939, the conference delegates at the Museum heard from various non-native speakers about the cultures, reserve economics, health, and education of the Indians. Federal government officials pointed out that Canada's Indian population was no longer in decline: since the late 1930s the population had increased annually by one per cent.

The press paid little attention to the meetings because, unfortunately, the timing of the conference could not have been worse. Three days before sessions started at the Museum, Germany invaded Poland, and two days later Britain declared war on Germany.

Throughout the first two weeks of September the press focused on the rapid German advance through western Poland. Midway through the conference, on 10 September, Canada declared war on Germany, and the day after the conference ended the Soviet Union invaded eastern Poland. The general public and press were too preoccupied to hear about the poor health conditions, unemployment, and the residential school system experienced by Indians.

On the last day of the conference delegates met to pass resolutions urging greater attention to "the psychological, social, and economic maladjustments of the Indian populations of the United States and Canada." A committee was established to oversee the publication of the conference's papers and the dissemination of information on North American Indians. And then a very dramatic defection took place. The Indian delegates broke from the main group and met separately to pass their own resolutions.

Members of the Indian delegation from the United States included Arthur C. Parker, an Iroquois anthropologist; D'Arcy McNickle, a distinguished academic; Louis Bruce, an Iroquois civil servant in New York State; David Owl, a Cherokee Christian missionary; and Ruth Muskrat Bronson, a Cherokee guidance officer with the Office of Indian Affairs in Washington. The delegates from Canada were Peter Kelly, a Haida United Church minister and an influential Indian leader in British Columbia; Teddy Yellowfly, the manager of the Blackfoot's coal mine in Alberta; Earl Calfchild, an interpreter from the Blackfoot band in Alberta; Canon Maurice Sanderson, an ordained Anglican minister from Ontario; Joe Peltier, a respected Indian leader from Manitoulin Island; Norman Lickers of the Six Nations Reserve near Brantford, the first Indian lawyer in Ontario; and Edith Brant Monture, the great-great-granddaughter of Joseph Brant, the famous Iroquois chief.

While appreciative of their invitation to the conference, the Indians resolved to have their own meetings. They did not need government officials, missionaries, white sympathizers, or Grey Owls to speak for them. As part of their resolution they stated: "We hereby go on record as hoping that the need for an All-Indian Conference on Indian Welfare will be felt by Indian tribes, the delegates to such a conference to be limited to bona fide Indian leaders actually living among the Indian people of the reservations and reserves, and further, that such conference remain free of political, anthropological, missionary, administrative, or other domination."

Canadians did not hear the Indian voice in September 1939, drowned out as it was by the outbreak of the Second World War, but

184

they did hear it after the war. The general acknowledgement of the strong contribution to the war effort made by Canada's native peoples and the injustice of their second-class status contributed to a growing public interest in native isues throughout the country.

Canada's native population continues to grow. Metropolitan Toronto now has a native population numbering in the tens of thousands. In the new multicultural Canada, native peoples no longer have to give up their cultural identity and assimilate into the larger society. Like the Indian delegation at the Royal Ontario Museum of Archaeology in 1939, today's native leaders speak for themselves without intermediaries. Dr. McIlwraith would applaud, and so would Grey Owl.

First Nations Sovereignty and Self-determination

Joe Sanders
Barrister and Solicitor

Absolute Sovereignty

Absolute sovereignty has two aspects: internal and external. Internal sovereignty is paramount power over all actions within, i.e. authority over all persons, things and territory within the reach of the sovereign power. It is the power that governments exercise to create laws within the society. External sovereignty means independence of control by any other sovereign power. It is the power that governments exercise in entering into treaties and to create international law.

In Europe, the concept of absolute sovereignty was significantly predicated upon ownership and possession of defined territory. In Africa, however, the situation was very different. There, tribes were regarded as absolutely sovereign regardless of the territorial factor. This was largely because of the topography of the land and partly because of the nomadic nature of the tribes.

When Europeans arrived in what is now known as the Americas, the First Nations peoples were the absolute "owners" of their possessions and lands. So-called "discovery," as de Vitoria argued, gave Spain no right to seize those lands. The European approach to absolute sovereignty was therefore inapplicable to the "American" situation as it was to the African.

In international law, the classic criteria that define a state are:
1. Population;
2. Territory;
3. Government; and,
4. Capacity to enter into international relations or treaties.[1]

It is a matter of historical record that, before the arrival of Europeans, First Nations possessed and exercised absolute sovereignty on the now-called North American continent. In what is now known as Canada, they lived in hundreds of tribal communities, from Newfoundland to Vancouver Island, made up of a variety of nations in at least ten linguistic groups. They decided their own citizenship. They had the use of the entire land. Although they had a wide variety and diversity of governmental systems, almost all of them regulated their activities and relations among their members with a degree of formality. The way they dealt with the Europeans is ample proof of their

186

capacity to enter into foreign relations: they entered into a number of treaties with the French and British Crowns, and many of the colonies survived because of the assistance they gave to the European settlers.

International law recognizes that social, political, or technical achievement in the contemporary sense is not a valid criterion for the rights to which aboriginal peoples are entitled.[2] Many distinguished European writers and international lawyers, from the Middle Ages onwards, recognized First Nations (or Indian) sovereignty.[3]

First Nations Sovereignty

Ownership of land in the Anglo-Canadian sense of title, i.e. "fee simple," was foreign to the thinking and systems of First Nations. Land was revered as a Mother from which life came and was to be preserved for future generations, as it had been from time immemorial. It was used for common benefit with no individual "owning" any more of it than another; but one nation's traditional hunting grounds were recognized as theirs by their neighbours. For the most part, the land was not delineated; but some nations in British Columbia, such as the Gitksan and the Nisga'a, had systems of identifying their boundaries and passing on custodial responsibilities. First Nations peoples believe that they live *with* the land, not simply *on* it.

European settlement in what is now known as Canada began with the arrival of the French at Port Royal in Acadia in 1605; but formal negotiations of an international or intergovernmental nature for land settlement and ownership purposes did not begin until the English superseded the French after the Treaty of Utrecht in 1713. "From the time of the first British settlement . . . the title of the Indians to lands occupied by them was conceded and compensation was made to them for the surrender of their hunting grounds".[4]

The *Royal Proclamation of 1763* set forth the Crown's policy on land negotiations. The Crown recognized that lands possessed anywhere (in what was then British North America) by First Nations are reserved for them unless or until they ceded land to the Crown.[5] That policy has never been revoked. (In fact, the rights and freedoms recognised in the *Proclamation* are constitutionalised by S.25 of the *Constitution Act 1982*).

The *Proclamation* could be regarded as the first major legal link between First Nations and the Crown. Under international law, a weaker power does not surrender its right to self-government merely by associating with a stronger power and taking its protection. By virtue of that *Proclamation*, First Nations become protected states of the British while being recognized as sovereign nations competent to maintain the relations of peace and war and capable of governing themselves under that protection. First Nations citizens became British-protected persons with the same civil rights as British subjects.

The international personality of First Nations was not relinquished by them. Although First Nations qualified as sovereign and independent under international law, successive Governments of Canada seem to have taken the position that circumstances changed over the years and that First Nations are no longer such; that they are subject to the will of the Crown.[6]

Thus, British, and later, Canadian citizenship were imposed upon First Nations citizens.[7] They were made subject to the jurisdiction of Canadian legislatures; like any citizen they could have had their rights and privileges altered and even taken away by legislative action despite any treaties agreed to between their forebears and the Crown.

Today, the Government of Canada officially rejects assimilation and termination for the aboriginal peoples, but it rejects also their full independence or absolute sovereignty.[8] Yet, at no time did First Nations willingly consent to the relinquishment of their sovereignty.

The Treaties

In international law, a treaty is primarily an executive act establishing relationships between recognized independent states acting in their external sovereign and equal capacities. Between 1781 and 1867 (Confederation), some First Nations signed certain treaties with the Crown under which they surrendered rights and privileges to certain lands. In turn, they were to obtain certain treaty rights. These treaties represented further legal links between those nations and the Crown, but, again there is no evidence that sovereignty was surrendered.

In 1867, the *British North America Act* (renamed the *Constitution Act 1867*) provided for internal self-government in Canada by the European settlers. First Nations were not a party to the Confederation which was established and to the drafting of the Constitution. However, subsection 91(24) provided that the federal Parliament would have the authority to legislate for "Indians, and lands reserved for the Indians" to the exclusion of the provincial legislatures. By virtue of that subsection, the Indian nations were placed under the

188

legislative power and jurisdiction of the federal government, as agent of the Crown, but not under its territorial "dominion."

Certain other treaties were executed between others of the First Nations and the Crown after Confederation (1867). In many cases, it appears that the treaties were imposed upon the First Nations, the leaders of which had little choice but to consent. The treaties were written in English, and the Crown's negotiators often misrepresented the contents. Today, it may be argued that many of those treaties are "unequal" or "unconscionable" or "unfair" both in substance and procedure. In any event, First Nations did not perceive the treaties as being a surrender of the sovereignty of their nations.

Unlike the colonies which became independent after the Second World War, there was no sudden act of independence for Canada. As a British colony, Canada gained its independence of Britain by a slow and gradual process between 1919 and 1931 in much the same way as Australia, New Zealand, and South Africa.

Once a state (in this case Canada) has been independent for a few years, it will have acted in such a way that it will be prevented in law from denying that it has succeeded to treaties made by the former colonial power (in this case Britain). Treaties create obligations as well as rights and a new state (in this case Canada) cannot succeed to the rights without the obligations. To say the least, the federal government's position on the treaties seems confused and confusing.[9]

Canadian law, since the latter part of the last century, has relegated the First Nations treaties with the Crown almost to the level of private law contracts thereby denying their status as treaties in the international law sense, although, as the Supreme Court of Canada repeated in the *Simon* case, they are unique and share some of the features of international treaties.

If the agreements were "treaties among sovereign nations" in the eighteenth and nineteenth centuries, how could their status be changed without First Nations consent by mere Canadian legal "diktat"? Treaties are to be interpreted as First Nations understood them, and they understood that their treaties were intended to preserve their existence and status as nations of peoples distinct from non-Indians.[10]

Indian Acts 1876-1951

Prior to 1876, the major legal links between First Nations and non-Indian society in Canada were through the *Royal Proclamation* of

1763, certain treaties with the Crown and subsection 91(24) of the *Constitution Act 1867.*

In effect, do those links mean that First Nations were nations protected by the Crown? The Crown owes some First Nations certain treaty rights and the federal government has arrogated to itself the authority to legislate *for* First Nations peoples and their lands to the exclusion of the provincial governments.[11]

Aside from those links, First Nations were not party to the Canadian Confederation by any voluntary act of their own. They were nations co-existing with the federal government and the provincial governments, although their powers to exercise sovereignty were being eroded by the Constitution and subsequent federal legislation.

In 1876 the federal government passed its first *Indian Act*, the first consolidation of the laws pertaining to Indians.[12] The *Indian Act* was passed by the federal government in the exercise of its exclusive legislative responsibility for Indians, and lands reserved for the Indians, but First Nations have had no input into it. In fact, First Nations citizens had no part in electing the politicians who legislated the *Indian Acts* since they were allowed to vote only in 1960.

For years the federal government has repeatedly stated that First Nations would have adequate time to consider their own priorities before any changes are brought into force regarding the *Indian Act.* Since 1987 the Department of Indian Affairs has been undertaking a review of the lands, revenues and trusts sections of the *Indian Act.* More recently, the Department reorganised in a way that it would be in a position to respond to proposals for alternatives to the *Indian Act* that might be put forward by some First Nation communities.

The Constitution and Self-Determination

For many years prior to 1982, the federal and provincial governments of Canada embarked upon a process of reform of their national Constitution, which resulted in the *Constitution Act 1982*. First Nations were not party to the drafting of the renewed Constitution. However, the non-Indian governments agreed that First Nations leaders should be invited to participate in subsequent constitutional conferences to identify and define their rights for inclusion in the Canadian Constitution.[13]

That was the first time, in their relationship with the Crown, that First Nations were being consulted about the Constitution, if to a very limited degree. They were, in effect, merely invited to establish and defend their rights. If they did not participate, non-Indian governments would probably have unilaterally identified and defined those rights.

That brings the argument to the matter of self-determination and sovereignty. In international law, the concept of self-determination encompasses the right of peoples "freely to determine, without external interference, their political status and to pursue their economic, social, and cultural development".[14] A people has been authoritatively described by the World Court as "a group of persons living in a given country or locality, having a race, religion, language and traditions of their own and united by the identity of race, religion, language and tradition in sentiment of solidarity, with a view to preserving their traditions, maintaining their form of worship, ensuring the instruction and upbringing of their children in accordance with the spirit and traditions of their race and rendering mutual assistance to each other".[15]

A people identifies itself as such provided the criteria are met. It requires no imagination to realize that Indians are distinct peoples within Canada. A people, therefore, has the right in international law to be free from external domination, free from discrimination on grounds of race, colour, creed, or political conviction, free to pursue their own economic, social, and cultural development, free to enjoy fundamental human rights and equal treatment, free to determine their own citizenship, free to form a government or governments of their own choosing.

A people's right to self-determination does not necessarily imply its independence, but rather its freedom to choose how it will be governed. That right also involves the further right to full compensation and restitution for the exploitation, depletion of, and damage to, their natural and other resources.[16]

While it rejected First Nations absolute sovereignty—which implies full independence as States—the federal government under Prime Minister Trudeau was prepared to discuss options to satisfy First Nations aspirations, as far as possible. On behalf of the federal government, he stated publicly that, "Some options, or variations of them, may be found in experience elsewhere in the world. As is so often the case, there is a substantial record of parallel experience in the U.S."[17]

In the law of United States, the absolute sovereignty of Indian nations is also denied. However, it is conceded that they are "domestic dependent nations," a term which encompasses two major elements: their inherent "sovereign" powers and the special trust relationship between the United States Government and the various Indian nations.

In a series of cases, ranging from 1831 to 1982, the United States Supreme Court has reiterated that the Indian nations in that country are "domestic dependent nations."[18] They have general authority, as "sovereign," to control economic activity within their jurisdictions. In other words, Indian nations in the United States are denied absolute sovereignty, independence, or international personality, but they have internal sovereignty for limited domestic purposes.

Qualified Sovereignty in International Law

Besides recognising absolute sovereignty, international law also recognises the concept of qualified sovereignty. Thus, a given political entity may be in a situation of legal dependency; that is, it may not be independent (or absolutely sovereign), yet, it may be regarded as having certain rights and duties before international law. It never entirely loses its international personality. It is, therefore, legally possible for Indian governmental power to exist; not only within the Canadian political system, but also with a measure of recognition by international law.[19]

In this regard, certain general models are available:

SPECIAL CASES: In the world today, the Holy See, Monaco, and San Marino are recognised as states with certain limited international roles while existing under the protection of other dominant powers with which they have close physical and economic ties and relations.

PROTECTED STATE: The relationship of protector and protected state occurs when two states enter into a valid treaty relationship under which the protector is afforded certain functions both internally and externally over the protected state. However, the protected state retains international responsibility for acts within its reserved jurisdiction. Brunei is an example of such a formerly protected state.[20]

ASSOCIATION OF STATES: By virtue of an international agreement, states may establish a confederation which is a very close form of cooperation with certain central institutions in common.

Finally with reference to Canada, certain specific models may be identified.

1. Recognition of First Nations Absolute Sovereignty or Independence

The federal government rejects recognition of First Nations absolute sovereignty[8]; and First Nations themselves have acknowledged the fact of the Canadian polity or political system.[19]

2. Constitutional Recognition of First Nations Qualified Sovereignty

(a) Qualified sovereignty may be *explicitly* recognized in the Canadian Constitution by way of an amendment to Section 35 of the *Constitution Act 1982*, which may or may not be elaborated by a special Charter of Rights for the First Nations; or

(b) Qualified sovereignty may be *implicitly* recognized by the constitutional recognition of First Nations government (or governments) with a spelling out of First Nations governmental powers and areas of jurisdiction in the same manner as the *Constitution Act 1867* defines the areas of federal and provincial jurisdiction.

3. Recognition of First Nations Qualified Sovereignty in Legislation (Indian Act Alternatives)

Qualified sovereignty may be *implicitly* recognized by an agreement with the federal government. Areas of respective legislative competence associated with First Nations and the federal government may be defined under subsection 91(24) of the *Constitution Act 1867*.

4. Indian Act Amendments

The federal government, in proper consultation with the First Nations, may amend the Indian Act to provide for First Nations governmental powers in certain areas of administration.

5. Assimilation

First Nations reject assimilation; so does the federal government.[17]

Endnotes

1. Art. I of the 1933 Montevideo *Convention on the Rights and Duties of States*.
2. Hugo Grotius, *The Law of War and Peace* at 61 (F. Kelsey trans. 1925).
3. Such eminent scholars included de Vitoria, de Vattel, Gentili, Grotius, Ayala, Heffter, Fiore, Solomon and Blackstone. They were the vanguard of the development of international law and

represented the thinking of international jurists in such imperial-
ist European powers as Spain, Germany, Holland, Italy, France
and Great Britain.

4. The Director of the Indian Affairs Branch in 1946 in a submission
   to a Joint Committee of the Senate and the House of Commons.

5. Part IV of the *Royal Proclamation 1763*.

6. In the *Sioui* case (1990), the Chief Justice of Canada, giving
   judgement on behalf of a unanimous Supreme Court, said: " . . .
   The Indian nations were regarded in their relations with the
   European nations . . . as independent nations."

7. See *Sero v. Gault* (1921), 50 O.L.R. 27; Cayuga Indians Claim
   (1926), Neilsen American and British Claims Arbitration Reports; and *Logan v. Attorney General* [1959] O.W.N. 316.

8. Prime Minister P.E. Trudeau at the First Ministers Conference
   on 16 March 1983. And, Prime Minister Mulroney in the House
   of Commons on 25 September 1990.

9. Before the so-called patriation of the Canadian Constitution,
   both the British and Canadian governments stated publicly that
   the rights and obligations under First Nations' pre-Confederation treaties with the Crown became the exclusive responsibility
   of the Canadian government at least as early as the *Statute of
   Westminster 1931*.

   Any special relationship which First Nations might have had with
   the Queen, they maintained, was now with the Crown in Canada,
   not with the Crown in Britain.

   Yet, on 13 May 1982, less than a month after the patriation of the
   Canadian Constitution, the Minister of Indian Affairs told a press
   conference in Ottawa that "the Indians have to show some act on
   the part of the (Canadian) government subsequent to Confederation clearly indicating the assumption of . . . responsibility."
   Does this mean that, in Canada's view, some of the treaties are
   still the responsibility of the British Crown?

10. A brief glimmer of hope that the treaties would be correctly
    regarded lay in the judgement of His Honour Judge C.T. Murphy
    in the District Court of the District of Manitoulin in the case of
    Hare and Debassige v. The Queen, on 9 September 1983 when he
    said: "In my view, those treaties should be treated with the same
    solemnity and seriousness as are treaties entered into with foreign
    sovereign states and as being as valid and binding as an Act of the
    Parliament of Canada . . . When one considers the true meaning
    of the word 'treaty' and the recognition that Indian treaties have

been accorded in the *Canada Act [S.35(1) Constitution Act 1982]*, one would be hard pressed to hold that a treaty entered into by the representatives of the Government of Canada with representatives of Canada's native peoples should be considered less seriously and with less respect or concern than a treaty entered into with a foreign government."

11. Provincial governments have no legislative responsibility for First Nations. Provincial laws of general application must not conflict with the terms of any treaty or any Act of the federal Parliament or any valid Band by-law.

12. The present *Indian Act* is the 1951 version, with some amendments.

13. Subsection 37(2) of the *Constitution Act 1982*.

14. *Declaration on the Principles of International Law Concerning Friendly Relations and Cooperation Among States in Accordance with the Charter of the United Nations*, G.A. Res. 2625, 25 U.N. GAOR, Supp. (No. 28), 121, U.N. Doc. A/8082 (1970).

15. *Advisory Opinion of the Permanent Court of International Justice concerning Greco-Bulgarian "Communities"* (1930) P.C.I.J., ser. B, No. 17, at 21.

16. United Nations *Declaration on Permanent Sovereignty over Natural Resources*, Res. 1803 (XVII), 1962. It emphasises that even foreign ownership of a means of producing a resource should not detract from the sovereignty of a state.

17. Prime Minister Pierre Elliot Trudeau at the First Ministers Conference on 16 March 1983.

18. See, eg., *Cherokee Nation v. Georgia*, 30 U.S. (5 Pet.) (1831); *Worcester v. Georgia*, 31 U.S. (6 Pet.) (1832).

On 24 January, 1983, the then U.S. President, Ronald Reagan stated, "Our new nation (i.e. the United States) continued to make treaties and to deal with Indian tribes on a government-to-government basis. Throughout our history, despite periods of conflicts and shifting national policies in Indian affairs, the government-to-government relationship between the United States and Indian tribes has endured. . . . Our policy is to re-affirm dealing with Indian tribes on a government-to-government basis for Indian tribes without threatening termination." Presidents Nixon and Bush have emphasized this position.

19. The First Nations *Treaty and Aboriginal Rights Principles* declare that: "Indian Governmental powers and responsibilities exist as a permanent, integral fact in the Canadian polity."

20. Brunei was a powerful state from the 16th to the 19th century, but it deteriorated and later became a British protected state. Under the protected status, the Sultan controlled internal affairs while Britain was responsible for defence and foreign affairs. The protected status terminated at the end of 1983.

Aboriginal Sovereignty
and Imperial Claims

Brian Slattery
Associate Professor of Law
Osgoode Hall Law School
York University

It is commonly assumed that indigenous American nations had neither sovereignty in international law nor title to their territories when Europeans first arrived; North America was legally vacant and European powers could gain title to it simply by discovery, symbolic acts, occupation, or treaties among themselves. It follows, on this view, that current indigenous claims to internal sovereignty or a "third order of government" have no historical basis. This paper argues that this viewpoint is misguided, and cannot be justified either by reference to positive international law or basic principles of justice. The author's view is that indigenous American nations had exclusive title to their territories at the time of European contact, and participated actively in the formation of Canada and the United States. This fact requires us to rewrite our constitutional histories and reconsider the current status of indigenous American nations.

The international legal history of North America has traditionally been presented as a series of military and diplomatic struggles among European states and their colonial offshoots, culminating in the grand treaty settlements of the 18th and 19th centuries in which the modern international boundaries of the United States and Canada were fixed.[1] The accounts differ in explaining exactly how the European powers originally gained sovereignty over North America, with some authors allowing for such supposed methods as discovery and symbolic acts, and others discounting these and arguing that effective occupation was necessary.[2] Despite these differences, the traditional accounts tend to assume that the original peoples of North America had no significant role to play in this high imperial drama. Indigenous peoples, it is thought, lacked sovereign status in law and so had no international title to the territories they occupied. On this view, the lands of North America were legally equivalent to vacant territories which could be appropriated by the first European state to discover or occupy them. The only role assigned to the original inhabitants of North America was subsidiary, as factual obstacles or aids to the spread of European sovereignty.

This approach is by no means dead. In a recent study of European claims to territory in America, L.C. Green concludes with this flat statement:

> Insofar as international law is concerned, there can be no doubt that the title to the land belonged, in the first instance, to the country of those who first discovered and settled thereon. ... Moreover, international law did not recognise the aboriginal inhabitants of such newly discovered territories as having any legal rights that were good as against those who "discovered" and settled in their territories. From the point of view of international law, such inhabitants became the subjects of the ruler exercising sovereignty over the territory. As such, they enjoyed no rights that international law would recognize, nor was international law concerned with the rights which they might enjoy or which they might claim under the national law of their ruler.[3]

These remarkable views, although prominent in histories of international law and diplomacy, are not restricted to that narrow genre. They permeate narratives of all kinds, from popular historical romances, through movies and television dramas, to newspaper editorials and legal decisions. Even when not explicitly stated, they show their influence in the structure of the story- line, the importance assigned to various episodes, and the terminology employed. Thus, such events as the fall of Quebec and the Treaty of Paris of 1763 are assigned a central place in the history of North America, while the peace treaties with the various native American nations in the same era receive only scant attention outside of specialist literature. The great Aboriginal-British war that engulfed the eastern and mid-western regions of North America in the period 1763-64 is dubbed "Pontiac's Rebellion," on the assumption that native Americans were rebelling against legitimate British rule rather than asserting their rights against invading forces.

The Eurocentric premises of traditional accounts have come under heavy attack in recent decades. The heightened political activism of Aboriginal groups, the large numbers of native claims reaching the courts, and the revival of interest in native American history, have all contributed to the development of more critical attitudes to the European penetration of the continent. This development is welcome and long overdue. Yet, while there is a growing consensus among historians and lawyers that the old legal framework is flawed, there is uncertainty and confusion as to how the situation may be remedied.

A historian, dismayed at the distortions caused by the old legal premises and daunted by the prospect of having to supply new ones, might well decide to avoid making any legal assumptions whatever and concentrate on the factual interplay of people and forces. By contrast, a lawyer or judge, bewildered at the complex historical panorama disclosed by the new scholarship, might think that the only safe route lies in a legal analysis that steers clear of historical materials. If only, says the historian, there were no law to distort our understanding of the historical forces; if only, says the lawyer, there were no history to muddy the purity of the law.

But history and law are not so easily severed. From early times, Aboriginal-European relations were profoundly shaped by legal conceptions on both sides, to the extent that they can hardly be understood otherwise. For example, the numerous treaties concluded between First Nations and colonial governments played an essential role in determining the various parties' expectations and actions, and moulding their understanding (and misunderstanding) of the other parties. These treaties necessarily figure prominently in any historical account of Aboriginal-European relations. Moreover, they are central to the self-understanding of many native American groups today, and an important basis for contemporary legal claims. It would be difficult to give an account of the treaties that is sensible and informative and yet avoids dealing with the basic issues of their legal status, character, and effects.

But here we encounter fundamental problems. What sort of legal authorities are relevant to an understanding of a treaty between Europeans and native Americans? This depends on our initial characterization of the pact. Is it equivalent to an international treaty between equal and sovereign entities? Or is it some other sort of international or quasi-international agreement, such as might arise between a sovereign nation and a dependent or protected nation? Is it, perhaps, not an international instrument at all, but a constitutional pact between a state and a body of its subjects, or even a species of domestic contract? More radically, is it perhaps not a true agreement in any sense, but a unilateral state act imposing terms on a group of subjects, closer in character to a statute?

These questions raise the issue of the relative status of the European and native American parties at the time of the treaty. Were they both sovereign international entities, or was one party subject to the other, or a protected entity? How do we go about answering this question? Is it sufficient to invoke standard European authorities on international law, or must we also consult non-European sources, including Aboriginal law and custom? Should we perhaps look beyond these sources to fundamental principles of justice, or "natural law"?

The question of native sovereignty is not, of course, simply historical or academic. As the recent armed confrontations at Kanesatake and Kahnawake vividly illustrate, issues of sovereignty are implicated in many current disputes between native Americans and governmental authorities over such matters as land claims, treaty rights, the application of customary law, and powers of self-government. Follow these disputes to their roots and you will often encounter the unresolved issue of indigenous sovereignty. Until some understanding on this matter is reached, it seems unlikely that the disputes will be resolved or fade away.

Nevertheless, the task of providing a legal framework for understanding the historical relations between Aboriginal peoples and incoming settler groups is remarkably difficult. My aim in this paper is to make a start. I will examine a number of standard approaches to the subject and show that for various reasons they are flawed or inadequate. I will then suggest approaches that hold out more promise.

Framing the Question

Let us begin by considering the traditional model of American international history.[4] This model involves a number of premises, which are grounded in a particular understanding of international law. The most fundamental of these holds that North America was juridically a vacant territory at the period of European exploration and settlement—in technical language, *terra nullius*—territory not belonging to any recognized international entity. On this view, European states were capable of directly appropriating American lands, securing what is known as an *original title*, that is a title not derived from any other state or legal entity. The authorities disagree as to how an original title could be obtained. Some argue that the first European state to "discover" or explore American lands gained title. Others say that a symbolic act of taking possession, such as the planting of a cross, a flag, or royal insignia, was necessary. Still others insist that none of these methods was valid, that the incoming European power had to occupy the territories in an effective manner before sovereignty vested, as by establishing settlements, a governmental apparatus, or at least the elements of factual control.

All these methods—discovery, symbolic acts, and effective occupation—presuppose that North America was legally vacant at the relevant time, that there were no existing rights capable of impeding the smooth flow of incoming sovereignty. In classic European thought, methods such as discovery, symbolic acts, or effective occupation cannot operate in territories that are already under the sovereignty of another power, no matter how small the territory or weak the incumbent power.[5] No one, for example, would seriously suggest that a visiting British official could gain title to Vatican City for the Queen simply by raising the Union Jack in St. Peter's Square. Where a territory is already held by a sovereign power, title to it can be won only by such methods as conquest, cession from the existing sovereign, or the continuous exercise of factual dominion for a period long enough to confer prescriptive title.[6]

The premise that America was legally vacant at the time of European contact has several corollaries. The first, as we have seen, holds that native American peoples did not have sovereignty over the territories they occupied or controlled. If they did, their lands would not be open to acquisition by discovery, symbolic acts, or occupation.

The second corollary goes further. It holds that native American peoples did not have any sort of lesser international title, short of sovereignty, sufficient to exclude others from their territories. This proposition meets the argument that, even if native groups did not have full sovereignty (such as states might hold), they did have sufficient territorial rights to prevent a legal vacuum from existing. It could, for example, be maintained that although a small band of Aboriginal hunters and fishers did not constitute a state, it nevertheless formed an independent political entity holding exclusive title to the territories it occupied. Were this the case, the lands in question would not be *terra nullius*.

The third corollary maintains that where the title of a European state to North American territories was not gained by an original appropriation it arose by succession to the title of another European state by virtue of conquest, cession, or prescription.[7] A title gained in any of the latter ways is termed a *derivative title* because it stems from some previous titleholder. The standard model of legal title assumes that derivative titles could not be secured from the native peoples, but only from other European powers.

Large parts of North America are commonly thought to be held under European-derived titles. According to traditional accounts, Acadia was transferred by cession from France to Great Britain in the Treaty of Utrecht of 1713 and the remainder of French Canada was conquered in 1759-60 and ceded to Britain by the Treaty of Paris of 1763. Twenty years later, the Treaty of Paris of 1783 drew the boundary between the newly independent United States and British territories to the North, recognizing the transfer of sovereignty that occurred during the American Revolution. This treaty was later supplemented by others, extending the international boundary between the United States and British North America westward to the Pacific. Native American peoples were not parties to any of these transactions, and under the traditional model, they played no legal role in the process.

To hold that a European state obtained title to a certain part of North America by succession to another European state presupposes that the previous state (or some more remote predecessor) held an original title that it could pass on to others. If Britain obtained New France by cession from the French Crown in 1763, France itself must have held a good title to the territory, otherwise it would not have been capable of ceding it to Britain, any more than a Parisian hustler can sell you the Eiffel Tower.[8] On this hypothesis, France's title was either original or derivative. The usual view is that France obtained an original title to New France by virtue of the explorations of Jacques Cartier and the settlements initiated by Champlain.

Such is the standard scheme. The whole structure depends on the premise that North America at the time of European encounter was legally a vacant land available for appropriation, despite the obvious fact that it was occupied and controlled by native peoples. The critical question is whether this basic premise is justified.

On purely historical grounds, it seems very doubtful that European imperial powers consistently regarded Aboriginal America as vacant territory. Any balanced survey of European state practice reveals that although most imperial powers indulged on occasion in lofty claims based on discovery, symbolic acts and occupation, these same powers often poured scorn on such claims when advanced by their European rivals. In short, they were not prepared to grant others the benefit of principles claimed on their own behalf. So, it may be doubted whether the supposed rules achieved true reciprocal acceptance, even among the nations that stood to benefit from them.[9]

Even if we assume that inter-European state practice was sufficiently uniform to support a doctrine of discovery, there is a wealth of historical evidence that some imperial powers, notably Great Britain and France, followed quite different practices in their direct dealings with native American peoples.[10] In effect, there were divergent streams of state practice, one inter-European, the other European-Aboriginal. One way of reconciling these differences is to say that the inter-European practice gave rise to a local rule which bound

202

European states among themselves, and yet had no effect on native American peoples, whose territorial rights were unimpaired.[11]

However, let us waive these objections and suppose that Spain, Portugal, Great Britain, France, and other European colonial powers consistently treated Aboriginal America as legally vacant territory and advanced claims to various parts of the continent on the basis of discovery, symbolic acts, or occupation. How can we determine whether such claims were well-founded?

In asking this question, we move into the realm of normative validity. Claims to title can of course be either valid or invalid. I can consistently claim ownership over the red Corvette in the window of my local car dealer, but if that claim is to be anything more than wishful thinking I have to show that it can be justified in some manner. Were the grandiose claims to North America advanced by such states as Britain and France in the 17th and 18th centuries just wishful thinking? By what standards can they be appraised?

According to the standard scheme, there are basically two ways of answering this question. The first looks to some existing body of "positive" or "conventional" law laid down by authority or accepted by the people in question, such as the domestic law of the claimant European state, the law of the Aboriginal nation whose lands are at stake, or rules of positive international law. The second approach detaches itself from any single system of positive law and attempts to find some universal or transcendent basis for assessing the matter, such as basic human values, inherent human rights, or fundamental principles of justice. This is sometimes called a "natural law" approach. Of course, the two approaches can be combined in various ways. You might, for example, rely primarily on positive law but resort to basic principles of justice as an ultimate test of validity. Or you might use principles of justice in the very process of determining what the positive rules are. For purposes of clarity, however, these two approaches will initially be considered separately.

My basic argument is that any approach which purports to rely *exclusively* on a body of positive or conventional law is necessarily afflicted by arbitrariness or circularity. The only possible approach is one that draws to some extent on basic principles of justice. In fact, so-called "positive law" cannot be severed from "natural law," nor the latter from the former: they are both aspects of the unitary phenomenon of law. I will argue that native American peoples held sovereign status and title to the territories they occupied at the time

203

of European contact and that this fundamental fact transforms our understanding of everything that followed. Finally, I will suggest that the best framework for understanding relations between Aboriginal nations on the one hand and Canada and the United States on the other is provided by a distinctive body of inter-societal law that was generated in the 17th and 18th centuries by interaction between native peoples and settler governments.

Positive Law

1. The Legal System of a Claimant Nation

It could be argued that claims to sovereignty over North American territories, whether advanced by European or Aboriginal nations, should be judged according to criteria supplied by the internal legal system of the claimant nation. If the claim meets those criteria then it is valid; if it fails to meet them, it is invalid.

There is an obvious difficulty with this approach, which has not prevented it from being surprisingly popular in practice. Where there are competing claims by different nations to the same territory (a common occurrence in North American history), this approach allows for each claim to be valid under the claimant's own laws. But since the claims are exclusive of each other, they cannot both be valid; one or the other (or both) must fail. For example, during the period 1713-1763, France, Great Britain, and Aboriginal nations had overlapping claims to the territories now located in New Brunswick and Nova Scotia. If we were to examine the particular claim of each competing nation, we might well find that it satisfied the requirements of that nation's domestic legal system, and so would be "valid" under that system. How should we go about resolving the resulting conflict?

If the standards of one domestic legal system are chosen over those of another without explanation, the solution is arbitrary. If reasons are supplied, they must be founded on principles that transcend the competing domestic systems involved, for to draw reasons just from one system or another is both circular and arbitrary. The question of which system of law should govern cannot be resolved by reference to principles secreted by one of the competing systems without assuming the supremacy of that system, which is the very question to be resolved. Where reasons going beyond the principles of a single system are sought or given, the approach necessarily takes on a

204

different character, one that looks to international law or basic principles of justice. These possibilities will be discussed below.

The attitude of British courts to the question of territorial claims advanced by the Crown resembles the approach considered above.[12] These courts have generally held that where the Crown has officially advanced an unequivocal claim of sovereignty over a certain territory, British courts should recognize and enforce that claim without further scrutiny, regardless of the degree of control actually exerted by the government, the legal pedigree of the claim, or the presence of competing claims by other states and peoples. This is considered part of the "act of state" doctrine.

The reasons generally given for this doctrine are prudential: it would be undesirable for the courts to review the acts of the executive in matters relating to the acquisition and loss of territory. On this view, these are high matters of state that should remain within the exclusive purview of the government; the executive must have the freedom to conduct foreign policy without fear of second-guessing by the judicial branch, which is ill-equipped to make decisions in these areas.

Whatever the merits of this argument in other contexts, it is doubtful whether it should induce modern Canadian or American courts to accept fictitious accounts of the manner in which their countries came into being, accounts that accept even the most extravagant imperial claims at face value and ignore the historical presence and viewpoints of indigenous peoples. When it comes to reconstructing the legal history of their own countries, courts cannot take refuge in the act of state doctrine without forfeiting their moral authority and acting as passive instruments of colonial rule. In this context, the act of state doctrine is mischievous and should be modified.

2. *International Law*

One possible way out of these difficulties is to look to international law for criteria capable of resolving the competing claims of European and Aboriginal nations. International law is in concept a body of rules governing relations among states and state-like entities, which among other things purports to determine the basis of sovereign title to territory. In principle, international law escapes from the objections against domestic legal systems, advanced above.

Nevertheless, international law has its own problems. In the absence of a universal legislature, international rules are either a matter of convention, based on agreement or customary practice, or they flow in whole or in part from basic principles of justice. To the extent that they stem from basic principles of justice, they transcend positive international law and will be considered below. Here I will treat international law as a body of exclusively conventional rules drawn from practice and agreement (henceforth described simply as "practice" for convenience).

At this point, a serious methodological problem arises. Assuming that practice is the basis for international norms, how does one ascertain which entities belong to the group whose practice generates the relevant norms? Remember that the question at stake is whether or not native American polities were ever sovereign entities. If the answer is affirmative, their practice must presumably be considered in determining the character of the international norms governing the acquisition of American territories. If the answer is negative, then their practice is arguably irrelevant.

The problem is this: it is logically impossible to determine the qualifications for membership in the international community by examining the practice of the members of that community. To proceed in this way assumes that one can identify in advance the members whose practice is relevant. But these entities can be identified only if one already knows the rules governing membership in the community—which is of course the very issue to be resolved.

An example may clarify the point. Suppose that around the year 1600 the world was made up of a large variety of factually independent political entities, varying greatly in population, territory, wealth, military power, political and social organization, culture, religion, learning, and technology.[13] A group of these polities, composed of A, B, C, D, and E, in practice treat one another as sovereign and equal, and recognize one another as members of an international community bound by certain rules. I will call this group the Arcadians. They regard the remaining political entities of the world, F through to Z, as failing to qualify for membership because of perceived deficiencies in religion, culture, and civilization. Polities F to Z, for their part, are not a homogeneous group. Polity F, for example, an ancient and powerful empire in an area remote from the Arcadians, considers itself the sole state worthy of the name, and regards all other political entities as inferiors, to be dealt with, if at all, as tributary or subordinate powers. Its relations with the Arcadians are infrequent. Polity G, an empire in closer proximity to the Arcadians, has more varied attitudes to outside powers, and is willing to deal with some on a basis of equality. But it usually insists on treating the Arcadians as inferiors, viewing them as infidels and barbarians. The remaining polities, H to Z, exhibit varying attitudes to outside powers. Many of them, however, show a pragmatic willingness to deal with other independent political groups on an equal basis, at least when it suits their purposes.

Which of these various political entities belong to the group whose practice generates the international rules governing the status and rights of political entities? It is clear that any selection process, if it is not purely random or arbitrary, must be governed by criteria concerning the nature and qualifications of a member. These criteria cannot be justified by reference to the practice of some select group among the entire field of polities without falling into logical circularity. Thus, for example, to argue that the practice of the Arcadians justifies the rule that only Arcadians are members of the international community is obviously self-serving. The question why one should restrict one's inquiry to the Arcadians cannot be answered by an inquiry restricted to those very entities.

Perhaps the solution lies in an empirical inquiry as to which polities *identify themselves* as belonging to a group bound by legal norms, on the theory that the group capable of generating international rules is self-identifying. This approach, however, is only capable of discovering a group of political entities that, like an exclusive club, has its own membership criteria and a distinctive body of rules *that bind exclusively the members*. The rules generated by such a group have no power to bind polities not belonging to the group. Just because the Arcadians agree among themselves that territorial rights to the rest of the world can be gained by discovery does not give a discovering Arcadian state any rights as against a non-Arcadian entity.

Moreover, several self-identifying groups of political entities might exist. Suppose that polities M through S make up a rival group called the Akkamites and that the rules of the Arcadians and the Akkamites differ on such matters as acquisition of territory. By what standards could it be decided which set of rules is correct? Or would one have to rest content with the trite observation that different groups have different rules? This conclusion, however, would bring our inquiry to an end, for it concedes that there are no universal international rules capable of resolving conflicting territorial claims.

It could be argued that we should look to the practice of *all* factually independent polities in the world in order to determine the rules governing the international community, including its membership rules. This is an attractive approach. However, its attraction lies in a tacit appeal to basic principles of justice. To the extent that it purports to be based simply on practice, it cannot escape the error of circularity encountered above. For example, suppose that the *predominant* practice among political entities in our hypothetical world is to recognize all

207

other autonomous political entities as holding sovereign status. It is not clear why one should prefer this body of practice over the more exclusive practice of the Arcadians and hold that it gives rise to norms binding on the Arcadians which they themselves do not accept.

So, the ultimate criteria for selecting those political entities whose practice is capable of generating international norms must be based on something other than international practice. But if the criteria cannot be justified by practice, they must be grounded in normative sources that lie beyond convention, that is, in fundamental principles of justice. Of course, the above arguments do not demonstrate the *existence* of principles of justice capable of solving the problems we have encountered. To the extent that these arguments have been successful, they have only shown the *need* for such principles. The matter will be pursued in the next section.

One practical point may be drawn here. To rely exclusively on European state practice to prove that Aboriginal America was vacant territory is, on its face, a misconceived procedure. It assumes that European practice standing alone could generate customary international rules binding on the rest of the world, and in particular, customary rules permitting European powers to appropriate large sectors of the occupied world for themselves.[14] One might as well try to show that the Barbary states had the right to prey on Mediterranean shipping by invoking their maritime practices in the 17th and 18th centuries, or cite the practices of ancient China and its neighbours to prove that the nations of the world owed tribute to the Middle Kingdom. At best, an exclusive appeal to European practice is capable of proving the existence of a customary rule binding European states among themselves, not one binding other nations and peoples.

Basic Principles of Justice

It will not be possible here to develop a full set of fundamental principles governing the original status of Aboriginal nations and the territories they occupied.[15] My aim is more modest: to sketch out a line of argument which shows that the premise that North America was legally vacant when Europeans arrived cannot be justified by reference to basic principles of justice. I will attempt to do this by blending two different approaches. The first examines the implications of the premise that North America was *terra nullius* when Europeans first arrived, and holds that this leads to unacceptable conclusions. The second argues from basic rights belonging to all human beings to the conclusion that native American territories were not legally vacant.

Were it true that native peoples did not hold any exclusive territorial rights at the era of European contact, North America would have been in a state of legal anarchy. No native group would have possessed territorial rights sustainable against any other native group, so that each group would have had as much right to areas held by its neighbours as to those under its own control, which is to say, no right at all.

My argument is that this conclusion contradicts a basic principle: every human society whose members draw the essentials of life from territories in their possession (whether collectively or individually) has a right to these territories as against other societies and individuals. I will call this the Principle of Territoriality.

In saying that the Principle entails a *right*, I mean a justifiable claim assertible against other groups and individuals. In attributing this right to a *group*, I assume that groups and not only individuals may hold rights, an assumption that could be disputed. Without attempting a full justification here, we may note that the concept of group rights is fundamental to the notion of state sovereignty, itself a cornerstone of modern international law. Someone who claims that a European state—a collective entity—had the capacity to acquire rights of sovereignty over American lands is hardly in a position to deny the existence of group rights.

I am not, of course, suggesting that the Principle of Territoriality is the only principle of justice relevant to questions of territorial rights, or that its concrete operation may not be modified in practice by other basic principles and values. I am simply saying that it is a principle of great weight that applies in the absence of serious countervailing considerations.

How is the Principle of Territoriality justified? The argument runs in outline as follows. Were the Principle untrue, a society would not have the right to protect the territories used by its members from external depredation and destruction, even though these lands are essential to survival.[16] But this conclusion contradicts a more fundamental principle: all human beings have rights to life and the necessaries of life as against all other people. This second principle furnishes the ultimate justification for the Principle of Territoriality. I will now show how in more detail.

We start with the premise, which will not be justified here, that every human being has the right to life and to the things necessary to sustain life—what may be called comprehensively the "right to well-being."[17] This right holds good against all other individuals and groups. It obliges others not only to respect the individual's well-being, in the negative sense of refraining from interfering with it, but also in some contexts to take steps to protect and advance it.

As a matter of experience, we know that an individual's well-being cannot be secured apart from a social group. The group need not be a large one, and may in fact be fairly small, limited to an extended family or several families. But some such group must exist to provide an individual with the basic characteristics and capacities of a human being. Even a hermit carries society to the desert, in the basic skills, capacities, ideas, and values that only an upbringing in human society can engender.

In order to be in a position to protect and advance the well-being of its members, a social group must be endowed with a collective moral capacity or status. In particular, it must have the capacity to act in the interests of its members, and the right to defend them from external attack. This collective status and right of self-defence are maintainable against all other groups and individuals. They are justified by reference to the individual's abstract right to well-being coupled with experience of what is necessary in practice to secure it. In summary, a society has a right to protect the well-being of its members against outside groups and individuals. This collective right cannot be denied without denying the basic rights held by the group's individual members.

But, as noted earlier, in most (perhaps all) societies, the well-being of their members depends upon individual and collective uses of territory. Whether a society recognizes private ownership of land or only collective ownership, whether it acknowledges the concept of land ownership at all or only rights of use or possession, the position is the same. Any society has the right to defend territories in its possession against outside intrusion, insofar as these territories are necessary to the well-being of the members.

Since native Americans had rights to life and the necessaries of life, it follows that the societies and groups to which they belonged had rights to the territories they occupied at the time of European contact, to the extent that they needed them to survive and flourish. These rights held good against other groups, including both Aboriginal and European nations. It cannot be argued that the right of native American groups to the lands used to sustain their members was automatically outweighed by the needs and ambitions of European states and their subjects without impliedly asserting that the lives of Europeans were more valuable than those of native Americans.

The rights held by a native group to its territories were necessarily secure against invasion by others, and were to that extent exclusive of other groups. It follows that in principle no outside group could gain control over or use the territories in question without the consent of those already in possession.[18] Even if the possessing group was not a fully sovereign entity (perhaps because it was too small or loosely organized), its territories would not be *terra nullius*. Otherwise, an outside state could legitimately seize the territories and expel the inhabitants or deprive them of secure access to their lands.

This position is similar to that advanced by Lindley in a classic work on the subject.[19] He argues that an area is not *terra nullius* when it is "inhabited by a political society, that is, by a considerable number of persons who are permanently united by habitual obedience to a certain and common superior, or whose conduct in regard to their mutual relations habitually conforms to recognized standards." Since he recognizes that a community composed of a number of families qualifies if the members conform to certain standards in their mutual relationships, his definition corresponds closely in practice to that advocated here, and would seem to include most and perhaps all native American societies.

Nevertheless, the emphasis in Lindley's approach is a little misleading. To tie territorial rights too closely to the size of a group or to the internal conduct of its members is to overlook the reason for attributing territorial rights to any society in the first place: namely to allow it to protect and advance the well-being of its members, both present and future. Human lives are not more valuable in a large, highly-structured society than in a small group of independently-minded hunters, and there would seem to be no less reason to attribute territorial rights to the latter than the former.[20]

Practical Implications

I have argued that the premise that North America was legally vacant when Europeans arrived cannot be justified by reference to positive or natural law. Attempts to justify it on either basis are afflicted by arbitrariness or circularity, or they conflict with basic principles of justice. I have also maintained that native American polities originally had exclusive rights to the territories they occupied and were entitled to defend them against invasion or intrusion.

A number of important consequences flow from these arguments, which I can only briefly describe here. First, and most obviously, it

211

cannot be true that the modern states of Canada and the United States trace their legal origins to "discoveries," symbolic acts, or acts of occupation carried out by European states. These modes of acquisition are operative only in legally vacant territories, and so could not apply to most of North America at the time of European contact. Accounts based on contrary assumptions are misguided.

Canada and the United States came into being, not simply through the activities of incoming European powers, but through a complex series of interactions among various settler groups and Aboriginal nations.[21] What forms those relations took—whether alliance, treaty, informal agreement, longstanding practice, or war—is a matter for detailed inquiry. But I suggest that the inquiry will reveal that Canada and the United States have more complicated constitutional structures than is sometimes assumed, structures based in part on inter-societal custom generated in the 17th and 18th centuries. Under these structures, Aboriginal nations continue to hold a residue of the sovereignty they once possessed. This conclusion has been broadly accepted in the United States,[22] although its significance has been underestimated. In Canada, the concept of internal sovereignty should come as no great novelty, for it has long been held that the provinces are autonomous within their constitutional spheres.

A second consequence affects our understanding of the genesis of international law. The fact that native American nations had international status and title to their territories suggests that they were capable of contributing to the formation of international custom, ordinarily considered a principal source of international law. The extensive records of treaties and other relations between Aboriginal nations and European governments, particularly in the period 1600-1800, indicates that these nations did in fact make such contributions, and that they did so at a crucial stage in the development of international law. So modern international law is not the exclusive product of European genius, as some texts fondly suggest. It stems from the activities and conceptions of a wide range of European and non-European nations, including the Aboriginal peoples of America.[23] Once again, this is a promising ground for historical investigation.

The third consequence is closely related to the previous two. The extensive relations between Aboriginal nations and the English colonies on the Atlantic seaboard in the 17th and 18th centuries gave rise to a distinctive body of inter-societal custom, recognized as binding among the parties. This custom was neither entirely English nor entirely Aboriginal in character, but incorporated elements from the legal cultures of all participants. Some of this custom contributed to the development of international law. But other parts were too local and specific for universal application. Important elements of this body of custom were incorporated in the embryonic constitutional law governing Britain's overseas territories, sometimes called "colonial law" or "imperial constitutional law."[24] This law was inherited by the United States and Canada upon independence, although it assumed variant forms in the two countries due to differences in constitutional structure. It now forms part of their basic common law.[25] Since imperial constitutional law applied not only in North America but also in other British possessions, the same basic principles were arguably incorporated in the basic law of such Commonwealth nations as New Zealand and Australia. In effect, the body of inter-societal law that developed on the Atlantic seaboard in the period 1600-1800 is the core of the law of Aboriginal rights, which in Canada has received explicit constitutional recognition.[26]

Above all, these reflections encourage us to find new ways of understanding our common and several histories, as native Americans, settlers and immigrants. For embedded in the past are the seeds of our future hopes.

Endnotes

1. See, for example, the monumental work by M. Savelle, *The Origins of American Diplomacy: The International History of Angloamerica, 1492-1763* (New York: Macmillan, 1967).
2. For a variety of views see, e.g., A.S. Keller, J. Lissitzyn & F.J. Mann, *Creation of Rights of Sovereignty through Symbolic Acts, 1400-1800* (New York: Columbia University Press, 1938); F.A.F. von der Heydte, "Discovery, Symbolic Annexation and Virtual Effectiveness in International Law" (1935) 29 *Am. J. Int'l Law* 448; J. Goebel, *The Struggle for the Falkland Islands* (New Haven: Yale University Press, 1927); L.C. Green, "Claims to Territory in Colonial America" in L.C. Green & O.P. Dickason, *The Law of Nations and the New World* (Edmonton: University of Alberta Press, 1989).
3. Green, *ibid.* at 125-26.
4. The best general account of the issues is still M.F. Lindley, *The Acquisition and Government of Backward Territory in International Law; Being a Treatise on the Law and Practice Relating to Colonial Expansion,* 1926 ed. (New York: Negro University Press, 1969).
5. As Grotius remarked with respect to Portuguese claims to the

East Indies, "discovery *per se* gives no legal rights over things unless before the alleged discovery they were *res nullius*. Now these Indians of the East, on the arrival of the Portuguese, although some of them were idolators, and some Mohammedans, and therefore sunk in grievous sin, had nonetheless perfect public and private ownership of their goods and possessions, from which they could not be dispossessed without just cause." H. Grotius, *Mare Liberum (The Freedom of the Seas)*, ed. by J. B. Scott, trans. R. Van Deman Magoffin (New York: Oxford University Press American Branch, 1916) at 13.

6. See, generally, Lindley, supra, note 4 at c. I - V; I. Brownlie, *Principles of Public International Law*, 4th ed. (Oxford: Clarendon Press, 1990) c. VII; D.P. O'Connell, *International Law*, 2nd ed. (London: Stevens & Sons, 1970) vol. I, c. XV. There are considerable differences in terminology and classification among the authorities. I follow here a simplified version of the classic terminology developed by European doctrinal writers in the 16th to 19th centuries.

7. For economy's sake, I will use "European states" to designate not only the imperial powers proper but also their colonial offshoots in North America.

8. *Nemo dat quod non habet*; one cannot give to another what one does not possess oneself. As was stated in the *Island of Palmas Case* (1928), 2 U.N.R.I.A.A. 829 at 842: "The *title alleged by the United States of America* . . .is that of *cession*, brought about by the Treaty of Paris, which cession transferred all rights of sovereignty which Spain may have possessed in the region. . . . It is evident that Spain could not transfer more rights than she herself possessed." (emphasis in original)

9. The matter is considered in more detail in: B. Slattery, *The Land Rights of Indigenous Canadian Peoples*, (Saskatoon: University of Saskatchewan Native Law Centre, 1979) at 66-125 [hereinafter *Land Rights*] and "Did France Claim Canada Upon 'Discovery'?" in J.M. Bumsted, ed., *Interpreting Canada's Past* vol. 1 (Toronto: Oxford University Press, 1986) at 2-26, an earlier version of which appeared in (1978) 59 *Can. Hist. Rev.* 139. For other discussions see: Goebel, *supra*, note 2 at 47-119; Lindley, *supra*, note 4; M.S. McDougal, H.D. Lasswell, & I.A. Vlasic, *Law and Public Order in Space* (New Haven: Yale University Press, 1963) at 830-44; von der Heydte, *supra*, note 2 at 452.

10. See, e.g., J.D. Hurley, *Children or Brethren: Aboriginal Rights in Colonial Iroquoia* (Saskatoon: University of Saskatchewan Native

Law Centre, 1985); P.C. Williams, *The Chain* (LL.M. Dissertation, Osgoode Hall Law School, York University, 1982); *Land Rights, ibid.* at 95-125.

11. A famous version of this view was espoused by Chief Justice Marshall of the United States Supreme Court in *Johnson v. M'Intosh*, 5 Law Ed 681, 8 Wheat. 543 (1823) and *Worcester v. Georgia*, 8 Law Ed, 6 Pet. 515 (1832). Thus, Marshall said of the principle of discovery: "It was an exclusive principle which shut out the right of competition among those who had agreed to it; not one which could annul the previous rights of those who had not agreed to it. It regulated the right given by discovery among the European discoverers, but could not affect the rights of those already in possession, either as aboriginal occupants, or as occupants by virtue of a discovery made before the memory of man." *Worcester v. Georgia,* at 544. See also O'Connell, *supra,* note 6 at 408-409. For a critical discussion of the Marshall view, see B. Slattery, *Ancestral Lands, Alien Laws: Judicial Perspectives on Aboriginal Title* (Saskatoon: University of Saskatchewan Native Law Centre, 1983) at 17-38.

12. The point is considered in *Land Rights, supra,* note 9 at 63-65; and K. McNeil, *Common Law Aboriginal Title* (Oxford: Clarendon Press, 1989) at 110-112.

13. I am not suggesting that this description is purely factual. Even the most "factual" accounts of the make-up of international society are grounded in certain ways of looking at things, which are tacitly normative and theoretical. However, this point does not affect my argument here.

14. As Chief Justice Marshall of the United States Supreme Court noted: "It is difficult to comprehend the proposition that the inhabitants of either quarter of the globe could have rightful original claims of dominion over the inhabitants of the other, or over the lands they occupied; or that the discovery of either by the other should give the discoverer rights in the country discovered which annulled the pre-existing rights of its ancient possessors." *Worcester v. Georgia, supra,* note 11 at 494.

15. For a thoughtful discussion, see D.G. Gormley, "Aboriginal Rights As Natural Rights" (1984) 4 *Can. J. Native Stud.* at 29.

16. Unless the Principle of Territoriality were replaced by another principle serving essentially the same purposes.

17. For a stimulating defence and elaboration of these rights, see the works of A. Gewirth, especially *Reason and Morality,* (Chicago: University of Chicago Press, 1978) and *Human Rights: Essays on Justification and Applications* (Chicago: University of Chicago

Press, 1982). For a critical discussion of Gewirth's arguments from a communitarian perspective, see B. Slattery, "Rights, Communities, and Tradition" (1991), 41 U.T.L.J. 447.

18. Prima facie, this would rule out acquisitions of territory by conquest. However, it may be argued that, for reasons associated with other basic values and principles of justice, territories illegitimately acquired may sometimes, by passage of time, be transformed into legitimate dominions — the process traditionally termed "prescription."

19. Lindley, *supra*, note 4 at 21-23.

20. For other opinions, see in particular C. Wolff, *Jus Gentium Methodo Scientifica Pertractatum*, 1764 ed. (Oxford: Clarendon Press, 1934) Prolegomena, para. 16, c. III, para. 309-313 at 156-160; E. de Vattel, *The Law of Nations or the Principles of Natural Law*, 1758 ed. (Washington: Carnegie Institution of Washington, 1916) vol. I, Book II, c. VII, para. 96-98; M. Shaw, *Title to Territory in Africa: International Legal Issues* (Oxford: Clarendon Press, 1986) at 31-38.

21. Compare the conclusion of the International Court of Justice regarding the status of Western Sahara at the period of its colonization by Spain, beginning in 1884: "the State practice of the relevant period indicates that territories inhabited by tribes or peoples having a social and political organization were not regarded as *terrae nullius*. It shows that in the case of such territories the acquisition of sovereignty was not generally considered as effected unilaterally through 'occupation' of *terra nullius* by original title but through agreements concluded with local rulers. . . . In the present instance, the information furnished to the Court shows that at the time of colonization Western Sahara was inhabited by peoples which, if nomadic, were socially and politically organized in tribes and under chiefs competent to represent them." *Western Sahara* (Advisory Opinion), [1975] I.C.J. Rep. 12 at 39.

22. See especially *Worcester* v. *Georgia*, *supra*, note 11.

23. For work that dispenses with a European centred methodology, see the pioneering legal-historical research of C.H. Alexandrowicz, notably: *An Introduction to the History of the Law of Nations in the East Indies* (Oxford: Clarendon Press, 1967) and *The European-African Confrontation: A Study in Treaty Making* (Leiden: Sijthoff, 1973).

24. The argument is elaborated in B. Slattery, "Understanding Aboriginal Rights" (1987) 66 *Can. Bar Rev.* 727.

25. The point was apparently accepted by the Supreme Court of Canada in *Roberts* v. *Canada*, [1989] 1 S.C.R. 322 at 340; see discussion in J.M. Evans and B. Slattery, "Case Note: Federal Jurisdiction — Pendent Parties — Aboriginal Title and Federal Common Law" (1989) 68 *Can. Bar Rev.* 817 at 831-32. See also, *Montana Band* v. *Canada* (1 February 1991), F.C.T.D., F.C.J. No. 102 (unreported).

26. Most recently in section 35(1) of the *Constitution Act, 1982* being Schedule B of the *Canada Act 1982* (U.K.), 1982, c.11 which recognizes and affirms the "existing aboriginal and treaty rights of the aboriginal peoples of Canada." Recognition has also been extended in a series of earlier constitutional instruments, notably the *Royal Proclamation of 1763*, R.S.C., 1985, App. II, No.1. Section 35(1) of the *Constitution Act, 1982* has recently been given a broad interpretation by the Supreme Court of Canada in *R.* v. *Sparrow*, [1990] 1 S.C.R. 1075.

The author is indebted to Michael Asch, Bruce Hodgins, Kent McNeil and Gail Sax for their helpful comments on an earlier draft of this paper.

Native Sovereignty in the United States: Developments During the Modern Era

Charles F. Wilkinson
Moses Lasky Professor of Law
School of Law
University of Colorado

I. Overview

In the early 19th century, the Supreme Court recognized an expansive Indian tribal sovereignty in the United States. During the next 100 years, however, the Court gave much less support to Indian rights.

From the late 1950s through the late 1980s, tribes achieved major victories in the Supreme Court. Then a conservative majority began to control the opinions and refused to extend tribal rights. Today, tribes in the United States will continue to use the courts, but the major advancements will probably come from Congress and from tribal governments operating in Indian country.

II. General Sources

A. *Felix S. Cohen's Handbook of Federal Indian Law* (Michie Bobbs-Merrill, 1982)

B. Wilkinson, *American Indians, Time, and the Law: Native Societies in a Modern Constitutional Democracy* (Yale University Press, 1987)

III. The Early Cases

A. The Marshall Trilogy

1. *Johnson v. M'Intosh*, 21 U.S. (8 Wheat.) 543 (1823) (Tribal land title and the doctrine of discovery)
2. *Cherokee Nation v. Georgia*, 30 U.S. (5 Pet.) 1 (1831) (Trust relationship)

3. *Worcester v. Georgia*, 31 U.S. (6 Pet.) 515 (1832) (Tribal sovereignty)

B. *The Assimilation Cases*

1. *United States v. McBratney*, 104 U.S. 621 (1882) (State criminal jurisdiction over non-Indians)
2. *United States v. Kagama*, 118 U.S. 375 (1886) (Federal criminal jurisdiction over major crimes by non-Indians; characterizing tribes as "weak," "helpless," and dependent on the United States)
3. *Lone Wolf v. Hitchcock*, 187 U.S. 553 (1903) (Congressional plenary power)

IV. Major Supreme Court Cases in Indian Law (1959-1986)

A. *Cases Limiting Tribal Rights*

1. *Oliphant v. Suquamish Indian Tribe*, 435 U.S. 191 (1978) (striking down tribal jurisdiction over crimes committed by non-Indians on a reservation)
2. *Montana v. United States*, 450 U.S. 544 (1981) (striking down the tribe's authority to regulate non-Indians' hunting and fishing on a state-owned navigable watercourse traversing the reservation)
3. *Arizona v. San Carlos Apache Tribe*, 463 U.S. 545 (1983) (upholding the dismissal of an action brought in federal court by an Indian tribe to adjudicate its reserved water rights when there is a concurrent adjudication of the same issue in state court)

B. *Cases Supporting Tribal Rights*

1. *Williams v. Lee*, 358 U.S. 217 (1959) (upholding exclusive tribal judicial jurisdiction over actions involving contracts entered into on an Indian reservation between a non-Indian plaintiff and an Indian defendant)
2. *Santa Clara Pueblo v. Martinez*, 436 U.S. 49 (1978) (holding the writ of habeas corpus to be the exclusive remedy available for alleged violations of the Indian Civil Rights Act)
3. *Washington v. Washington State Commercial Passenger Fishing Vessel Ass'n*, 443 U.S. 658 (1979) (upholding the Pacific Northwest tribes' treaty right to take up to 50 percent of the harvestable fish passing through the tribes' usual and accustomed fishing places)
4. *Central Machinery Co. v. Arizona State Tax Comm'n*, 448 U.S. 160 (1980) (striking down the imposition of a state gross receipts tax

on on-reservation sales by a non-Indian to a tribe, where the non-Indian seller is not licensed to trade with Indians and has no permanent place of business on the reservation)

5. *Merrion v. Jicarilla Apache Tribe*, 455 U.S. 130 (1982) (upholding the tribe's authority to impose a severance tax on oil and gas production on reservation land)

6. *New Mexico v. Mescalero Apache Tribe*, 462 U.S. 324 (1983) (upholding exclusive tribal regulatory jurisdiction over hunting and fishing by members and nonmembers within the reservation)

7. *County of Oneida v. Oneida Indian Nation*, 105 S. Ct. 1245 (1985) (upholding the tribe's federal common law right of action for a violaton of its possessory rights to aboriginal lands that occurred in 1795)

V. Major Supreme Court Cases in Indian Law (1987-Present)

A. *Oregon Employment Division, Department of Human Resources v. Smith, 110 S.Ct. 1595 (1990) (First Amendment's Free Exercise Clause does not protect members of Native American Church from criminal prosecution for religiously motivated use of peyote.)*

B. *Duro v. Reina*, 110 S.Ct. 2053 (1990) (An Indian Tribe may not assert criminal jurisdiction over a nonmember Indian.)

C. *Brendale v. Confederated Bands and Tribes of Yakima Indian Nation*, 109 S.Ct. 2994 (1989) (Indian Tribe has zoning authority over fee lands owned by nonmembers of tribe in reservation's closed area, but not over such lands in reservation's open area.)

D. *Wyoming v. United States*, 109 S.Ct. 2994 (1989) (Affirmed without written decision the ruling of the Wyoming Supreme Court, *In Re Rights to Use Water in Big Horn River*, 753 P.2d 76 (Wyo., 1989), which among other issues, awarded the Wind River tribe 477,000 acre-ft. of water.)

E. *Cotton Petroleum Corp. v. New Mexico*, 109 S.Ct. 1698 (1989) (State may impose severance taxes on the same on-reservation production of oil and gas by non-Indian lessees as is subject to the Tribe's own severance tax.)

F. *Mississippi Band of Choctaw Indians v. Holyfield*, 109 S.Ct. 1597 (1989) (Tribal court has exclusive jurisdiction over adoption of Indian children born off-reservation to unmarried mother domiciled on reservation pursuant to 25 USCS sec. 1911[a].)

G. *Lyng v. Northwest Indian Cemetery Protective Association*, 485 U.S. 439 (1988) (Free exercise clause of First Amendment does not bar Federal Government from allowing timber harvesting and construction of road through National Forest area used by Indians for religious purposes.)

H. *Iowa Mutual Insurance Co. v. LaPlante*, 480 U.S. 9 (1987) (Diversity Jurisdiction may not be exercised by a Federal District Court over a dispute where the same parties and the same dispute is pending in Indian Tribal Court.

I. *United States v. Cherokee Nation of Oklahoma*, 480 U.S. 400 (1987) (Tribe had no right to be compensated under the Fifth Amendment for Federal Government's exercise of navigational servitude in riverbed held in fee simple by Indian Nation.)

J. *Amoco Prod. Co. v. Gambell*, 480 U.S. 531 (1987) (Alaska National Interest Lands Conservation Act section that would significantly restrict Alaskan natives' use of lands for subsistence did not apply to outer continental shelf.

K. *Hodel v. Irving*, 481 U.S. 704 (1987) (Section of Indian Land Consolidation Act, barring inheritance of Indian land allotments, held unconstitutional as authorizing a seizure of property without just compensation.)

L. *California v. Cabazon Band of Mission Indians*, 480 U.S. 202 (1987) (California not allowed to apply state and county gambling laws to regulate tribal bingo and card game enterprises on reservations.)

M. *Kerr-McGee Corporation v. Navajo Tribe*, 471 U.S. 195 (1987) (Navajo Tribe may tax business activities conducted on its land without first obtaining the approval of the Secretary of the Interior.)

VI. Major Federal Legislation (1986-Present)

A. Enacted Legislation

1. P.L. 99-303 (An act to amend Section 1153 of Title 18, United States Code, to make felonious sexual molestation of a minor an offense within Indian country. Approved 5/15/86.)
2. P.L. 100-497 (Indian Gaming Regulatory Act- A bill to regulate gaming on Indian lands. Approved 10/17/88.)

3. P.L. 100-588 (Archaeological Resources Protection Act 1979, Amendment - A bill to amend the Archaeological Resources Protection Act of 1979 to strengthen the enforcement provisions of the Act. Approved 11/03/88.)
4. P.L. 100-358 (Indian Housing Act of 1988 - A bill to amend the U.S. Housing Act of 1937 to establish a separate program to provide housing assistance for Indians and Alaska Natives. Approved 6/29/88.)
5. P.L. 100-579 (Native Hawaiian Health Care Act of 1988 - A bill to improve the health status of Native Hawaiians. Approved 10/31/88.)
6. P.L. 100-442 (Indian Financing Act of 1974, Amendment - A bill to amend the Indian Financing Act of 1974. Approved 9/22/88.)
7. P.L. 100-241 (Alaska Native Claims Settlement Act Amendments of 1987 - A bill to amend the Alaska Native Claims Settlement Act to provide Alaska Natives with certain options for continued ownership of lands and corporate shares received pursuant to the act. Approved 02/03/88.)
8. P.L. 100-581 (Indian Reorganization Act, Amendment - A bill to establish procedures for review of tribal constitutions and bylaws or amendments thereto pursuant to the act of June 18, 1934 (48 Stat. 1987). Approved 11/01/88.)
9. Pub. L. 101-185 (National Museum of the American Indian Act - A bill to authorize the establishment with the Smithsonian Institution of the National Museum of the American Indian, to establish a memorial to the American Indian, and for other purposes. Approved 11/28/89. Rick West appointed director.)

B. *Proposed Legislation*

1. Federalism

   S.2512 by DECONCINI (D-AZ) — New Federalism for American Indians Act of 1990 (A bill to establish a New Federalism for American Indians.) Introduced: April 25, 1990. Recent Action: Referred to Senate Select Committee on Indian Affairs.

2. Death Penalty

   S.1970 by BIDEN (D-DE) — Federal Death Penalty Act of 1989 (A bill to establish constitutional procedures for the imposition of the sentence of death.) Recent Action: Inouye(D-Hi) amendment, providing that the death penalty provisions of the bill not apply to crimes committed in any portion of Indian Country that

223

elects to make the procedures inoperable (opt-in clause), passed by the Senate (7/05/90).

3. Gambling/Gaming

H.R.1075 by OBERSTAR (D-MN) — Indian Gaming Regulatory Act, Amendment (A bill to amend the Indian Gaming Regulatory Act to classify electronic or electromechanical facsimiles of certain games of chance as Class II gaming.) Introduced: February 22, 1989. Recent Action: Referred to House Committee on Interior and Insular Affairs.

4. Grave Sites/ Repatriation

a. H.R.1646 by UDALL (D-AZ) — Native American Grave and Burial Protection Act (A bill to provide for the protection of Indian graves and burial grounds.) Introduced: March 23, 1989. Recent Action: Referred to House Committee on Interior and Insular Affairs.
   Similar Bill in the Senate: S.1021 by MCCAIN (R-AZ) — Native American Grave and Burial Protection Act. Introduced: May 17, 1989. Recent Action: Public Hearings held by Senate Select Committee on Indian Affairs.

b. H.R.1381 by BENNETT (D-FL) — Native American Burial Site Preservation Act of 1989 (A bill to prohibit the excavation of Native American burial sites and removal of the contents.) Introduced: March 14, 1989. Recent Action: Referred to House Committee on Interior and Insular Affairs.

c. S.1980 by INOUYE (D-HI) — Native American Repatriation of Cultural Patrimony Act (A bill to provide for the repatriation of Native American group or cultural patrimony.) Introduced: November 21, 1989. Recent Action: Public Hearings held by Senate Select Committee on Indian Affairs.

d. S.1781 by INOUYE (D-HI) — Native American Language Act (A bill to establish as the policy of the United States the preservation, protection, and promotion of the rights of native Americans to use, practice, and develop native American languages.) Introduced: October 23, 1989. Recent Action: Received in the House after passage in the Senate, referred to House Committee on Education and Labor.

5. Religion

   a. H.R.1546 by UDALL (D-AZ) — American Indian Religious Freedom Act of 1989 (A bill to amend the American Indian Religious Freedom Act of 1978.) Introduced: March 21, 1989. Recent Action: Public hearing held by House Committee on Interior and Insular Affairs.

   b. S.1124 by MCCAIN (R-AZ) — American Indian Religious Freedom Act Amendments of 1989 (A bill to provide a means to ensure that the management of Federal lands does not undermine and frustrate traditional Native American religious practices.) Introduced: June 6, 1989. Recent Action: Public Hearings held by Senate Select Committee on Indian Affairs.

   c. S.1979 by INOUYE (D-HI) — Free Exercise of Religious Practices by Indians, Alaska Natives and Native Hawaiians (A bill to remove certain barriers to the free exercise of, and to ensure equal respect for, and treatment of, traditional religious practices by Indians, Alaska Natives and Native Hawaiians.) Introduced: November 21, 1989. Recent Action: Referred to Senate Select Committee on Indian Affairs.

6. Environment

   a. H.R.3065 by DICKS (D-WA) — Federal Nuclear Facility Environmental Response Act (A bill to create a Federal nuclear facility environmental response fund and to require the Secretary of Energy and the Administrator of the Environmental Protection Agency to cooperate with affected States and Indian tribes.) Introduced: August 1, 1989. Recent Action: Joint Referral to several House Committees.
   Similar bill in the Senate: S.1462 by ADAMS (D-WA) — Federal Nuclear Facilities Environmental Response Act. Introduced: August 1, 1989. Recent Action: Public Hearings held by the Senate Committee on Environment and Public Works.

   b. S.1289 by MCCAIN (R-AZ) — National Indian Forest and Woodland Enhancement Act (A bill to improve the management of forests and woodlands and the production of forest resources on Indian lands.) Introduced: July 11, 1989. Recent Action: Ordered reported with an amendment by Senate Select Committee on Indian Affairs.

   c. S.2075 by MCCAIN (R-AZ) — Indian Environmental Regulatory Enhancement Act of 1990 (A bill to authorize grants to improve the capability of Indian tribal governments to regulate environmental quality.) Introduced: February 6, 1990. Recent Action: Received in the House after passage in the Senate, referred to House Committee on Interior and Insular Affairs.

7. Economic

a. H.R.3339 by UDALL (D-AZ) — Indian Economic Development Act of 1989 (A bill to encourage Indian economic development.) Introduced: September 25, 1989. Recent Action: Referred to House Committee on Ways and Means.

Similar Bill in the Senate: S.1203 by MCCAIN (R-AZ) — Indian Economic Development Act of 1989. Introduced: June 20, 1989. Recent Action: Public Hearings held by Senate Select Committee on Indian Affairs.

b. H.R.4987 by DORGAN, BYRON (D-ND) — Indian Development Investment Zone Act of 1990 (A bill to encourage Indian economic development.) Introduced: June 7, 1990. Recent Action: Joint Referral to House Committee on Ways and Means and to the House Committee on Interior and Insular Affairs.

c. S.321 by INOUYE (D-HI) — Indian Preference Act of 1990 (A bill to revise provisions of law that provide a preference to Indians.) Introduced: January 31, 1989. Recent Action: Received in the House after passage in the Senate, referred to House Committee on Interior and Insular Affairs.

d. S.1650 by DOMENICI (R-NM) — Indian Employment Opportunity Act of 1989 (A bill to reduce the 22 percent unemployment rate on Indian reservations by amending the Internal Revenue Code of 1986 to provide Indian Employment Opportunity tax credits to employers within Indian reservations.) Introduced: September 20, 1989. Recent Action: Public Hearings held by Senate Select Committee on Indian Affairs.

e. S.1821 by MCCAIN (R-AZ) — Indian Housing Opportunity Act of 1989; American Indian and Alaska Native Housing Grant Program (A bill to increase housing opportunities for Indians.) Introduced: October 31, 1989. Recent Action: Referred to Senate Select Committee on Indian Affairs.

8. Treaty Rights

a. H.R.4033 by OBEY (D-WI) — Indian Treaty Conflict Reso-

226

lution Act of 1990 (A bill to establish an Office of Indian Treaty Conflict Resolution.) Introduced: February 21, 1990. Recent Action: Joint Referral to the House Committee on Interior and Insular Affairs and the House Committee on the Judiciary.

Similar Bill in the Senate: S.2196 by KOHL (D-WI) — Indian Treaty Conflict Resolution Act of 1990. Introduced: February 27, 1990. Recent Action: Referred to Senate Select Committee on Indian Affairs.

b. H.J.Res.287 by DAVIS, ROBERT (R-MI) — (Joint resolution to establish a Presidential Commission to review the exercise of Indian treaty rights on off-reservation lands.) Introduced: June 1, 1989. Recent Action: Referred to House Committee on Interior and Insular Affairs.

9. Health

a. S.2645 by INOUYE (D-HI) — Urban Indian Health Equity Act (A bill to improve the health status of the urban Indian population and to enhance the quality and scope of health care services, disease prevention activities, and health promotion initiatives targeted at the urban American Indian population.) Introduced: May 16, 1990. Recent Action: Referred to Senate Select Committee on Indian Affairs.

b. S.192 by MATSUNAGA (D-HI) — (A bill to require the Secretary of Veterans' Affairs to provide for the conduct of a comprehensive study of the psychological problems of Native Americans who are Vietnam veterans.) Introduced: January 25, 1989. Recent action: Public Hearings held by Senate Committee on Veterans' Affairs.

10. Civil Rights

S.517 by HATCH (R-UT) — Indian Civil Rights Act Amendments of 1989 (A bill to provide Federal court authority to enforce rights secured by the Indian Civil Rights Act of 1968.) Introduced: March 6, 1989. Recent Action: Referred to Senate Committee on the Judiciary.

11. Law Enforcement

a. H.R.498 by RHODES, III (R-AZ) — Indian Law Enforcement Reform Act (A bill to clarify and strengthen the authority for certain Department of Interior law-enforcement services, activities, and officers in Indian country.) Introduced: January 4, 1989.

227

Recent Action: Returned to the House from the Senate with Senate amendments.

b. H.R.4032 by OBEY (D-WI) — Indian Treaty Law Enforcement Assistance Act (A bill to establish within the Office of Justice Programs of the Department of Justice an Indian Treaty Law Enforcement Assistance Program.) Introduced: February 21, 1990. Recent Action: Referred to House Committee on the Judiciary.

c. S.1783 by MCCAIN (R-AZ) — Indian Child Abuse Prevention and Treatment Act (A bill to regulate Indian child protection and prevent child abuse on Indian reservations.) Introduced: October 24, 1989. Recent Action: Received in the House after passage in the Senate, public hearings held by House Committee on Interior and Insular Affairs.

d. S.2340 by MCCAIN (R-AZ) — Indian Child Protective Services and Family Violence Prevention Act (A bill to develop and improve child protective service programs on Indian reservations and to strengthen Indian families.) Introduced: March 27, 1990. Recent Action: Public Hearings held by Senate Select Committee on Indian Affairs.

12. Water

Several bills are pending. *See generally*, American Indian Resources Institute, *Handbook of Tribal Water Settlements* (1989)

VII. Alaska Natives

A. General Sources

1. David S. Case, *Alaska Natives and American Laws* (University of Alaska Press, 1984)
2. *Felix S. Cohen's Handbook of Federal Indian Law*, Ch. 14A (Michie Bobbs-Merrill, 1982 ed.)

B. Aboriginal Title in Alaska as of the 1960s

1. *Tee-Hit-Ton Indians v. United States*, 348 U.S. 272 (1955) (Aboriginal title not compensable under 5th Amendment if extinguished)
2. *County of Oneida v. Oneida Indian Nation*, 470 U.S. 226 (1985) (Indian title remains valid if not extinguished)

C. Alaska Native Claims Settlement Act of 1971

1. Lazarus & West, *The Alaska Native Claims Settlement Act: A Flawed Victory*, 40 Law & Contemp. Prob. 132 (1976)
2. Robert D. Arnold, *Alaska Native Land Claims* (The Alaska Native Foundation, 1978)

D. The Berger Commission

Thomas R. Berger, *Village Journey: The Report of the Alaska Native Review Commission* (Hill & Wang, 1985)

E. The "1991 Amendments"

Act of Feb. 3, 1988, Pub. L. No. 100-241, 101 Stat. 1788

F. The Modern Movement for Sovereignty

1. *Native Village of Stevens v. Alaska Management & Planning*, 757 P.2d 32 (Alaska, 1988) (Stevens Village and most other Native Villages are not tribes possessing sovereign immunity or other sovereign powers.)
2. *State of Alaska v. Native Village of Venetie*, 856 F.2d 1384 (9th Cir. 1988) (Implicitly rejecting *Stevens Village* and finding that tribal status of Alaska Native Villages to be determined by principles of Federal Indian law as applied in the Lower 48 States)
3. *Native Village of Noatak v. Hoffman*, 896 F.2d 1157 (9th Cir. 1990) (Three Native Villages are recognized tribes for purposes of federal court jurisdiction under 28 U.S.C.A. { 1362 and the suit is not barred by the State of Alaska's sovereign immunity under the 11th Amendment.)

VIII. Hawaiian Natives

A. General Sources

Felix S. Cohen's *Handbook of Federal Indian Law* Ch. 14C *(Michie Bobbs-Merrill, 1982 ed.)*

B. International Sovereign Status of the Hawaiian Kingdom Until the Overthrow of 1893 and the Annexation of 1898

C. Native Lands

1. *General Sources*

   a. Linda S. Parker, *Native American Estate: The Struggle Over*

Indian and Hawaiian Lands (University of Hawaii Press, 1989)

   b. Maivan Clech Lam, *The Kuleana Act Revisited: The Survival of Traditional Hawaiian Common Rights in Land*, 64 Wash. L. Rev. 233 (1989)

2. *The Great Mahele of 1848*
3. *The Kuleana Act of 1850*
4. *The Hawaii Homes Commission Act of 1921*
5. *The Statehood Land Trust*

D. *Applicability to Hawaiian Natives of Federal Indian Law as Applied on The Mainland*

1. Hawaiian Natives as within Congress' Authority under the Indian Commerce Clause *Felix S. Cohen's Handbook of Federal Indian Law* 207-212, 802-804 (1982 ed.)
2. *Keaukaha-Panewa Community v. Hawaiian Homes Commission*, 739 F.2d 1467 (9th Cir. 1984) (Hawaiian Admission Act imposed trust obligation, based in federal law, on State of Hawaii with regard to lands administered for the benefit of Hawaiian Natives.)
3. *Price v. State of Hawaii*, 764 F.2d 623 (9th Cir. 1985) (Plaintiff group not a tribe for purposes of 28 U.S.C.A { 1362, but court found that tribal status of Hawaiian Native groups would be determined by principles of federal Indian law as applied on The Mainland.)

IX. Assessing Future Courses of Action

See generally, American Indian Resources Institute, *Tribal Governance* (1990) and *Integrated Resource Management* (1990).

A. *Litigation*

B. *Federal Legislation: Setting a National Tribal Agenda*

C. *State Legislation*

D. *State-Tribal Negotiations*

E. *Economic Development Agreements with Private Industry*

F. *Tribal Action*

1. Research and Development
2. Tribal Courts

3. Tribal Administrative Agendas
4. Land Acquisition Programs
5. Health and Education Programs

A Critique of
Federal Government Land Claims Policies

The Assembly of First Nations

Introduction

First Nations in Canada have had their aboriginal and treaty rights recognized and affirmed within Canada's Constitution since 1982. The accumulation of case law by the Supreme Court of Canada has assisted in defining the federal government's responsibilities toward the aboriginal peoples. Section 35 of the *Constitution Act, 1982*, requires that all laws and policy in Canada must be consistent with the recognition and affirmation of aboriginal and treaty rights. Despite this legal foundation, the federal government's approach to aboriginal matters has remained fundamentally unchanged and continues to be a source of frustration for the aboriginal peoples of this country.

The federal government attempts to present its land claims policies in the best light possible, both in Canada and abroad, despite its obvious failure to adequately address the land rights issues of Canada's aboriginal peoples. This self-promotion is in direct contrast to the fundamental problems and difficulties, both historic and contemporary, which First Nations experience on a continual basis when attempting to address their rights with governments in this country.

The underlying source of this contradiction is to be found in the opposing objectives of aboriginal peoples and the Government of Canada. Whereas the First Nations have sought to have their rights recognized and implemented, the federal government's primary goal has always been to extinguish the "burden" of aboriginal rights and minimize its legal obligations.

Such policies have relegated First Nations to dealing with bureaucrats on matters of fundamental importance to their survival. The range of issues involved are inherently political in nature and go to the heart of the relationship of First Nations with the Canadian State. There should no confusion as to the source of the problem; land rights matters must be addressed from a proper legal perspective and within the political arena. The federal government's conflict of interest and selective use of the law must be addressed. The bureaucratic approaches designed by Indian Affairs and Justice officials have proven to be completely inappropriate for dealing with such important matters.

This fundamental contradiction has been a major contributor to the enormous frustration felt throughout native communities today. Many claims do not meet the narrowly defined criteria set down in these policies and are rejected despite the strong sense of injustice felt by the claimant. If a claim does manage to get accepted under the narrow confines of the government's two policies, the claimant must deal with the slow pace of negotiations and lack of progress which have characterized the land claims process in this country.

This has lead to a great deal of frustration on the part of First Nations, which are left with no alternative but to address their grievances either through the courts or by direct action. The courts have often not been found to be a reasonable course of action for many due to the prohibitive costs and the fact that many native people feel the courts are likely to be biased against them or are simply an alien forum which cannot address their concerns properly. A growing number of native communities have found that they must take direct action on the ground, through roadblocks or other forms of protest, in order to get governments to take notice of their concerns.

One of the most obvious criticisms of the process is the conflict of interest the federal government has in attempting to deal with these matters. On the one hand the federal government has a fiduciary or trust-like responsibility toward aboriginal peoples to act in their best interests, while at the same it seeks to act in its own best interests. Clearly the interests of the two parties are not the same and often directly conflict. Therefore how can one party to such disputes control the resolution process and expect it to result in fair and just settlements?

Through these policies the federal government sets itself up as the judge and jury in dealing with claims against itself. It sets the criteria, decides what claims are acceptable, and controls the entire negotiation process, including funding support. Clearly, in the democratic world there are few examples of such a grievance procedure being so totally controlled by one party to a dispute. Seventeen years of experience have shown this to be an inadequate dispute resolution mechanism.

One point often overlooked by those not familiar with the subject is the fact that since the early 1980s the federal government has segmented its approach to land claims into two separate policies. The specific claims policy is a narrowly defined type of claims process designed to address breaches of federal obligations. A comprehensive

233

claims policy was established ostensibly to deal with claims arising from unsurrendered aboriginal ownership of lands and resources.

These new policy formulations were a departure from the original land claims policy statement of 1973 which identified three types of claims the government was prepared to consider. These included specific and comprehensive claims, as well as a third category which was dropped with the new policy formulations of the early 1980s. That third category was referred to as "claims of another nature" and would have encompassed many of the claims that have been rejected by the federal government under the existing comprehensive and specific claims policies. Regardless of the importance attached by First Nations to outstanding rights issues, the federal government continues to deny these important matters an appropriate resolution process.

1. Comprehensive Claims

The Government of Canada's comprehensive claims policy has become increasingly narrow since it was split from specific claims in the early 1980s. Despite federal assertions to the contrary, the policy has not been opened up over the past few years; it has had its contents increasingly defined to the point where every aspect and matter for negotiation is subject to debate and disagreement. The priorities of First Nations have been excluded from the policy, while the governments objectives are made ever the more prominent.

The recommendations of the Coolican Task Force, which reviewed the comprehensive claims policy in 1985, were practically ignored in the formulation of the new policy announced in 1986. Although the task force report encompassed many of the concerns expressed by First Nations, only a few limited changes were made to the policy. These included some very narrow alternatives to extinguishment of aboriginal title and extending the list of matters open to negotiation to off-shore areas.

Obviously, this left First Nations in wonderment at the waste of the entire consultation process, which took well over a year and resulted in such minimal change. It did confirm however, the government's priorities; the foremost being obtaining "finality" through settlement agreements, thereby providing the "certainty" required for resource development to proceed. The policy still requires the full release and surrender of rights to lands in the settlement area. The change merely provides for the possible retention of aboriginal title to some portion of land upon settlement.

The announcement of a revised policy also provided the government an opportunity to clarify its intent to exclude self-government from comprehensive land claim agreements and the constitutional protection to be accorded such settlements. Any self-government arrangements must be negotiated separately and be consistent with existing Indian Affairs policy. Existing policy on self-government is extremely limited in nature and may prejudice existing aboriginal sovereignty. Upon settlement the claimant would be subject to all levels of non-aboriginal government such as provincial, territorial, and municipal laws. This would not serve as an enhancement of aboriginal governments.

What First Nations require is the recognition and affirmation of aboriginal rights in a manner consistent with Section 35 of the Constitution. This includes enhancing the special relationship of First Nations with the Crown, aboriginal hunting and fishing rights, the recognition of aboriginal title to lands and waters within traditional territories, and the jurisdiction required to control and protect the traditional homeland from third party incursion. While the federal government contends that its comprehensive claims policy is intended to address claims to aboriginal rights, in practice it is being used to extinguish aboriginal rights and replace these with "benefits" established under settlement legislation. Constitutionally recognized rights such as land title, hunting, and fishing, as well as self-government, are to be eliminated under existing policy in exchange for much narrower land claim settlement rights. In effect, it is coercing native peoples to surrender constitutionally protected rights in exchange for legislated rights.

It was made abundantly clear in the 1986 policy statement that Canada intends to address only land and resource matters, as defined by the federal government. This is clearly not a policy intended to recognize and affirm existing aboriginal rights. Third party interests and the rights of non-natives to have access to First Nations lands and resources receive more protection than do aboriginal rights under existing policy. First Nations are again expected to ignore the fundamental relationship of the land to all their rights. In order to negotiate, the claimant must to some degree ignore the intimate connection between rights and land.

It is difficult to see how one constitutionally protects provisions of an agreement dealing with land, resources, wildlife, and environment, while at the same time excluding the very basis of First Nations jurisdiction over those same matters. First Nations find it fundamentally unjust that they are being required to surrender the very rights they are seeking to protect through the claims negotiation process. To the First Nations a policy that does not affirm their aboriginal rights amounts to an extinguishment policy.

In its submission to the Coolican Task Force in November of 1985 the Assembly of First Nations called for the elimination of the artificially imposed distinction between comprehensive and specific claims and their replacement with a First Nations Rights Policy. AFN called for the establishment of a First Nations Rights Policy based on the principles of the inherent rights and title of First Nations, consistent with the spirit and intent of the constitutional entrenchment of aboriginal and treaty rights.

Such an approach is reasonably compatible with many of the objectives of First Nations. It would provide for a process by which the many outstanding matters which are inherently interrelated could be dealt with in one forum, rather than in a piecemeal fashion as at present. The theme of one rights policy for the implementation and review of all rights was far too advanced for the limited perception of federal officials accustomed to segmenting and isolating specific issues.

A. Conflicting Objectives: Avoiding the Issues

The stated objective of the federal government's comprehensive land claims policy is to establish certainty of rights concerning land and resources. However, in reality the only certainty the government is truly concerned with is its own right to promote the exploitation of lands and resources. When it comes to certainty for native people, the government seeks to limit rights as much as possible. While restricting comprehensive claims negotiations to dealing only with land and resource matters, it denies constitutional entrenchment of self-government arrangements required to put aboriginal jurisdiction over these very matters into practice.

One of the more misleading aspects of the government's stated policy is its contention that negotiations are based on claims of aboriginal title and that the option of not surrendering aboriginal title to at least a part of a claimant's territory is available. One only needs to refer to recent agreements-in-principle with the Dene-Métis of the Northwest Territories and Council for Yukon Indians to see that aboriginal title is severely limited or clearly surrendered in these documents. Nowhere within these agreements is there an explicit acknowledgement that aboriginal rights and title exist. There is no positive affirmation of aboriginal title to be found anywhere in the text.

For example, the only place aboriginal title and rights are specifically mentioned in the General Provisions of these agreements-in-principle is under the Certainty clause. These clauses are basically surrender provisions by which claimants "cede, release and surrender to Her Majesty the Queen in Right of Canada, all their aboriginal claims, rights, titles and interests, if any" to the lands specified.

The fact is, federal land claims policy criteria are inconsistent with the developing law on aboriginal rights in this country. Landmark cases such as the recent *Guerin* (1984) and *Simon* (1985) decisions are ignored in the criteria for its comprehensive claims policy. For instance, the *Guerin* decision confirmed the federal government's fiduciary duty to aboriginal peoples and the responsibility it has for protecting aboriginal and treaty rights. In *Sparrow* (1990) the Supreme Court of Canada said that Section 35 of the *Constitution Act, 1982* is a solemn commitment to aboriginal peoples which must be given meaningful content by government legislation, practices, and policies. The federal government has yet to respond in any significant manner to the requirements delineated in these decisions.

A clear example of the federal government's application of pseudo-legal concepts is the idea that aboriginal title can be "superseded by law"; meaning that any aboriginal title or rights which may have existed has been extinguished by the accumulation of legislation over the lands in question. The Micmacs of Nova Scotia had their comprehensive claim rejected in 1977 on this basis, even though they had never signed a treaty or agreement surrendering their traditional territories. It should be noted that this concept was also used in the reasoning for the rejection of the Mohawk comprehensive claim in 1975.

The Supreme Court of Canada confirmed the position held by aboriginal peoples all along, when it stated, in the *Sparrow* decision, that although aboriginal rights could be arbitrarily extinguished by the Crown prior to 1982, the intent of the legislation must have been "clear and plain." First Nations will expect that the federal government will abandon its illegal "supersession by law" concept as grounds for extinguishment.

It is ludicrous for the federal government to continue forcing First Nations to go to court every time aboriginal rights are an issue, rather than obeying the law as declared by the Supreme Court by dealing with aboriginal peoples fairly. Federal policy must be changed to reflect the state of the law in a cooperative rather than adversarial fashion.

B. An Arbitrary Process: The Predetermined Agenda

If by chance a comprehensive claim is accepted, it is added to a waiting list. It is federal policy that only six claims can be negotiated at any one time. Some claims presently being negotiated were accepted as much as fifteen years ago. This means that claimants on the waiting list have no way of protecting their rights and interests while awaiting their turn at negotiations. At the present rate the wait could take over fifty years or more. Ongoing development and third party alienation of aboriginal lands and resources continues unabated whether or not the government has acknowledged a claim.

From the federal government's perspective this may not be strange when one considers that nowhere in the current claims process does the federal government intend to acknowledge that any aboriginal rights exist; in fact, the federal government also considers that it is granting land rights to aboriginal people under land claims agreements. The main reason the federal government is negotiating comprehensive claims is because aboriginal rights are a burden on Crown title and their objective is to release that burden.

The federal government maintains that participation in the process is voluntary and that First Nations cannot be forced into agreements. In reality, the only alternative to the process is the court system, which is expensive, adversarial in nature, and without any assurance that the federal government will honour the court's decision. A more dramatic way of drawing attention to the problem is direct action, which raises a host of other problems. Even if success is achieved through the courts, negotiations must follow to give effect to the court's decision.

Once in the negotiation process set up under the policy, the claimant must comply with the restricted subject matter for negotiation set down by the government, leaving many vital items off the table. Arbitrary deadlines set down by Cabinet and the general "take it or leave it" attitude of government officials toward claimants reflect the coercive strategy of the federal government.

C. Financial Support: A Means of Control

Another means by which the government controls the negotiation process is through financial support to claimants. Loan funding is provided to cover negotiation costs such as professional and technical staff, but the use of these funds is very closely monitored. Any use of loan funds deemed inappropriate by federal officials may result in reductions or suspension of funding. Ultimately, priorities are more

238

or less dictated by the federal government, with funding cuts being the big stick to ensure compliance.

The government's contention that loans are interest free is inaccurate. All loans become interest bearing upon the approval of agreements-in-principle. Although the interest rate applied may be equal to the current treasury bill rate, it serves to further complicate an already complex schedule of payments. The experience of claimants has been that upon final settlement repayment of loans and interest is calculated and scheduled into the compensation package in a manner more advantageous to the federal treasury than to the claimant.

The loan funding process is one of the more repulsive aspects of the policy, as the repayment of such loans represents a deduction from the compensation obtained by the claimants through negotiations. This is especially unfair in that the prolonged time-frame and inevitable ensuing expense of these negotiations is not the result of the claimants' actions, but of the federal government's complex negotiation requirements under its policy.

D. Self-Government: Narrowing the Options

Another aspect of the policy which causes problems for aboriginal peoples is the exclusion of self-government arrangements under claims agreements, thereby excluding constitutional protection for self-government. Also, the federal government's insistence that all laws of general application must apply to lands dealt with under a claim is offensive to claimants and inconsistent with their thrust toward self-government.

The exclusion of self-government agreements from the constitutional protection to be accorded land claims agreements ignores the importance of jurisdiction in land and resource matters. Why else would a First Nation get involved in the process, if not to clarify its rights in this regard. Land claims settlements mean little if the aboriginal control over lands and resources to be retained is not addressed. It would seem the conflict over such matters would be likely to continue.

The imposition of provincial or territorial laws of general application, combined with the limited authority provided to claimants on management boards, leaves little to be discussed in eventual self-government discussions and renders self-government an empty shell. The fact that the comprehensive claim negotiations are restricted to land and resource matters results in a piecemeal approach to jurisdictional matters which aboriginal peoples wish to deal with on a more substantial basis.

E. Progress to Date: A Record of Deception

With regard to Canada's claims to success in reaching comprehensive claim settlements, it should be noted that the Crees of Quebec are currently bringing forward litigation to have their settlement declared null and void, due to noncompliance by federal and provincial governments. Since settlement legislation was passed under the terms of the *James Bay and Northern Quebec Agreement* (1975), the Crees have been in a continual battle with the federal government to live up to its obligations under the agreement. Again there has been an ongoing process of denial on the part of the federal government, despite the clear and plain intent of written agreements and legislation. Quebec's plans for James Bay II was the breaking point for the Crees of Quebec.

The experience of this claimant group demonstrates some of the problems claimants have come to expect, even after land claim agreements are supposedly finalized. This experience and the historical experience of aboriginal peoples in dealings with governments in Canada are some of what is behind the mistrust pervading relations between First Nations and Canada.

2. Specific Claims

The federal government alleges its specific claims policy is "working," although federal officials admit it may not be working to everyone's satisfaction. They continue to refuse to acknowledge that it needs a complete overhaul. Despite the record of failure of the policy, the Minister continues to speak of improvements and speeding up the process. It will be impossible to improve or speed up the process until the conflicting objectives of the First Nations and the Government of Canada are resolved.

A. Reducing Federal Liabilities

The Government of Canada states that its specific claims policy deals with claims against the federal government related to the administration of land and other Indian assets and to the non-fulfilment of specific treaty provisions. Federal policy restricts matters to be addressed under specific claims to outstanding obligations or breaches of legislative requirements and treaty provisions. This generally amounts to whether the federal government will accept that there exists a rigorously defined legal obligation on its part and then a process of negotiating compensation.

240

It is in the area of specific claims that the deficiencies of government claims policy become most apparent. The strict legal criteria applied to specific claims have rendered the policy useless for resolving a large number of claims. Even more appalling is the selective use of legal interpretations to reduce or reject claims while blatantly ignoring crucial developments in case law. It appears that the federal government feels free to consider only legal concepts which are advantageous to itself, rather than applying the law as declared by the courts.

Officials administering this program have admitted in the past that it cannot address the full range of grievances First Nations may have against the Government of Canada. A major weakness of the policy is the lack of provision for addressing treaty rights matters. Although the department says it would be willing to entertain claims based on the non-fulfilment of specific treaty provisions, it has in the past maintained the position that the Minister has no mandate to address treaty rights, such as hunting and fishing.

Apart from the many claims that cannot be addressed by this process, the problems experienced at every stage of negotiation of any claim is alarming. Even some First Nations that have agreed to settle their claims are not fully satisfied that their concerns were adequately dealt with, but agreed to settle in order to get something for their efforts.

B. A Growing Backlog Speaks for Itself

The federal government's statistics on specific claims are misleading. Besides the 578 specific claims which it admits have been submitted, there may be as many as 1,000 more claims currently being developed. No more than forty-four claims have been settled since the policy was brought into effect in 1973. Not a great record over seventeen years, amounting to an average of little more than two per year. Of these claims about fifteen were the so-called B.C. "cut-off" claims, which were similar in nature and the substance of which were basically dealt with together.

The most appalling misrepresentation is the federal government's statement that 205 claims have been "resolved." Included in this figure are claims that have been rejected and certainly not resolved as far as First Nations are concerned.

As for the 275 claims the department says are at various stages, including negotiation, one only needs to ask how many of these claims were in active negotiations this year? The answer could not be more than a dozen, and it is doubtful that many of those progressed significantly.

241

The department also states that ninety-eight claims are being either reassessed by the claimant, in litigation or have been suspended by the department. No less than twenty-two claims previously submitted to the specific claims process are now in litigation. That doesn't include the claims First Nations decided to pursue through litigation without submitting them under a policy they know doesn't work. It is estimated there may be up to fifty more claims in litigation.

Suspended claims are those specific claims the department has decided to strike from its case load. Claims are usually suspended because a claimant has not responded to departmental requests for information by a certain date. Yet, when claims sit at the Department of Justice year after year, no adequate explanation for the delay is given to the claimant. They are expected to wait, with no progress possible until Justice decides to address the claim.

The settled specific claims listed in the department's public information are only those involving larger sums of money or land. This does not portray the majority of claims settled, which are much less dramatic. The fact is, with a few exceptions, the federal government appears unable to deal with large claims.

C. Negotiations: Take It or Leave It

There have always been many difficulties with the process itself as administered by the Department of Indian Affairs and Northern Development (DIAND). From the first stage of research and development of a specific claim to its submission to the federal government, there are financial limitations due to the limited funds available. Once a claim is submitted there are the endless clarification requirements entailing costly and time-consuming legal and policy wrangling. Throughout this preliminary process federal lawyers are involved at every step, ensuring a continuous and expensive debate of the legal merits of a claim.

If a claim survives this rigorous process, and both the claimant First Nation and DIAND Specific Claims Branch agree on the components of the claim submission, it is then sent on to the Department of Justice. After an extended period, usually taking a year or more, the claim is either accepted or rejected by the Minister based upon the Department of Justice's analysis and advice.

If by chance a claim is accepted, it is seldom clear just how much responsibility the federal government is accepting. This is left to further wrangling within the negotiation process itself. Only a limited number of claims can be negotiated at any time, so when a claim is accepted it goes on the waiting list, usually for years. Once negotiations do commence, they generally degenerate to a protracted debate over the method of calculating compensation.

An example occurred when the Department of Indian and Northern Affairs' Specific Claims Branch conducted an internal review of its operations a couple of years ago. As a result of this review it was decided that some new, more "rigorous" principles would be applied to the handling of such claims.

One of the more disconcerting changes brought in at that time was the concept of "discounting" with regard to calculating compensation. Discounting is done by the Department of Indian Affairs in conjunction with the Department of Justice and involves reducing the amount of compensation to be offered on a claim by a percentage equal to the federal government's assessment of the chances for success a claim would have if submitted to the courts. Therefore, if a claim was assessed as having a 50 percent chance of being successfully litigated, the government would cut the compensation by 50 percent.

This ludicrous concept is just an example of the confounding impediments First Nations run into when attempting to resolve claims under this policy. This new more "rigorous" interpretation of the policy has failed to significantly improve the paltry annual average of claims settled.

Again, as with comprehensive claims, financial support is provided through loans which the claimant is expected to repay from eventual compensation. Claimants are at a disadvantage because they do not have the financial, administrative, or legal resources to draw upon, except through this loan funding, which is very closely monitored and controlled by the department. Meanwhile the federal government has the resources of the entire federal bureaucracy to draw upon. Often, another round of wrangling takes place over how much of the claimant's negotiation loans will be reimbursed if a settlement agreement is reached.

If negotiations fail to reach agreement on a settlement package, there is no independent mechanism for breaking such a deadlock. The only alternative is costly litigation or direct action efforts aimed at bringing public attention to the issue.

D. The Flawed Policy: A Reflection of the Colonial Legacy

In summary, the federal government's specific claims policy is inadequate in almost every respect. Its criteria, process, and costs have resulted in very few settlements, causing some First Nations to reject it as a viable mechanism to address their grievances. Many others, who are into the process at one stage or another, get discouraged waiting for progress on even relatively minor claims.

As pointed out earlier, many of these problems exist due to one important aspect of the policy: it is administered by DIAND, with legal support from Justice, which puts the federal government in a conflict of interest. The fact that the federal government has appointed itself judge and jury in dealing with claims against itself further erodes any credibility this policy might ever have had among aboriginal peoples and is contrary to the principles of natural justice. It is basically an extension of the racist and paternalistic attitude toward aboriginal peoples that is characteristic of Canada's colonial traditions.

The adversarial nature of native claims puts the government in a poor position when it attempts to control the exclusive arena for negotiated settlements of First Nation grievances and outstanding matters. The federal government has not attempted to provide for appeal mechanisms when claims are rejected or negotiations fail. Over the years, First Nations have unsuccessfully proposed that arbitration or mediation mechanisms be put in place as part of the process. Clearly this is one policy area requiring fundamental review with a view to making it consistent with the current aspirations of First Nations and the constitutional rhetoric of the federal government.

Conclusion

The First Nations of Canada do not view their rights in terms of "claims." We more properly view the claims process as one of the few mechanisms available for implementing our constitutionally protected rights. Although there is a consensus that such policies fall far short of what is required, many First Nations have had little choice but to use the claims process as a limited device with which to engage the federal government in negotiations on matters integral to their survival and development.

First Nations and the Government of Canada do not view claims in the same way. While First Nations need a claims process that will result in the proper recognition of their rights, the federal government continues to impose completely inappropriate policies, designed to minimize the implementation or limit the recognition of aboriginal and treaty rights. The policy approach of the federal government in the area of native claims reflects this government's intent to limit any expansion of federal responsibility towards Indians, especially with regard to expenditures.

A fundamental difference between the federal government and First Nation perceptions of claims is the artificial division of federal policies into "specific" and "comprehensive" claims. Two narrowly defined policies have been developed which are inadequate to meet the needs and priorities of First Nations. Most First Nations view their claims within the greater context of constitutionally protected aboriginal and treaty rights, and their political relationship with Canada.

This arbitrary division of claims into two limited policy frameworks excludes many claims from the process. They simply fall between the cracks, not fitting neatly within either policy. The policies also fail to address rights issues which clearly have a basis in law. There is little recourse for First Nations that find their claims in this situation, beyond pursuing costly litigation or developing direct action strategies.

There are few options available for dealing with matters which so clearly have an impact on both the history and future development of not only Indian communities, but Canada as a whole. First Nations want a settlement of their outstanding grievances through a process which is based on principles of fairness and justice. Most of the Canadian public support this objective. It can only be accomplished through a process that takes account of the importance First Nations attach to the recognition and implementation of aboriginal and treaty rights already recognized in the Constitution.

Experience shows that attempts to address First Nations concerns within federal claims policies are consistently doomed to failure as long as the fundamental issues involved are ignored. Government officials and bureaucrats do not have the authority to deal with matters of this nature. It is only through a political process that the rights of First Nations can be effectively implemented. Half measures, such as the present claims policy approach, only leave more questions to be dealt with later.

Of course, if the government's only objective is to minimize its legal and financial obligations and to provide certainty with regard to land tenure, thereby ensuring resource development, then the present framework might go some way towards that. However, it does not even meet that objective adequately, and resulting agreements are a recipe for future acrimony and continuing dissatisfaction. Such an approach puts off far too many issues to be addressed later, thereby counteracting whatever benefits might be achieved in the present.

The fact that litigation is the only legal alternative to negotiations under existing claims policies serves to reinforce the adversarial nature of First Nations/Canada relations contrary to the declaration of the Supreme Court of Canada in the *Sparrow* decision. This situation also does little to enhance the present government's desired image of Canada as a champion of human rights. It gives the appearance of a country that pays scant attention to the provisions of its own Constitution and the decisions of its Supreme Court, let alone international law on human rights. The absence of inexpensive, speedy, fair, and effective mechanisms by which Canada's aboriginal peoples may pursue their rights and titles is contrary to the standards expected of a democractic society that respects the rule of law.

The federal government must meet the challenge and deal with First Nations on common ground in a spirit of cooperation as declared by the Supreme Court of Canada. The objectives and priorities of First Nations must be respected if satisfactory solutions amenable to all parties are to be found. For there to be fair and just settlements, there must be a recognition of the inseparable connection land claims have with the greater framework of aboriginal and treaty rights in Canada.

The implementation of aboriginal and treaty rights will require that great care be given to how land rights are vindicated. Land claims should not be considered in isolation from the greater context within which they must fit. In terms of land claims policy formulation, due consideration must also be given to the needs and objectives of First Nations.

Such important policy frameworks should not be dictatorily or unilaterally imposed and First Nations told "take it, or leave it." Surely more appropriate policies can be devised which will truly ensure that all can live with the settlements reached. Fair and just settlements require that all parties have a say in developing the process by which such agreements are to be reached. In the spirit of the *Sparrow* decision, proper consultation should take place between the federal government and the relevant First Nation whenever matters that directly affect the latter are involved.

Assembly of First Nations
August 1990

Appendix No. 1

Canada's Land Claims Policies: Issues and Problems

1. *Conflict of Interest*
   - Canada's fiduciary duty requires advocacy, not adversarial approach
   - Indian perception not given favourable interpretation in most cases
   - federal government acts as judge and jury in claims against itself
   - role of Justice department to protect government interests compromises fairness in assessment of claims
2. *Lack of Guiding Principles for Policy*
   - government policy not based on mutually acceptable principles to guide development and implementation
   - underlying principle of current policy appears to be based on minimizing federal liabilities
3. *Current Policy*
   - focus on claims against government rather than recognition and implementation of aboriginal and treaty rights
   - lawful obligations defined through narrow policy framework rather than by accepted legal principles
   - -policy based on technical issues rather than concepts of equity and current moral standards
   - exclusion of pre-Confederation claims and treaties from policy
   - federal government's fiduciary responsibility not accounted for under policy
   - policy cannot address rights and treaty issues, even though such are legal rights
   - loss of hunting and fishing rights, whether aboriginal or treaty, cannot be addressed under current policy
   - onus is on claimant to demonstrate claim, rather than on ensuring that government fulfills its responsibilities
   - policy did not require consent of First Nations
4. *Current Process*
   - policy and process completely dictated and controlled by federal bureaucrats
   - research and development of claims closely controlled and monitored by Indian and Northern Affairs
   - arduous requirements for claims submission inconsistent with role of fiduciary or advocate
   - validation process questionable and secretive

- no consistency with case law developments or selective use of only interpretations favourable to federal government interests
- unilateral and arbitrary approach to validation and compensation has never been acceptable and has been constant source of frustration
- no disclosure of legal opinions from Justice, while full disclosure of legal position of claimant required
- role of Justice at every stage of process, from claim submission, negotiation, and settlement is a major hindrance to progress
- federal negotiators' lack of authority and subservience to Justice personnel undermines negotiation process
- attitude of many federal officials offensive to First Nations and their representatives, reflecting a lack of respect and concern for matters of the utmost importance to the survival of First Nations
- funding controlled by federal government through same department that defines and implements policy
- First Nation negotiation costs funded through loans from government and represent first charge against settlement compensation
- funding levels to support all aspects of policy inadequate and unfair to First Nations, which do not have the massive technical support network the federal government has to draw upon

5. *Settlements*
- no appeal mechanism when negotiations reach a deadlock except to go to court, which then entails suspension of negotiations and costly, unfunded effort by First Nation
- if claim goes to court, government reserves the right to use all technical defenses, despite the fact they may have unfair advantage by means of their access to all relevant research material used by claimant to develop claim, including legal opinions
- compensation arbitrarily dictated by federal government on the basis of unknown principles, which appear to have no relationship to common law or the concept of equity—ie. loss of use, "degree of doubt," "technical breach," special value, return of lands, "third party interests," etc.
- role of fiduciary to indemnify the beneficiary ignored
- requirement that claimant extinguish all claims or rights in echange for settlement is far too sweeping a release of federal responsibilities
- claimants cannot integrate settlement process with self-government or economic development initiatives

6. *Policy Development*
    - lack of consultation for real cooperative and effective policy development
    - no consent from First Nations sought on final policy announcements
    - arbitrary time limits set by federal government
    - no open and realistic commitment to policy reform

Self-Determination and the Treaties

Lawrence Courtoreille
Regional Chief for Alberta
Co-Chair, National Committee
on Treaties

The connection between self-determination and the treaty relationship is an important one, which has deep roots in the constitutional and historical fabric of what we know today as Canada. The treaty-making process itself was an exercise of sovereignty on the part of the First Nations, since we couldn't have entered into treaty in the first place without the proper political authority and jurisdiction. For the First Nations, the treaty-making process itself was an act of governance, where we formalized political relationships with the Europeans or with other First Nations.

From the Crown's perspective, the treaty-making process was not only an exercise of its own political authority; it was also a clear recognition of the political authority of the First Nations. It was an acknowledgement of our right to self-determination. Otherwise, why would the Crown have sought our consent and cooperation through treaty?

The position of the First Nations has always been that our right of self-determination is an inherent one, given by the Creator. In terms of specifics, however, the treaty-making process was used by the First Nations to formalize our relationship with the Europeans. This took many shapes, depending on the context: there are peace and friendship treaties, concluded to cease hostilities and/or forge alliances; trade treaties, concluded to secure the terms of commerce; and other treaties which dealt with a whole host of matters related to the sharing of lands, resource rights, education, justice, etc.

It is important to point out that items *not* dealt with specifically in any particular treaty were retained by the First Nations for themselves, and remain in the domain of inherent, aboriginal rights. The right of self-determination is one of these rights. In many regions, although the *Indian Act* was imposed after treaties were signed, it was without the consent of those First Nations affected, and in fact, traditional systems of governance continued despite constraints imposed from the outside (for example, the regulation of traditional harvesting, education, etc.)

Acceptance of the federal government's "community based self-government" policy is a denial of our treaty-making power, and undermines our treaty and aboriginal rights.

We must look to a fresh approach to these issues that is consistent with our history, consistent with our principles, and consistent with our treaties. We won't find room for this approach in current government policy.

If we don't look for serious alternatives, we run the risk of terminating ourselves, and undermining the treaty relationship that our grandfathers worked so hard to protect. We can't lose sight of the fact that the fight for our inherent, aboriginal and treaty rights goes on side by side with our fight for self-determination. What we do in one area stands to affect all of the other areas. What one First Nation does may affect the prospects for all of the other First Nations.

For the future, we hope that our Nations will show the teamwork that is necessary to build a strong alternative to the existing policies and positions of the federal government. This is the only way that we will be able to challenge them effectively and get on with the business of true Nation building.

Aboriginal Governments in Canada: An Emerging Field of Study

Frank Cassidy
University of Victoria
Institute for Research on Public Policy

Introduction

For the past several years aboriginal governments in Canada have been the focus of greatly increased attention by the press, the academic community, and governments. Despite considerable interest, research about aboriginal government has yet to emerge in a defined, bounded, and self- generating manner. This has not been an entirely unfortunate state of affairs. The lack of definition has enabled various researchers and commentators to respond to the quick pace of change, as constitutional matters, government policies, and the institutions of aboriginal government have all taken, in varying degrees, paths of development different from those that might have been foreseen. At the same time, a new body of work has set the stage for a progression of knowledge and insight in a more coordinated and interrelated manner. It may be possible to foresee the emergence of an identifiable field of study and to speculate in a disciplined manner about some of its key research tasks.

This article attempts to bring together many of the diverse strands that should be joined if Canadians—aboriginal and non-aboriginal— are to understand aboriginal government as a comprehensive and development phenomenon. Fourteen areas needing study are cited under three major headings. The effort is offered as an exploration, a search of territory not fully charted. It is not intended to be exhaustive. Rather it is a first step, a step that needs to be taken with some caution and then refined. The next steps might involve a more detailed review of the literature and a thorough review of research currently underway. These steps should involve discussion and debate among those concerned with the subject. They need to involve cooperative approaches to research on the part of scholars, aboriginal peoples, and their governments.

Such tasks should not be undertaken by scholars in isolation from the realities and development of aboriginal governing forms. It is useful for many reasons to define the research field, but it would not

252

be useful to detach this field from its subject. This, of course, can happen in the study of politics; and it would be particularly unfortunate in the field of aboriginal government. The study of aboriginal governments should not turn into one more effort to impose a non-indigenous outlook on Canada's First Nations, to study aboriginal peoples primarily as the subjects of government policies and the product of fluctuations in a social, economic, and political order seemingly beyond their control.

A major portion of the effort by political scientists and other scholars to study aboriginal governments should be rooted in an understanding of the efforts of aboriginal peoples to create and re-create their governments. It is important, for example, to make a special effort to identify, circulate, and build upon related research that is currently being undertaken in aboriginal communities and by aboriginal governments and organizations. The initiatives of aboriginal peoples and their governments are the real basis of the energy for change and growth in this policy area, and they should be treated as such. Federal and provincial policies and initiatives also need continuing attention, but the research emphasis needs to move more to the manner in which these policies and initiatives provide a context for the emergence of aboriginal government.

The following section reviews research on aboriginal governments in Canada in the last fifteen years. Next, a conceptual framework that can be used to guide scholarly thinking about more systematic approaches to research is briefly outlined. Then, the three clusters of subject matter that flow from this framework are explored in more detail. Finally, a few comments are made about the ways in which the aboriginal government research agenda should be addressed in the near future.

An Emerging Research Agenda

The wider policy environment has been the subject of much of the research by social scientists, historians, and others on aboriginal governments. Bartlett, Hawley, and Manitowabi, for example, have described and analyzed the *Indian Act* and its relationship to reserve-based band government.[1] Daugherty and Madill have examined the Act's historical development.[2] Weaver, Getty and Lussier, Coopers and Lybrand, Taylor, and Doerr have stressed the role of federal policies.[3] Cardinal, Manual and Posluns, Adams and others have focussed on the perspectives of aboriginal peoples in the face of these policies.[4] Ponting and Gibbins have surveyed the views of the Canadian public on Indians and Indian issues.[5] Many other studies have stressed the broader context of the public policy issues concerning aboriginal peoples in Canada.

Intergovernmental relations have received increasing attention from scholars over time. Reiber, Cassidy, Bartlett, Nahwegabow, and Gibbins and Ponting have examined the federal and provincial implications of aboriginal government, with particular reference to jurisdictional concerns.[6] Recently, there has been a sharpening focus on the roles and responsibilities of the provinces, reflecting their accelerating involvements with Indian peoples and their governments. Long and Boldt in association with Little Bear have edited an interesting collection entitled *Governments in Conflict? Provinces and Indian Nations in Canada*.[7] Hawkes has also edited a collection on the topic, *Aboriginal Peoples and Government Responsibility: Exploring Federal and Provincial Roles*.[8] This collection contains several important chapters, including one on the special federal-provincial self-government legislation in relation to the Sechelt Band in British Columbia and one on fiscal arrangements and self-government.

There has been no dearth of work on questions of aboriginal title and rights. Lysyk, Sanders, Berger, Jobson and King, Ayers and Slattery as well as a score of other authors have written on these matters.[9] Boldt, Long, and Morse have drawn together the efforts of many authors in two landmark collections entitled *The Quest for Justice: Aboriginal Peoples and Aboriginal Rights* and *Aboriginal Peoples and the Law: Indian, Métis and Inuit Rights in Canada*.[10] Muller-Wolle and Pelto, Hemmingson, and Dyck have writen about related matters, placing Canadian developments in an international context.[11]

In a widely discussed article in the *Canadian Journal of Political Science*, Boldt and Long explored alternative models of self-determination for Canada's Indians, suggesting that the doctrine of sovereignty is not compatible with the core values comprising Indian culture. On this basis, they concluded that interpretations of the governing experiences and aspirations of Indian peoples that focussed on the concept of "stateless nationhood" may offer those peoples a far better basis than sovereignty for achieving the goal of self-determination. In the same issue Flanagan followed with a critique of their argument to which Boldt and Long subsequently replied.[12] This discourse is not finished. The effort to understand the meaning of aboriginal government in terms of the basic concepts of political theory has just begun. Cassidy has examined the nature of aboriginal citizenship in Canada.[13] Opekekew has explored the interplay of

254

collective and individual rights in light of the concept of self-determination for aboriginal peoples.[14] Much more work of this nature has to be done, particularly by political theorists.

To a significant degree, aboriginal governments have been viewed within the context of constitutional issues and processes. Asch has addressed the political rights of aboriginal peoples in Canada in *Home and Native Land*, one of the most significant books in the field.[15] Dacks, Robertson, Keith and Wright, and Drury have each focussed on aboriginal government in Canada's North in terms of the constitutional issues relating to territorial government.[16] McMurtry and Pratt, McNeil, Zlotkin, Schwartz, Sanders, Robinson and Quinney, Nakatshura, Stevenson, and Barsh and Henderson have also contributed to the constitutional debate.[17]

Moving from the wider policy environment to the components of governance, one can perceive a recent intensification of research. Until the mid-1980s, the dynamics of aboriginal government received far less research attention than wider policy matters such as federal and provincial policy, aboriginal rights and title, and constitutional matters. *Indian Self-Government in Canada*, the 1983 Report of the House of Commons Special Committee and commonly known as the *Penner Report*, has been a very influential document in this sense, as it has focussed the attention of many scholars, policy-makers and field-based researchers on such key issues as financing, education, health, and child welfare.[18] Gibbins and Ponting, Tennant, and Weaver have provided insightful reviews of the report.[19]

Asserting that the aboriginal perspective on aboriginal government was "largely missing" from the literature, Little Bear, Boldt, and Long published a widely-read collection of readings, *Pathways to Self-Determination*, in 1984. It emphasized such matters as the cultural and ideological foundations, the legal, political, and economic environments, and the economic and organizational requisites for self- government.[20] Boldt and Long's *Quest for Justice* was an important sequel to this collection.[21]

Focussing on the elements of governance, Cassidy and Bish have conducted research across Canada, analyzing jurisdiction, citizenship, policy-making, service production, and finance issues on the basis of selected case studies of Indian government.[22] Cassidy has explored the implications of the 1985 *Indian Act* amendments for Indian governments.[23] Taylor has provided a description of an early instance of band-based self-government at Walpole Island in Ontario in the 1960s, and Graham Allen has written about the special legislation regarding the Sechelt Band.[24] Sinclair has brought together an

255

interesting set of documents focussing on the practical dynamics of resource management.[25] With particular reference to land claims cases in British Columbia, Cassidy and Dale have highlighted the involvement of aboriginal governments throughout North America in resource management and development.[26] The 1988 report of the Commission of Inquiry on the Westbank Band in British Columbia, conducted by John Hall, included a great deal of general information on Indian government and revealed the development and challenges of band government in a particular community.[27]

The community setting of aboriginal governments has not yet received the attention it requires from scholars and other analysts. Siggner has done some of the most useful work on the socio-demographic conditions of Indian people since the pathbreaking Hawthorn Report, and Holmes has focussed on the effects of the 1985 amendments to the *Indian Act* on Indian women.[28] Driben and Trudeau, Frideres and Brody have focussed on community life, or what Frideres terms "the political economy of natives in Canadian society" as seen from the vantage point of these people.[29] In 1986, Ponting published a selection of readings on Indian self-government, *Arduous Journey: Canadian Indians and Decolonization*, which he characterized as "a significant departure from my past concentration on national-level developments in Ottawa." Ponting devoted particular attention in this book to "Indian attempts to generate more power and more self-sufficiency at the grassroots of Indian communities."[30] From a somewhat different perspective, Gibbins and Ponting's wideranging essay for the Macdonald Commission was an attempt to carry on a similar type of analysis; it speculated about the impact of self-government on the internal vitality of aboriginal communities as well as on many other matters.[31]

Treaty and land claims questions have been the subject of much insightful research. Wildsmith and Upton have analyzed pre-Confederation treaties.[32] Purich, Zlotkin, Price, and Fumoleau have provided insightful contributions on post-Confederation treaties.[33] Raunet, Watkins, Richardson, Berger, and Cassidy and Dale have stressed the land claims question in its modern context.[34] Berger's *Village Journey: A Report of the Alaska Native Review Commission* has been influential in Canada.[35] The Coolican Report, *Living Treaties, Lasting Agreements: Reports to the Task Force to Review Comprehensive Claims Policy*, provided a good summary and set of recommendations concerning federal land claims policies, particularly in relation to self-government matters.[36] An especially compelling account of the claims process in James Bay, *Negotiating a Way of Life*, has been contributed by LaRusic.[37] Daniels has done some important work on Métis people and non-status Indian land claims.[38] With regard to the question of Métis rights, Flanagan and McKenzie also have made contributions.[39]

There have been a small number of concerted efforts to bring together the several strands of research and thinking on aboriginal governments. By far the most comprehensive effort has been made by the Institute of Intergovernmental Relations at Queen's University. Within the context of the constitutional reform process as it relates to aboriginal peoples, the Institute has published more than twenty background, position, and discussion papers as well as reports on related workshops and an annotated bibliography. The Institute's work has been pivotal. Hawkes, the director of the project, Lyon and Boisvert have provided general insights into the constitutional debate and into the nature and variety of aboriginal government.[40] For the first time sustained analysis has taken place in a coordinated and interrelated manner on such matters as jurisdiction (Cowie), financing (Malone), education (Paquette), resource management (Bartlett), aboriginal government off a land base (Weinstein), existing self-government arrangements in Canada (Peters), public administration (Franks) as well as the international context of aboriginal government (Sanders, Morse).[41] Interestingly, as the Queen's research has progressed, it has moved from a perspective that stressed larger constitutional issues to one that emphasizes the components of governance at the community level.

Over the past several years one of Canada's major research institutes, the Institute for Research on Public Policy (IRPP), has published several scholarly works on public policy issues which concern aboriginal peoples in Canada.[42] The IRPP's early efforts stressed the role of federal, provincial, and corporate policies and the conditions of aboriginal peoples in urban settings.[43] It then considered the basic relationships betwen aboriginal peoples and Canada as a nation-state.[44] The Institute has continued to address these items. In more recent years, it has turned to a direct analysis of the activities of aboriginal peoples and governments in their own communities, with particular reference to economic development and governing institutions.[45]

While much work has been going on in independent research institutes, the federal government, and the universities, it also has been progressing in tribal and band councils and other organizations of aboriginal peoples. The Western Constitutional Forum, the Nunavut Constitutional Forum, the Makivik Corporation, the Inuit

257

Committee on National Issues, the Walpole Island Band in Ontario, the Dakota-Ojibway Tribal Council in Manitoba, the Federation of Saskatchewan Indians, the Union of British Columbia Indian Chiefs, the Association of Métis and Non-Status Indians of Saskatchewan, the Dene Nation, the Council for Yukon Indians, the Gitksan and Wet'suwet'en Tribal Council and the Carrier Sekani Government Commission in British Columbia, the Mohawk, the Native Council of Canada, and the Assembly of First Nations, to name just a few, have undertaken impressive research agendas.[46] To date, not a large amount of this research has been circulated formally. When this happens, research on aboriginal government sponsored by aboriginal peoples may well turn the field around, as it forcefully focusses on the issues that are most pressing for these peoples.

A Framework for Understanding

Since the early 1980s, the form and character of research on aboriginal governments has begun to take shape, and as it has, a dominant theme has begun to emerge. Simply stated, this theme is that aboriginal governments are first and foremost created and re-created by aboriginal peoples themselves. Aboriginal governments cannot be understood primarily as "creatures" of federal policies and programmes; nor can they be projected as achievements of constitutional reform. To the contrary, if aboriginal governments are to be understood, they can be understood most usefully as products of aboriginal peoples living and working to form the political structures they require to meet the challenges of economic development, health, education, social services, resource management, and any number of common concerns in their communities and on their lands.

For aboriginal peoples, the "self" in self-government means much more than delivering programmes and administering policies designed by other governments and non-aboriginal people. It means defining, through the practice of government, how aboriginal governments can be used to come to terms with important problems and objectives in aboriginal communities, what the various aspects of aboriginal government look like and how they function in relationship to one another, and how aboriginal governments affect and are affected by the wider public policy environment in Canada and internationally.

To begin to understand aboriginal governments, it is necessary first of all to understand the movement for aboriginal self-government. Aboriginal self-government in Canada can be defined as a diverse range of efforts by aboriginal peoples to gain and exercise decisive control over, and to redesign where necessary, the activities, institutions, and financial arrangements of those governments that exist in their communities and regions. Self-government can take many forms. Some would argue that it can occur only following full constitutional recognition of the inherent right of aboriginal peoples to govern themselves. Others would contend that self-government can take place within the current framework of federal-provincial powers, that it can be a matter of degree and not just a fundamental state of being. Still others would maintain that it is an existing reality, that it is continuing to emerge in a variety of ways, and that this reality has yet to be fully recognized and accommodated in the Canadian constitutional order.

Whatever approach one takes, it is necessary to recognize that self-government is an outgrowth of many kinds of activity. As self-government emerges, it can involve or be made possible by expanded operations under the *Indian Act* or special legislation; by the reassertion of traditional institutions; through arrangements concerning service delivery and financing with federal, provincial, and/or municipal governments; through expanded resource management and economic development; and by the implementation of arrangements flowing from land claims agreements and the redesign of public government in Canada's North. The movement toward self-government can involve all of these approaches and more. In the future, aboriginal governments may even be founded on the exercise of constitutionally entrenched powers. Whatever form it takes—and in a particular setting it may take several forms—aboriginal self-government represents the efforts of aboriginal peoples to control their own affairs in their own ways. Given the multiple dimensions of this effort across Canada, research on aboriginal governments is no simple matter.

Such research might well be informed by a conceptual framework that revolves around three clusters of subject matter: aboriginal communities and their governments, the components of governance, and the wider policy environment. These clusters need to be related in a systematic fashion. As each changes, the others change. With regard to aboriginal communities and their governments, five principal areas of concern can be identified: social and cultural trends, economic development, the land question, history and tradition, and the political decision-making patterns in aboriginal communities. These areas of interest strongly influence the shape of aboriginal governments. They produce many of the critical issues and challenges

259

facing these governments. They determine, to a significant extent, what political decisions have to be made and by whom.

A second cluster of topics that need to be understood if aboriginal governments are to be the focus of relevant and disciplined research, relates to the components of governance itself. These topics include the structural forms of aboriginal governments, policy-making and administration, service and programme production and delivery, the financial basis of aboriginal governments, and responsibility as well as accountability patterns. These matters are fundamental to government in any form. They determine where it takes place as well as how it is organized and financed. They point to the fact that aboriginal governments, like all governments, are created to meet people's needs by providing public goods. They show how people can maintain control over their governments.

A third group of themes in this field of inquiry concerns the wider policy environment of aboriginal governments. Here such matters as citizenship and aboriginal rights issues, the legal/constitutional basis of aboriginal governments, intergovernmental relations, and aboriginal government as an international phenomenon predominate. These themes relate to larger contextual matters, including the nature of aboriginal citizenship and rights in the Canadian political order, the legal/constitutional setting for aboriginal governments in the Canadian federal system, the relations of aboriginal governments with other governments, be they federal, provincial, or municipal, and the international dimensions of the efforts of indigenous peoples to confront and live with modern nation-states.

Taken together these three clusters of themes offer a starting point for understanding aboriginal governments in Canada. Research is proceeding on many of these matters, and in areas where it has not yet commenced, the rapid development of the field suggests that studies are likely to appear in the near future. Each cluster of themes is examined in more detail below.

It should be stressed that these issues are not mutually exclusive. For example, if the institutions of aboriginal government are to be understood, then the international context as well as the intergovernmental setting of these institutions must be examined. These institutions also must be viewed within the context of specific government responsibilities such as justice, health, and education, and they must be seen in a historical as well as legal light. This fusing of issues and dimensions reflects the multifaceted nature of aboriginal government and the challenges it presents to scholars as well as policy-makers.

Aboriginal Communities and Their Governments

Governments are shaped by and in turn shape the physical and social settings in which they are created and operate. These settings present governments with the bulk of those matters about which decisions need to be made. Each affects, to an extent, how these decisions are made and implemented. In relation to their immediate community settings, aboriginal governments need to respond to issues and forces that arise from social and cultural trends, economic develoment, the land question, history and tradition, and political decision-making patterns.

Social and Cultural Trends

The aboriginal population is changing greatly in its numbers and characteristics.[47] In general, it is younger than the rest of the Canadian population. Levels of education and other characteristics also differ dramatically when the two populations are compared. These demographic differences raise questions about the treatment of aboriginal people within the Canadian justice and corrections systems.[48] They indicate the relative need for such services as health, child care, and education. They point to a significance of adult literacy as a matter of self-government. They portray a labour force with very different characteristics from the general Canadian labour force.

Particular social groupings will often take on critical cultural roles that have a political impact. Elders hold a particularly important place in aboriginal communities.[49] They play significant educational, historical, and political roles as they pass on the wisdom of their peoples. More research is necessary by scholars and others into their roles and, in particular, into the socio-economic conditions they experience. There is also a need to focus on the roles of women in aboriginal communities, the social circumstances they experience, and the key cultural responsibilities they retain.[50]

Cultural issues and their relation to aboriginal government deserve careful attention. This is particularly true of matters relating to language in general and in its effect on political discourse in particular. When aboriginal peoples discuss and debate critical political issues with other Canadians, the two groups may fail to communicate because key words may mean very different things to each. Words such as "government," "politics," and "sovereignty" do not readily translate into aboriginal languages. As a result, their use to describe and analyze aboriginal government can be misleading. A much greater scholarly awareness of this possibility and more research

261

attention to the words, images, and concepts that various aboriginal peoples use to describe their political ways are necessary.

Economic Development

Economic development and aboriginal self-government are closely linked.[51] Without economic development, aboriginal governments may be reduced to the administration of a welfare state that no one, most particularly aboriginal peoples, wants. In this context, many questions arise. What does an aboriginal economy look like? What kinds of economic development entities are most appropriate and effective in aboriginal communities? What is the role of traditional and subsistence economies—which are not necessarily the same—and what is their role in the future? What are the relative roles of capital, labour, and technical expertise? These questions are being asked as aboriginal communities seek to develop resources, create employment, reduce poverty, and provide an economic foundation for self-government. They need to be the focus of cooperative research efforts on the part of scholars, public policy analysts, aboriginal peoples, and various governments.

Over the next several years, the economic disparities between aboriginal communities in Canada will widen, and there is a need to recognize that in many cases these communities will face radically different economic challenges. Some bands such as the Fort Nelson, Westbank, and Sechelt bands in British Columbia are developing an extensive economic base, as have several bands in Alberta. Other bands face poverty and isolation from their traditional economic pursuits as well as from the economic mainstream. Economic development in such communities will be difficult. The implications for aboriginal government in these differing kinds of communities need to be explored in a more comprehensive fashion.

The Land Question

The aboriginal land question takes many forms. On the Prairies and in other parts of Canada it involves disputes about Canada's treaty responsibilities and its failures or achievements in fulfilling them.[52] In British Columbia, parts of the North and other places, aboriginal land claims remain an open question in the absence of treaties or land claims agreements. In northern and northeastern Quebec and the western Arctic, land claims agreements have produced circumstances that are just becoming clear.[53] Development agreements in the Northwest Territories and the Yukon will have a huge impact on aboriginal government in coming years. Throughout the country the management of reserve lands, specific claims, and aboriginal government off a land base need to be the focus of research.

Federal and provincial governments have made significant efforts to disconnect the more fundamental issues of aboriginal government from land claims and treaty questions. The report of the federal Task Force on Program Review in 1985, for example, suggested that land claims negotiations await clearer self-government policies and programmes.[54] Federal and provincial legislation specifically indicated that self-government for the Sechelt band could be considered apart from the land question.[55]

In those parts of the country where land claims are unresolved, many bands and tribal groups tie together self-government and comprehensive claims. The Gitksan and Wet'suwet'en hereditary chiefs of northwestern British Columbia, for example, assert their claim to the sole jurisdiction and ownership of their territories.[56] On this basis, among other things, they maintain that the provincial government cannot issue forest-cutting licences for their lands and that the federal government does not have the right to control fishing in their rivers.[57]

Specific claims that concern Canada's obligations relating to treaty and reserve lands also affect aboriginal governments, since they raise questions about the management of the land base.[58] In general, the management of reserve lands and the rights of federal, provincial, and Indian governments to these lands are related to the drive of aboriginal peoples for more self-government. Many aboriginal people in Canada do not live on reserve lands. For these people, whether they be status or non-status, government is also a very important matter. In particular, the meaning of self-government for Métis people and aboriginal peoples in the territories needs to be analyzed and understood.[59]

The land and the resources it holds are central to the culture of aboriginal peoples in Canada. Land and resources have economic value and political significance, but most importantly they represent a way of life and a spiritual commitment for many aboriginal people. As such, land and resource management issues need to be elevated on the aboriginal government research agenda.

History and Tradition

Historically, aboriginal governments were part of an integrated social order. Unlike the European-style governments of the past few hundred years, they were not composed of institutions and processes that were distinct from other institutions and processes serving religious, family, or social functions. Nevertheless, these governments fulfilled key political functions in their societies. To a lesser or greater extent they kept order. They provided for the authoritative resolution of disputes. They maintained the boundaries and integrity of their territories. They represented the collective will of the people.[60]

When Europeans and later Canadians began to move into aboriginal lands, the governments of aboriginal peoples interacted with the new settlers in a variety of ways. By the mid-nineteenth century, through the *Indian Act* and other means, Canada began to impose new governing forms on aboriginal peoples. Throughout the twentieth century, these governing forms have developed; in some cases, they have replaced traditional forms, while in others, they stand side by side with traditional forms. In still others, traditional and more modern forms operate in isolation or opposition.

The historical development of aboriginal governments and their interaction with Canadian governing forms as well as with the Canadian political, social, and economic systems, need much more attention from political scientists and historians. The current movement for self-government is not a development that can be traced just to increased educational achievements among aboriginal peoples or to more awareness on the part of other Canadians. It is a movement which has its roots in the past and which seeks to structure the future in terms of the lessons of history.

In many communities there is a particular need to undertake more research on the traditional nature of aboriginal government.[61] What role do such institutions as the clan and potlatch play in governance? How are traditional chiefs selected, and what is the nature of their authority compared to that of chiefs and councils selected under the *Indian Act*? How does the aggregation of political interests take place in traditional ways? How do traditional systems of justice and related enforcement systems work? Scholars can work in partnership with people in aboriginal communities and their governments to obtain answers to these questions. The resulting insights will provide increased understandings of the actual workings of band and tribal councils as well as the emerging character of aboriginal governments. For example, what may seem to be disputes about health or educational matters in many communities may also be contests between different interests within traditional systems. Or what may seem to be "reasonable" in light of general Canadian norms may be foolish or inappropriate when judged by traditional criteria. Even more significantly, as aboriginal government develops in many communities, there will be efforts to merge traditional and modern governing forms or to make one subordinate to another. To understand these efforts, it will be necessary for researchers to pay more attention to the history and traditions of aboriginal governments than has been the case to date.

Political Decision-Making Patterns

Politics is the process by which people make decisions about those issues that they cannot address without recourse to authoritative means of compliance or agreement within a given domain. In any political system it is important to know what decisions are political decisions, who makes decisions, how decisions are made, and where decisions are made.

These are particularly difficult questions for aboriginal communities, which are asking basic questions about their political and constitutional order. Thinking about aboriginal governments means thinking about the role of politics in everyday life. How "political" do aboriginal communities, which often have a small number of people, need to be if they are to be self-governing? How do different interests in aboriginal communities develop and exert influence on governments? What is political and what belongs to other realms of activity? How does consensual decision-making take place, and what is the role of conflict in aboriginal decision-making? The expertise of political scientists in such matters could be useful to aboriginal peoples and their governments.

The political context in aboriginal communities is a critical determinant of the possibilities for self-government. It might be argued that the 1983-1987 constitutional process failed to entrench aboriginal rights to self-government because Canadians were unwilling to make room for aboriginal governments in the political order. It also might be argued that the emerging political will among aboriginal peoples in Canada will not be satisfied with anything less than a recognition of the inherent right to aboriginal government. The political realities in aboriginal communities need to be understood if aboriginal governments are to be fully comprehended.

The Components of Governance

Aboriginal governments come in many shapes and sizes. In relation to some public functions, they work in one way; in relation to others, they work in other ways. The manner in which governments are structured, managed, and financed, the ways they design and deliver

265

services and are kept responsible and accountable determine to a great extent how effective, efficient, and equitable they are. Under this heading, the following matters need study: structural forms, policy-making and administration, specific service and programme sectors, finance and responsibility, and accountability patterns.

Structural Forms

There is a need to study the nature and interaction of aboriginal governing forms. The relative roles of band councils, citizens' committees, traditional institutions, general assemblies, administrative mechanisms, and elders' councils need to be understood and assessed. A particular area that needs attention is the interaction of band councils, tribal councils, and other governing authorities, whether they be purely traditional or more recent in origin.[62] Attention needs to be given to the division of governing functions as well as the structural interdependencies relating to service delivery in various aboriginal governments. Economic development corporations, school boards, and the various entities created by land claims settlements are examples of governing forms that are assuming increased importance in aboriginal communities. The tribal council—a governing structure exhibiting great diversity—needs to receive special emphasis.

The band council is not an indigenous form of government in many Indian communities. Band councils to a significant extent are creatures of the *Indian Act*, but they also may be institutions of self-government. It could be said that in many instances band councils are a living contradiction. They are a part of the Canadian governing framework, but they are also structural forms of aboriginal governance. In some instances, as at Walpole Island in Ontario, band councils have replaced more traditional institutions. In other instances, as in the case of the Six Nations Reserve in Ontario or the Carrier Sekani peoples of northern British Columbia, their legitimacy as alternatives to the traditional structures of government is hotly contested.[63]

Policy-Making and Administration

Most band and tribal councils have a portfolio system whereby responsibilities for specific tasks are given to individual council members who then work with a committee. Given the size and complexity of the functions aboriginal governments perform, the portfolio system seems an inevitable development. There are problems with the system, however, as it tends to overload elected or appointed authorities with too many responsibilities and to isolate one programme area from another. More attention needs to be given to how band and tribal councils organize themselves and the various administrative mechanisms they use to produce effective and efficient decision-making.

There is a general need to study band and tribal council management systems and to answer such questions as: What are the most prevalent organizational cultures of aboriginal governments? How do these organizational cultures change and develop in light of the larger inter-cultural context of aboriginal governments? What is the role of management training and development? Questions such as these need to be explored in case studies as well as in more general research.

Specific Service and Programme Sectors

Aboriginal governments often emerge in practice, through the development of specific service and programme sectors. In some communities, greater self-government comes about as people take more control over health, child welfare, education, and other social services. In other communities, policing or housing becomes a catalyzing issue. More than occasionally, disputes concerning fishing, hunting, and forestry lead to active involvement in resource mangement and development. If aboriginal governments are to be understood, then individual as well as collective challenges and dynamics in specific sectors need to be studied.

Each sector in which aboriginal governments design and deliver services is a microcosm of aboriginal government in practice. There is a particular need to study the traditional dimension, the intergovernmental setting and financial aspects of aboriginal governments. There is also a strong need to focus on the problems and possibilities involved in the design of culturally sensitive service delivery systems, particularly where two or more levels of government and close coordination with other service providers are involved. The evolution of specific programme needs in aboriginal committees as well as the matter of eligibility criteria for various programmes merit much more attention. So, too, do the roles of professionals and the influence they exert on the governing process.

Finance

As the old saying goes, "he who pays the piper calls the tune." Given their limited or contested land bases and the social and economic conditions in their communities, most aboriginal governments have

267

severely constrained access to financial resources. They have to rely on the federal government and on their ability to assemble funding from many sources, sources which often have contradictory goals and requirements. Recently, there has been a move toward alternate funding arrangements by Indian and Northern Affairs Canada (INAC). Bands have also been given new taxing powers as a result of changes to the *Indian Act*.

These developments have been greeted positively for the most part, but they have been introduced within a context of fiscal restraint. This context has raised questions about the ultimate aims behind changes, for example, in the financial arrangements for band governments. Just as significantly, questions concerning the nature of intergovernmental financial transfers have arisen. There is some general recognition that band governments need to have more control over finances if they are to have more control over their own affairs. There are also, however, requirements that line agencies such as INAC must face as they are held accountable by Parliament and central agencies (notably Treasury Board). In the ensuing tug of responsibilities, aboriginal governments can and do get caught in the middle.[64] Financial procedures can determine programme priorities and directions. All of these matters must be the subject of research, particularly by social scientists who study public finance.

Responsibility and Accountability Patterns

A special research focus needs to be placed on matters of responsibility and accountability. How do aboriginal governments maintain answerability for their financial activities? How do they remain politically accountable to their communities? How can community accountability patterns, often customary and implicit in other areas, be reconciled with the procedures that federal and provincial agencies follow to establish programme standards and expenditure patterns?

Traditional government in aboriginal communities is government which takes place within the context of family relationships. To serve the community responsibly political leaders serve the needs of their family. Responsibility is assured through education, the careful selection of leaders, and adherence to community norms. To some extent this is generally true of governance in Canada, but responsibility is increasingly measured through recourse to formal accountability measures. Behaving responsibly, behaving in the public interest, is measured and assured through the use of formal management systems audits, treasury boards, and regular inspections. Moreover, stronger lines are being drawn all the time between public and private affairs.

Service to the family can be seen as a conflict of interest. The implications of separation of family and governance as well as the emphasis on formal accountability procedures as the guarantee of responsibility need to be understood within the context of aboriginal government. The possibility of other approaches more congruent with traditional patterns needs to be explored in cooperative efforts by scholars who study governmental accountability and responsibility and people more directly involved in the affairs of aboriginal governments.

The Wider Policy Environment

Government and politics take place within a broader context and cannot be separated from this context. Concepts such as citizenship and civil and human rights touch upon the core of political order. Indeed, this core is defined by a framework of law and within an intergovernmental system. More so than provinces and municipalities, aboriginal governments also function within an international order in which indigenous peoples interface with the modern nation-state. As far as aboriginal governments are concerned, it is critical that research systematically pursue citizenship and aboriginal rights issues, the constitutional and legal framework, intergovernmental relations, and the international context.

Citizenship and Aboriginal Rights Issues

The passage of the Bill C-31 amendments to the Indian Act in 1985 led to several developments regarding Indian status and band membership.[65] Provision was made for the restoration of Indian status to many Indian women as well as to others who were denied status because of prior discriminatory aspects of the Act. Bill C-31 also enabled bands to assume greater control over their membership and to move toward more self-government. These developments raise many questions about the rights of status Indians and the nature of citizenship in Indian governments. Bill C-31 may be seen as a compromise between the individual rights that all Canadians, aboriginal and non-aboriginal, have and the collective rights of aboriginal peoples to determine and implement their own forms of government. These collective rights need to be clarified, and the roles of aboriginal citizens in aboriginal governments need to be explored. The viability and legitimacy of trade-offs between individual and collective rights need to be evaluated, especially by legal scholars and political scientists.

269

More generally, the nature of aboriginal rights and their relationship to aboriginal government require further illumination.[66] What are the implications of an aboriginal right to self-government for resource management and development and for provincial and federal jurisdiction in relation to aboriginal peoples? The definitions of aboriginal rights which were current among legal authorities only ten or fifteen years ago are considered by many aboriginal people and their governments to be excessively narrow. Broad definitions of aboriginal rights will have broad implications for aboriginal governments.

The Constitutional and Legal Framework

The question of the constitutional status of the right to aboriginal self-government has been dominant in the 1980s. It is likely to continue to be a priority. This question sets the issue of aboriginal government in terms of first principles. Constitutional progress has been difficult to achieve, however. Efforts have been made to change the *Indian Act*, suggesting that despite the general dissatisfaction with it on all sides, this Act might remain a critical legal basis for Indian governments in future years.

Special legislation allowing particular Indian governments to opt out of the *Indian Act* will also be a feature on the self-government landscape in the near future, as some bands and tribal councils seek what they interpret to be more or less short-term and practical solutions to the problems of governance. Many of the aboriginal governments that choose this route will not do so because they believe that the sole source of jurisdiction for their governments is federal and provincial. They will seek to pursue a firmer basis for aboriginal government and, as they do so, they will call not only for more fundamental change at the constitutional level, but also for changes based on international law. The associated issues need to be studied by scholars as practical matters of government.

Intergovernmental Relations

At some point in the future, the right of aboriginal peoples to self-government may be entrenched in the Constitution. Without a constitutional recognition of the right to self-government and lacking independent jurisdiction of some kind, aboriginal governments have little choice but to seek, conclude, and implement intergovernmental agreements that assure the provision of education, health care, and other services. The nature of such agreements as well as the negotiating and implementation processes which accompany them need to be studied. The difficulties and advantages of bilateral, sequential bilateral, interlocking bilateral, and trilateral agreement processes need to be compared. Experiences involving these processes need to be shared and analyzed. Political scientists could make an important contribution to this effort.

To date, much of the analysis of aboriginal governments has stressed the effects of federal programmes. Although the focus is now shifting to the policies and programmes of aboriginal governments, there will be a continuing need to analyze and interpret the outcome of federal government activities. In particular, federal self-government, economic development, and land claims policies as well as financing programmes and efforts to encourage devolution of the administration of services need to be examined in light of their impact upon aboriginal governments.

Relationships between provinces and aboriginal governments only began to receive attention recently. Many provinces have developed administrative and policy formation mechanisms to deal with the challenges presented by aboriginal governments. These mechanisms vary greatly in their mandates and modes of operation. A comparative study from a political science perspective is badly needed. So too is a study of how aboriginal governments occupy jurisdictional ground that is normally provincial, as in the operation of child welfare and educational services. Links between aboriginal government and the territories also present many significant questions. Indeed, the political future of the territories may be bound to the drive of aboriginal peoples within them for more autonomy.

The International Context

Aboriginal governments are not just a Canadian phenomenon. Aboriginal peoples in Australia, the United States, Greenland, Finland, and many other countries have confronted and are confronting conditions and challenges which are in many ways similar to those faced by aboriginal peoples in Canada.[67] Great diversity exists, but there is knowledge that can and should be drawn upon if Canadians are to learn about the interface of traditional and nation-state systems, economic development, and the variety of legislative alternatives for recognizing aboriginal self-governing systems. Every issue identified in this short essay can be examined in an international light. What may not seem possible here and now may well have been or be possible elsewhere. The lessons may be ready for the learning.

Conclusion

The above is a brief overview of the emerging research agenda on aboriginal governments in Canada. If the field is to develop in a more disciplined and self-developmental manner, then this agenda should be discussed and debated. Researchers—academic and non-academic, governmental and independent, aboriginal and non-aboriginal—should communicate more actively. Developing ideas must be shared. New information technologies should be used to create an awareness of what has been done and what is being done.

The task that has been laid out is a challenging one that will take time to address in a meaningful way. What should be done to encourage further research? A good part of the answer to this question involves organization and process. Beyond the specific concerns that need to be addressed, there is a need to bring scholars and analysts together, to ask them to share their work and ideas. This can be done in several ways. Electronic networks can be established to link aboriginal governments and organizations; universities; research institutes; and the federal, provincial, and territorial governments. People from each of these organizations also can be involved in roundtables, workshops, and conferences that focus on research efforts. Held more or less systematically across the country, such sessions could focus on the issues that have been outlined in this article, doing so in a relatively non-adversarial way.

There are other tasks that need to be undertaken. An inventory of past, current, and ongoing research should be developed. The most important aspects of this research need to be made more readily available to scholarly and more general audiences. Aboriginal governments, in particular, are doing a significant amount of research. Much of value could be exchanged amongst these governments and others. A series of occasional papers, including research by various aboriginal governments, could be initiated by an organization such as the Institute for Research on Public Policy.

There needs to be a significant financial contribution to the field of aboriginal government research by the federal government, particularly to aboriginal governments and organizations. At present, Indian and Northern Affairs Canada, through its Self-Government Community Negotiations Program, provides funding for Indian communities to undertake self-government research, but such funding is limited to band and tribal councils. It is granted for relatively short periods, always for one year or less, and the funding is tightly controlled. In an important sense, INAC can direct the research

272

agenda for a particular Indian government by exercising influence through the power of the purse. Moreover, such research is tied to the requirement that the funded Indian government indicate some level of interest in progressing toward special federal and perhaps provincial self-government legislation. As the research progresses, this requirement becomes more explicit and prohibitive.

Given the hesitancies of many Indian people toward special self-government legislation under the existing Constitution as an alternative to constitutional entrenchment of a pre-existing and independent aboriginal right to self-government, the INAC approach to funding aboriginal government research is inappropriate and inadequate. It also ignores the research needs of non-status aboriginal peoples. The federal government needs to fund research concerning aboriginal governments, particularly by or through aboriginal governments and organizations. As it does so, it should establish clear funding levels which would provide the basis for a significant approach to an important task, provide funding through an agency more neutral than INAC, allocate funding on the basis of real consultation with the representatives of aboriginal governments and organizations, not tie funding to its own self-government goals and programmes, and encourage cooperative and community-based research on the part of the scholarly community and aboriginal peoples and their governments.

As measures such as these and others described above are undertaken, it is important to bear in mind the matter of diversity. There is tremendous diversity among aboriginal communities and in forms of aboriginal government across the country. This diversity will not recede as the movement for aboriginal self-government grows. It will increase as aboriginal peoples express themselves politically about who they are and what they want to be. Such diversity does not yield easy generalization, and generalization is one of the building blocks in any field of study. Nevertheless, diversity and respect for diversity are at the core of aboriginal government.

As the research agenda for aboriginal government becomes clearer, it will be important for scholars who are not members of aboriginal communities to retain a focus on the needs, experiences, and goals of aboriginal peoples. The study of public policy should not be detached from the aspirations and requirements of the public. Nor should it be isolated from government. With reference to aboriginal governments, this is particularly important. Self-government cannot be imposed. It has to be asserted and nurtured by those who will govern themselves. Research concerning aboriginal govern-

273

ments by political scientists and other scholars should reflect the nature of aboriginal self-government. Unless this occurs, what is called research on aboriginal governments will become one more chapter in the long history of the denial of self-government.

Endnotes

1. Richard H. Bartlett, *Subjugation, Self-Management and Self-Government of Aboriginal Lands and Resources in Canada* (Kingston: Queen's University Institute of Intergovernmental Relations, 1986); Donna Lea Hawley, *The Indian Act Annotated* (Calgary: Carswell, 1984); and Mark Manitowabi, *The Governing of Indian Reserves: Authorities of the Band and the Minister under the Indian Act* (Ottawa: Indian and Northern Affairs Canada, 1980).
2. Wayne E. Daugherty and Dennis Madill, *Indian Government Under Indian Act Legislation 1868-1951* (Ottawa: Indian and Northern Affairs Canada, 1980).
3. Sally M. Weaver, "Indian Policy in the New Conservative Government, Part 1: The Neilson Task Force of 1985," *Native Studies Review* 2 (1988), 1-44; Ian A.L. Getty and Antoine S. Lussier (eds.), *As Long as the Sun Shines and the Water Flows: A Reader in Canadian Native Studies* (Vancouver: University of British Columbia Press, 1983); Coopers and Lybrand, *Federal Expenditures and Mechanisms for Their Transfer to Indians. A Research Project for the Special Committee of the House of Commons on Indian Self-Government* (Ottawa: Coopers and Lybrand, 1983); John Leonard Taylor, *Canadian Indian Policy During the Interwar Years, 1918-1939* (Ottawa: Indian Affairs and Northern Canada, 1984); Audrey Doerr, "Indian Policy," in G. Bruce Doern and V. Seymour Wilson (eds.), *Issues in Canadian Public Policy* (Toronto: Macmillan, 1974), 36-54.
4. Harold Cardinal, *The Rebirth of Canada's Indians* (Edmonton: Hurtig, 1977); George Manuel and Michael Posluns, *The Fourth World: An Indian Reality* (Toronto: Collier-Macmillan, 1974); Howard Adams, *Prison of Grass: Canada From a Native Point of View* (Toronto: General Publishing, 1975).
5. J. Rick Ponting and Roger Gibbins, *Out of Irrelevance: A Socio-Political Introduction to Indian Affairs in Canada* (Toronto: Butterworths, 1980). See also J. Rick Ponting, "Public Opinion on Aboriginal Peoples' Issues in Canada," *Canadian Social Trends* (Winter 1988), 9-17.

6. Jesse A. Reiber, *Fundamental Concerns Regarding Indian Local Government: A Discussion Paper of Potential Problems and Research Areas* (Ottawa: Indian and Northern Affairs Canada, 1977); Frank Cassidy, *On The Inherent Jurisdiction of Indian Governments* (Victoria: Institute for Research on Public Policy, 1988); David C. Nahwegabow, *Federal-Provincial Implications of Various Concepts of Indian Self-government* (Ottawa: Indian and Northern Affairs Canada, Corporate Policy Branch, 1983) and Roger Gibbins and J. Rick Ponting, "An Assessment of the Probable Impact of Aboriginal Self-Government in Canada," in Alan Cairns and Cynthia Williams (eds.), *The Politics of Gender, Ethnicity and Language in Canada*, research studies for the Royal Commission on the Economic Union and Development Prospects for Canada, Vol. 34 (Toronto: University of Toronto Press for Minister of Supply and Services Canada, 1986), 171-245.

7. J. Anthony Long and Menno Boldt, in association with Leroy Little Bear (eds.), *Governments in Conflict? Provinces and Indian Nations in Canada* (Toronto: University of Toronto Press, 1988).

8. David Hawkes (ed.), *Aboriginal Peoples and Government Responsibility: Exploring Federal and Provincial Roles* (Ottawa: Carleton University Press, 1989).

9. Kenneth M. Lysyk, "The Rights and Freedoms of the Aboriginal Peoples of Canada ss. 25, 35, 37," in Walter S. Tarnopolsky and Gerald Beaudoin (eds.), *The Canadian Charter of Rights and Freedoms: Commentary* (Toronto: Carswell, 1982), 467-88; Douglas E. Sanders, "Prior Claims: An Aboriginal People in the Constitution of Canada," in Stanley M. Beck and Ivan Bernier (eds.), *Canada and the New Constitution: The Unfinished Agenda*, Vol. 1 (Montreal: Institute for Research on Public Policy, 1983), 225-80; Douglas E. Sanders, "The Rights of the Aboriginal Peoples of Canada," *Canadian Bar Review* 61 (1983), 314-38; Thomas R. Berger, "Native History, Native Claims and Self-Determination," in Paul Tennant (ed.), *British Columbia: A Place for Aboriginal Peoples? A Special Issue of B.C. Studies* (Vancouver: University of British Columbia Press, 1983), 10-23; Thomas R. Berger, "Native Rights and Self-Government," *Canadian Journal of Native Studies* 3 (1983), 363-75; Keith Jobson and Richard King (eds.), *Aboriginal Title, Rights and the Canadian Constitution* (Victoria: University of Victoria Press, 1983); Brian Slattery, "The Constitutional Guarantee of Aboriginal and Treaty Rights," *Queen's Law Journal* 8 (1983), 232; Nancy E. Ayers, "Aboriginal Rights in the Maritimes," *Canadian Native Law Reporter* 2 (1984),

1-84; and Brian Slattery, "Understanding Aboriginal Rights," *Canadian Bar Review* 66 (1987), 727-83.

10. Menno Boldt and J. Anthony Long, in association with Leroy Little Bear (eds.), *The Quest for Justice: Aboriginal Peoples and Aboriginal Rights* (Toronto: University of Toronto Press, 1985); and Bradford W. Morse (ed.), *Aboriginal Peoples and the Law: Indians, Métis and Inuit Rights in Canada* (Ottawa: Carleton University Press, 1985).

11. Ludger Muller-Wolle and Pertti J. Pelto, "Political Expressions in the Northern Fourth World: Inuit, Cree, Sami," *Etudes Inuit Studies* 3 (1979), 5-72; Rick H. Hemmingson, "Jurisdiction of Future Tribal Courts in Canada: Learning From the American Experience," *Canadian Native Law Reporter* 2 (1985), 1-35; and Noel Dyck (ed.), *Indigenous Peoples and the Nation-State: "Fourth World" Politics in Canada, Australia, and Norway*, Social and Economic Papers No. 14 (St. John's; Memorial University of Newfoundland Institute of Social and Economic Research, 1985).

12. Menno Boldt and J. Anthony Long, "Tribal Traditions and European-Western Political Ideologies: The Dilemma of Canada's Native Indians," *Canadian Journal of Political Science* 18 (1985), 367-74; Menno Boldt and J. Anthony Long, "A Reply to Flanagan's Comments: 'The Sovereignty and Nationhood of Canadian Indians: A Comment on Boldt and Long'," *Canadian Journal of Political Science* 19 (1986) 151-53.

13. Frank Cassidy, *Indian Status and Band Membership: Citizenship, Self-Government, and the Revised Indian Act* (Victoria: Institute for Research on Public Policy, 1988).

14. D. Opekekew, "Self-Identification and Cultural Preservation: A Commentary on Recent Indian Act Amendments," *Canadian Native Law Reporter* 2 (1986), 1-25.

15. Michael Asch, *Home and Native Land: Aboriginal Rights and the Canadian Constitution* (Toronto: Methuen, 1984).

16. Gurston Dacks, "The Case Against Dividing the Northwest Territories," *Canadian Public Policy* 12 (1986), 202-13; Gurston Dacks, *Liberal-Democratic Society and Government in Canada* (Yellowknife: Western Constitutional Forum, 1983); Gordon Robertson, *Northern Provinces: A Mistaken Goal* (Montreal: Institute for Research on Public Policy, 1985); R.F. Keith and J.B. Wright *Northern Transitions: Second National Workshop on People, Resources and the Environment North of 60 Degrees* (Ottawa: Canadian Arctic Resources Committee, 1978); C.M. Drury, *Constitutional Development in the Northwest Territories: Report of the Special Representa-*

tive (Hull: Minister of Supply and Services Canada, 1979).
17. William R. McMurtry and Alan Pratt, "Indians and the Fiduciary Concept, Self-Government and the Constitution: Guerin in Perspective," *Canadian Native Law Reporter* 3 (1986), 19-46; Kent McNeil, "The Constitution Act, 1982, Sections 25 and 35," *Canadian Native Law Reporter* 1 (1988), 1-13; Norman Zlotkin, *Unfinished Business: Aboriginal Peoples and the 1983 Constitutional Conference* (Kingston: Queen's University Institute of Intergovernmental Relations, 1983); Brian Schwartz, *First Principles, Second Thoughts: Aboriginal Peoples, Constitutional Reform and Canadian Statecraft* (Montreal: Institute for Research on Public Policy, 1986); Douglas E. Sanders, "The Indian Lobby," in Keith Banting and Richard Simeon (eds.), *And No One Cheered: Federalism, Democracy and the Constitution Act* (Toronto: Methuen, 1983), 301-32; Eric Robinson and Henry Bird Quinney, *The Infested Blanket: Canada's Constitution and the Genocide of Indian Nations* (Winnipeg: Queenston House, 1985); Shaun Nakatshura, "A Constitutional Right of Indian Self-Government," *University of Toronto Law Review* 43 (1985), 72-99; Brian Stevenson, "Political Integration and Self-Government: Hegemonic and Counterhegemonic Discourse" (unpublished M.A. thesis, Department of Political Science, University of Victoria, 1986); and R.L. Barsh and J.W. Henderson, "Aboriginal Rights, Treaty Rights and Human Rights: Indian Tribes and Constitutional Renewal," *Journal of Canadian Studies* 17 (1982), 55-81.
18. Canada, House of Commons, Report of the Special Committee, *Indian Self-Government in Canada* (Ottawa: Minister of Supply and Services Canada, 1983).
19. Roger Gibbins and J. Rick Ponting, "The Paradoxical Nature of the Penner Report," *Canadian Public Policy* 10 (1984), 221-24; Paul Tennant, "Indian Self-Government: Progress or Stalemate?," *Canadian Public Policy* 10 (1984), 211-15; and Sally Weaver, "A Commentary on the Penner Report," *Canadian Public Policy* 10 (1984), 215-21.
20. Leroy Little Bear, Menno Boldt and J. Anthony Long (eds.), *Pathways to Self-Determination: Canadian Indians and the Canadian State* (Toronto: University of Toronto Press, 1984).
21. Boldt and Long, *The Quest for Justice*.
22. Frank Cassidy and Robert L. Bish, *Indian Government: Its Meaning in Practice* (Victoria: Oolichan Books and the Institute for Research on Public Policy, 1989).
23. Cassidy, *Indian Status and Band Membership*.

24. John Leonard Taylor, *Indian Band Self-Government in the 1960's: A Case Study of Walpole Island* (Ottawa: Indian and Northern Affairs Canada, Treaties and Historical Research Centre, 1984); W. Graham Allen, "Bill C-93: Sechelt Self-Government Legislation," paper prepared for Indians and the Law 111, Continuing Legal Education, Vancouver, April 1986; and W. Graham Allen "Sechelt Indian Self-Government," paper prepared for Self-Government Project: First Nations' Government Structures and Powers Conference, University of British Columbia, May 1988.

25. William F. Sinclair, *Native Self-Reliance Through Resource Development* (Vancouver: Hemlock Printers, 1984).

26. Frank Cassidy and Norman Dale, *After Native Claims? The Implications of Comprehensive Claims Settlements for Natural Resources in British Columbia* (Victoria: Institute for Research on Public Policy and Oolichan Books, 1988).

27. John E. Hall, Commissioner, *The Report of the Commission of Inquiry Concerning Certain Matters Associated with the Westbank Indian Band* (Ottawa: Minister of Supply and Services Canada, 1988).

28. Andrew J. Siggner, "Socio-Demographic Conditions of Registered Indians," *Canadian Social Trends* (Winter 1986), 2-9; H.B. Hawthorn, *A Survey of the Contemporary Indians of Canada*, 2 vols. (Ottawa: Queen's Printer, 1966) and J. Holmes, *Bill C-31 — Equality or Disparity: The Effects of the New Indian Act on Native Women* (Ottawa: Canadian Advisory Council on the Status of Women, 1987).

29. Paul Driben and Robert S. Trudeau, *When Freedom is Lost: The Dark Side of the Relationship Between Government and the Fort Hope Band* (Toronto: University of Toronto Press, 1983); James S. Frideres, *Native Peoples in Canada* (3rd ed.; Scarborough: Prentice-Hall Canada, 1988); and Hugh Brody, *Maps and Dreams* (Markham, Ontario: Penguin, 1983).

30. J. Rick Ponting (ed.), *Arduous Journey: Canadian Indians and Decolonization* (Toronto: McClelland and Stewart, 1986).

31. Gibbins and Ponting, "An Assessment of the Probable Impact of Aboriginal Government in Canada."

32. Bruce H. Wildsmith, "Pre-Confederation Treaties," in Bradford W. Morse (ed.), *Aboriginal Peoples and the Law: Indian, Métis, and Inuit Rights in Canada* (Ottawa: Carleton University Press, 1985); and Leslie Upton, *Micmacs and Colonists: Indian-White Relations in the Maritime Provinces* (Vancouver: University of British Columbia Press, 1979).

33. Donald J. Purich, "Indian History, Aboriginal Rights and Prairie Treaties," *Canadian Native Law Reporter* 3 (1986), 1-18; Norman K. Zlotkin, "Post-Confederation Treaties," in Morse, *Aboriginal Peoples and the Law*, 272-307; Richard Price (ed.), *The Spirit of the Alberta Indian Treaties* (Montreal: Institute for Research on Public Policy and Indian Association of Alberta, 1979); and Rene Fumoleau, *As Long as This Land Shall Last: A History of Treaty 8 and Treaty 11, 1870-1939* (Toronto: McClelland and Stewart, 1973).

34. Daniel Raunet, *Without Surrender, Without Consent: A History of the Nishga Land Claims* (Vancouver: Douglas and McIntyre, 1984); Mel Watkins, *Dene Nation: The Colony Within* (Toronto: University of Toronto Press, 1977); Boyce Richardson, *Strangers Devour the Land* (Toronto: Macmillan, 1975); Thomas R. Berger, *Village Journey: The Report of the Alaska Native Review Commission* (New York: Hill and Wang, 1985); Berger, "Native History, Native Claims and Self-Determination"; Thomas R. Berger, *Northern Frontier, Northern Homeland: The Report of the Mackenzie Valley Pipeline Inquiry*, 2 vols. (Toronto: Lorimer, 1977); and Cassidy and Dale, *After Native Claims?*

35. Berger, *Village Journey*.

36. Report of the Task Force to Review Comprehensive Claims Policy, *Living Treaties: Lasting Agreements* (Ottawa: Indian and Northern Affairs Canada, 1985).

37. Ignatius E. LaRusic, *Negotiating a Way of Life: Initial Cree Experience With the Administrative Structures Arising From the James Bay Agreement* (Ottawa: Indian and Northern Affairs Canada, Policy, Research and Evaluation Group, Research Division, 1979).

38. Harry Daniels (ed.), *The Forgotten People: Métis and Non-Status Indian Land Claims* (Ottawa: Native Council of Canada, 1979).

39. Thomas Flanagan, "The Case Against Métis Aboriginal Rights," *Canadian Public Policy* 9 (1983), 331-32 and Wayne McKenzie, *Métis Self-Government in Saskatchewan, 1855 and After: Native Society in Transition* (Regina: University of Regina Canadian Plains Research Centre, 1986).

40. David C. Hawkes, *Aboriginal Self-Government: What Does It Mean?* (Kingston: Queen's University Institute of Intergovernmental Relations, 1985); David C. Hawkes, *Negotiating Aboriginal Self-Government: Developments Surrounding the 1985 First Ministers' Conference* (Kingston: Queen's University Institute of Intergovernmental Relations, 1985); David C. Hawkes, *The*

Search for Accommodation (Kingston: Queen's University Institute of Intergovernmental Relations, 1987); Noel Lyon, *Aboriginal Self-Government: Rights of Citizenship and Access to Governmental Services* (Kingston: Queen's University Institute of Intergovernmental Relations, 1984); and David A. Boisvert, *Forms of Aboriginal Self-Government* (Kingston: Queen's University Institute of Intergovernmental Relations, 1985).

41. All of the following have been published by the Institute of Intergovernmental Relations at Queen's University in Kingston, with the year of publication appearing in parenthesis: Ian B. Cowie, *Future Issues and Coordination between Aboriginal and Non-Aboriginal Governments* (1987); Marc Malone, *Financing Aboriginal Self-Government in Canada* (1986); Jerry Paquette, *Aboriginal Self-Government and Education in Canada* (1986); Richard Bartlett, *Subjugation, Self-Management* (1986); John Weinstein, *Aboriginal Government Off a Land Base* (1986); Evelyn J. Peters, *Existing Aboriginal Self-Government Arrangements in Canada: An Overview* (1987); C.E.S. Franks, *Public Administration Questions Relating to Aboriginal Self-Government* (1987); Douglas E. Sanders, *Aboriginal Self-Government in the United States* (1985); and Bradford W. Morse, *Aboriginal Self-Government in Australia and Canada* (1985).

42. Rick Marshall, *Getting Back to Self-Government: A Survey of the Institute's Major Publications on Policy Issues Concerning Native Peoples* (Victoria: Institute for Research on Public Policy, 1988).

43. E. Breton and G.G. Akian, *Urban Institutions and People of Indian Ancestry: Suggestions for Research* (Montreal: Institute for Research on Public Policy, 1978); Raymond Breton and Gail Grant (eds.), *The Dynamics of Government Programs for Urban Indians in the Prairie Provinces* (Montreal: Institute for Research on Public Policy, 1984).

44. Price, *The Spirit of the Alberta Indian Treaties*; and Schwarz, *First Principles, Second Thoughts*.

45. Cassidy and Dale, *After Native Claims?*; Cassidy and Bish, *Indian Government: Its Meaning in Practice*; and Fred Wien, *Rebuilding the Economic Base of Indian Communities: The Micmac in Nova Scotia* (Montreal: Institute for Research on Public Policy, 1986).

46. Western Constitutional Forum, *Partners for the Future: A Selection of Papers Related to Constitutional Development in the Western Northwest Territories* (Yellowknife: Western Constitutional Forum, 1985); Dacks, *Liberal-Democratic Society and Government in Canada*; Lesley Malloch, *Dene Government Past and Future: A Traditional Dene Model of Government and Its Implications for*

280

Constitutional Development in the Northwest Territories Today (Yellowknife: Western Constitutional Forum, 1984); Peter Jull, *Nunavut* (Ottawa: Nunavut Constitutional Forum, 1983); Makivik Corporation, *The Future of Inuit in Canada's Economic Union: Northern Partnership or Neglect?* Brief to the Royal Commission on the Economic Union and Development Prospects for Canada (Montreal: Makivik Corporation, 1983); Inuit Committee on National Issues, *Completing Canada: Inuit Approaches to Self-Government* (Kingston: Queen's University Institute of Intergovernmental Relations, 1987); Sheila Van Wyck (ed.), "Walpole Island: The Struggle for Self-Sufficiency: A Panel Presentation" (Occasional paper No. 3, Walpole Island Research Centre, 1984); Dakota-Ojibway Tribal Council, *Paper on Indian Self-Government* (Manitoba: Dakota-Ojibway Tribal Council, 1983); Delia Opekekew, *The First Nations: Indian Government in the Community of Man* (Saskatoon: Federation of Saskatchewan Indians, 1982); Union of British Columbia Indian Chiefs, *Self-Determination First Nations: Our Right to Choose* (Vancouver: Union of British Columbia Indian Chiefs, 1982); Association of Métis and Non-Status Indians of Saskatchewan, *Métis Self-Detemination; A Discussion Paper* (Regina: Association of Métis and Non-Status Indians of Saskatchewan, 1984); Dene Nation, *Denendeh: A Dene Celebration* (Yellowknife: Dene Nation, 1984); Scott Clark and John Cove, *Some Preliminary Options for the Structure of a New Gitksan-Carrier Government: A Discussion Paper* (Hazelton, B.C.: Gitksan-Wet'suwet'en Tribal Council, 1985); Robert L. Bish, *A Practical Guide to Issues in Gitksan and Wet'suwet'en Self-Government* (Victoria: University of Victoria and Gitksan and Wet'suwet'en Tribal Council, 1985); Frank Cassidy, *Everything Must be Done in Public* (Prince George, B.C.: Carrier Sekani Government Commission, 1988); Native Council of Canada, *Native Self-Government and the Delivery of Educational, Cultural, Social and Economic Services: An Interim Report* (Ottawa: Native Council of Canada, 1982); Native Council of Canada, *Bill C-31 and the New Indian Act: Applying for Status* (Ottawa: Native Council of Canada, Indian Act Secretariat, 1986); Native Council of Canada, *Bill C-31 and the New Indian Act: Protecting Your Rights* (Ottawa: Native Council of Canada, Indian Act Secretariat, 1986); Martin Dunn, *Access to Survival: A Perspective on Aboriginal Self-Government for the Constituency of the Native Council of Canada* (Kingston: Queen's University Institute of Intergovernmental Relations, 1986); and Assembly of First Nations, *Answers to Your*

281

Questions About First Nations' Self-Government (Ottawa: Assembly of First Nations, 1985).

47. Siggner, "Socio-Demographic Conditions of Registered Indians."
48. Frideres, *Native Peoples in Canada* and Canadian Bar Association, *Report of the Canadian Bar Association Committee on Aboriginal Rights in Canada: An Agenda for Action* (Ottawa: Canadian Bar Association, 1988).
49. See Tom Porter, "Traditions of the Constitution of the Six Nations," in Little Bear, Boldt and Long, *Pathways to Self-Determination*, 14-21.
50. Holmes, *Bill C-31—Equality or Disparity*.
51. Cassidy and Dale, *After Native Claims?*; and Sinclair, *Native Self-Reliance Through Resource Development*.
52. Price, *The Spirit of Alberta Indian Treaties*.
53. Cassidy and Dale, *After Native Claims?*
54. *Improved Program Delivery: A Study Team Report to the Task Force on Program Review April 1985* (Ottawa: Supply and Services Canada, 1986).
55. Allen, "Bill C-93: Sechelt Self-Government Legislation."
56. Cassidy, *On the Inherent Jurisdiction of Indian Governments*.
57. Ibid.
58. Bradford W. Morse, "The Resolution on Land Claims," in Morse, *Aboriginal Peoples and the Law*, 617-83.
59. Weinstein, *Aboriginal Government Off a Land Base*.
60. Marie Smallface Marule, "Traditional Indian Government: Of the People, By the People, For the People," in Little Bear, Boldt and Long, *Pathways to Self-Determination*, 36-45.
61. Cassidy and Bish, *Indian Government: Its Meaning in Practice*.
62. Ibid.
63. Ibid.
64. Malone, *Financing Aboriginal Self-Government in Canada*.
65. Holmes, *Bill C-31—Equality or Disparity*.
66. Canadian Bar Association, *Report of the Committee on Aboriginal Rights in Canada*.
67. Morse, *Aboriginal Self-Government in Australia and Canada*; and Sanders, *Aboriginal Self-Government in the United States*.

282

L'Institut de recherches politiques.

Une présence nationale

Créé en 1972, l'Institute de recherches politiques est un organisme national et indépendant à but non lucratif, possédant des bureaux d'un bout à l'autre du Canada.

La mission de l'Institut est d'améliorer la politique d'État au Canada en encourageant un processus politique plus général, mieux informé et plus efficace et en contribuant à la mise en application de ce processus. Pour remplir cette mission, l'Institut:

- identifie les questions importantes auxquelles devra faire face le Canada dans un avenir à long terme et entreprend des recherches indépendantes sur ces questions;
- favorise la dissémination générale des résultats-clés des activités de recherches (celles menées par l'Institut et d'autres);
- encourage le débat impartial et la critique de questions de politique d'État, de manière à provoquer la participation de tous les secteurs et de toutes les régions de la société canadienne, et établit la liaison entre la recherche et les mécanismes d'apprentissage social et d'élaboration de politiques.

Direction de l'Institut

L'Institut est diregé par un Conseil d'administration, conseillé par des représentants des gouvernements fédéral, provinciaux et territoriaux et d'autres organismes nationaux de recherche, ainsi que par des groupes d'experts venant de l'extérieur, qui se réunissent en comités consultatifs pour aider le Comité de recherches. Le président, en tant qu'administrateur en chef, est responsable de la mise en pratique et de l'administration des politiques et des programmes de l'Institut, ainsi que de la direction du personnel.

Indépendance et neutralité

L'indépendance de l'Institut est assurée par les revenue d'un fonds de dotation auquel ont souscrit les gouvernements fédéral et provinciaux, ainsi que le secteur privé. L'Institut obtient en outre des subventions et des contrats de la part des gouvernements, des entreprises et des fondations, pour soutenir les activités de ses programmes et pour mener à bien des projets de recherche particuliers.

La décision de diffuser l'information au nom de l'Institut est la responsabilité ultime de la président. Elle bénéficie à cette fin des conseils du personnel de l'Institut et de ceux des lecteurs extérieurs, quant à l'exactitude et à l'objectivité d'un manuscrit. Seuls sont publiés les manuscrits qui traitent de façon compétente d'un sujet digne de l'intérêt du public. Les publications de l'Institut paraissent dans la langue de l'auteur et sont accompagnées d'un résumé rédigé dans les deux langues officielles.

The Institute for Research on Public Policy

56

A National Presence

Founded in 1972, the Institute for Research on Public Policy is an independent, national, non-profit organization with offices across Canada.

- The mission of the Institute is to improve public policy in Canada by promoting and contributing to a policy process that is more broadly based, informed and effective.

In pursuit of this mission, the Institute:

- identifies significant public policy questions that will confront Canada in the longer term future, and undertakes independent research into those questions;
- promotes wide dissemination of key results from its own and other research activities;
- encourages non-partisan discussion and criticism of public policy issues in a manner which elicits broad participation from all sectors and regions of Canadian society, and links research with processes of social learning and policy formation.

Governance of the Institute

The Institute is governed by a Board of Directors, advised by representatives of federal, provincial and territorial governments and of other national research organizations, and by panels of external authorities, drawn into *ad hoc* advisory committees formed to assist the Research Committee. Implementation and administration of the Institute's policies and programs and management of the staff are the responsibility of the president, who is the chief executive officer.

Independence and Neutrality

The Institute's independence is assured by an endowment fund, to which federal and provincial governments and the private sector have contributed. The Institute receives grants and contracts from governments, corporations and foundations, both to support program activity and to carry out specific research projects.

The president bears final responsibility for the decision to disseminate information under the Institute's imprint. She is advised on the accuracy and objectivity of a manuscript by both the Institute staff and outside reviewers. Publication of a manuscript signifies that it is deemed to be a competent treatment of a subject worthy of public consideration. Publications of the Institute are in the language of the author, with an executive summary in both official languages.